Fleur – The Dog That Refused to Die

*'Buy a pup and your money will buy
Love unflinching that cannot lie'*

'The Power of The Dog'
Rudyard Kipling

Fleur – The Dog That Refused to Die

By
Andrew & Wendy Morris

Bookaholics Publishing, 2019.

FLEUR
the dog that REFUSED to die

Published by Bookaholics Publishing
imprint of
Estuary Media Group Ltd
19, Carters Garth Close, Grainthorpe, Louth,
Lincolnshire, LN11 7HT

ISBN: 978-1-9160289-0-6

Copyright © Wendy Morris, 2019

Wendy Morris is recognised as author and copyright holder of this book and its full contents. No reproduction of part or whole of this book with prior permission.

Page design by Pageset Ltd, High Wycombe, Buckinghamshire HP11 1JR.
Printed by Ridgeway Press, Breach House, Easton Royal Pewsey Wiltshire SN9 5LU.

CONTENTS

~ • ~

Chapter		Page
1	Meet Fleur – A dog with a golden heart	1
2	Meanwhile, another story unfolds	17
3	The rescue that had to happen	25
4	It was not that simple	37
5	Will Fleur make it?	47
6	The journey to…where?	61
7	At last – the arrival!	73
8	Settling in the new arrival	83
9	The heartbreak of another setback	99
10	Where there's life, there's hope	113
11	Fleur and hope fade fast	123
12	The last chance for a brave little dog	135
13	News of Fleur's 'death'	145
14	Good news at last	155
15	Home, sweet home	163
16	More tears in the Morris home	171
17	Stardom for Fleur	189
18	Fleur has the final word	211

FABULOUS FLEUR

~ • ~

foreword by
BEVERLEY CUDDY
(editor of *Dogs Today magazine*)

I HAVE MET thousands of remarkable dogs in the last 28 years of editing Dogs Today magazine, but I'll never, ever forget Fleur.

There was no scrolling past her tragic photos when they popped up on my Facebook newsfeed. She had been so very cruelly and carelessly damaged.

Yes, I vaguely knew that things were horrendous for dogs in Romania, but looking into Fleur's sad eyes made it very real and urgent. The urge to save Fleur united so many of us dog lovers.

When I first met her, I was surprised by how tiny she is – she's really elegant. When the stains were washed away, she became a silvery white and seemed to glow. I called her the Kate Moss of the dog world, as she appeared on almost as many magazine front covers!

But Fleur's real beauty always came from within. Fleur refused to die, despite all the odds being cruelly stacked against her.

Wendy and Andrew unconditionally loved her and gave her a wonderful life in Hampshire, but they didn't know that she was still dying inside. Fleur would need another miracle. Her odds for surviving this time were only 1%. Was such a slim chance better than nothing? Could love conquer all?

She somehow loved and trusted people, despite what had happened in that 'kill shelter'.

You can't change the world for every dog – but we can try. And they, in turn, change us.

Fleur taught me that we must never give up hope. Wendy and Andrew Morris never did.

Thank you to everyone who donated, shared or just prayed for a miracle. Just as suffering knows no borders, so a dog's love for us is limitless, too.

Fleur is the poster girl for all rescued dogs.

Chapter One

MEET FLEUR – A DOG WITH A GOLDEN HEART

~ • ~

THE HOSPITAL WAS as busy as ever. In some parts the daily routine was in full swing with patients looking on as doctors and their trainees huddled in the centre of the ward, comparing notes and occasionally glancing over their shoulders at the occupant of bed A19. The other patients were relieved.

In another part of the hospital the routine was different. This was A & E where the smell of disinfectant just about eased into the nostrils ahead of the aroma of illness. Yes, it was routine but the patients already slumped into the waiting room chairs were an unscripted miscellany of aches, breaks and fakes. Worn-out staff smiled, consoled and comforted. The receptionist coped.

And then there was the main entrance where voluntary receptionists pointed people in all directions. Those people and their friends and families milled around the area looking at at direction signs, wondering if the shop sold Rich Tea Biscuits, avoiding the ragged-looking man leaning against the pillar.

This was routine too. Most people were looking up at signs or looking ahead at the corridors that would eventually lead them to the right department. They could be forgiven for not looking down. They could be forgiven for not noticing that there was something, or someone, in their midst which was decidedly not routine.

It was not every day that a dog walked into the hospital. But then Fleur was not an everyday dog. Fleur was a dog with a mission. She was there to see someone special, someone she could relate to. Someone who was as ill as she had been. Fleur was there to give them hope.

Perhaps, we are running ahead of ourselves. Fleur would know doubt like to tell you her story in her own way – and why not? Like most dogs, Fleur is good at communication. The trouble with humans is that we take a while to understand the language of looks, sounds, postures and movements. Some of us never actually learn that language at all which canbe very frustrating for a dog that is eager to please, eager to give, eager to be a close friend. Fleur is all of those things.

Her story began in Romania and she was born when it was the best of times for some but mostly the worst of times. Imagine a freezing cold night with hunger pangs gnawing at the stomach while the skin or fur is doing its best not to shiver away any chance of sleep.

Here, Fleur takes over the story.

I don't know if it was the rumbling from our empty stomachs that had woken us on that typically cold night. The blizzard meant Shimeka snuggled up and we were like pups again. In my dreams we had been safe, our bony old mum licking us roughly with her raspy tongue. The kind little boy who used to play with me shared his food without even a growl.

I felt Shimeka's muscles suddenly tense, ready to fight. She hated people. Mum always warned us to keep away from men because they can be cruel.

For as long as I can remember we had lived in fear of being captured. She said one of our ancestors must have bitten Mr ChowChessCo for him to want to lock all of us away.

Shimeka said she would bite him when she found him. The only human I have ever met was very kind to me but if Mum gave us a warning we always knew it was worth listening to.

Despite the cold, last night's sleep had been the best for a long time. I'd felt safe hearing my big sister's heartbeat. The rest of the litter took after mum and those black coats had made them easy for the dog catchers to spot when the snow came. Shimeka and I were mainly white, only a few splodges of black – Mum said maybe the paint ran out while we were being made.

We hope the others are safe. Sometimes I wonder if we should just try to get caught by the dog catcher too, so we can all be together, but Shimeka says she would rather starve to death than be a man's slave. Shimeka was like that but she was a great older sister.

I remember that night so well. Shimeka was suddenly alert. We held our breath, noses twitching as we sense danger on the wind. Shimeka's hearing is much better than mine, it has saved us before. My stupid ears flop down, but hers stand proud. I watched in awe as they swivelled, locating the source of the noise that had disturbed her. I licked my nose to sharpen its sensitivity. Yes, there was definitely something in the air.

Mother taught us the three Fs. But today there was nothing to fight, and flight wouldn't make sense – under the car we are safe. I don't think I told you that we were sleeping under a car becaue we couldn't find anything else. It wasn't the best but at least we were sheltered, could see movement around us and we could escape in any direction. The other F? Well, freezing was often our only option, especially in the long Romanian winter.

We both twitched our noses again. Blood, we could definitely smell fresh blood. And fear.

And death. And possibly breakfast.

Shimeka was already out from under our car and hunting it down.

Mum had always warned us about the long grass that bites, to stay clear of the cold smell of metal and the sweet smell of men, but our bellies were shouting louder – our noses were telling us there was a feast.

The splash of red in the snow marked the spot. We were very lucky no one else had heard the snap of the trap. Shimeka greedily ripped the rabbit's legs free and I gulped down what she left. There wasn't time for us to chew our food, it was too dangerous to be outside in daylight but what a start to the day for us, if not the poor rabbit. Or the man. He would be very angry that his trap was now empty.

Euphoric, we trotted back to the old car that had become our den, licking our lips more than was strictly necessary. The dry snow crunched beneath our feet, leaving very clear tracks. Shimeka always went first, her strides were longer than mine. She stopped abruptly, head cocked, something was very wrong. Someone was coming, coming fast.

We both dived through the hedge totally blind to what was the other side, desperate to get off the road. I was tumbling down a steep slope. Thankfully the snow was very deep in this gulley and my landing was soft. I looked around and I was alone. If I couldn't see Shimeka, maybe the man couldn't either, I hoped.

The growl of a truck stopped next to the empty trap. I could hear the man curse as he discovered our meagre leftovers. He must be hungry, too. I heard a crack, like a man's fire stick. But it wasn't. It was Shimeka, she had landed on top of a frozen ditch. She had fallen through and she was desperately trying to scramble out. The man had heard the noise, too. He rushed to grab Shimeka with a long pole.

See, Mum was wrong, men can be kind. He was going to try to save her.

The man expertly looped a noose around Shimeka's neck and pulled.

He was very strong. Shimeka's eyes were bulging, she wanted to bite him. I could hear her muffled swearing. The loop tightened around her neck when he pulled her from the water.

I scrabbled back up the bank. I'd seen the terror in Shimeka's eyes. I want to tell her not to bite the man, but now he was dragging her limp body through the snow. She looked dead. I wanted to get closer, to sniff, to make sure.

The man opened the van and the cage inside and threw Shimeka in so she landed with a sickening thud. He released her noose and it was suddenly around my neck. I didn't struggle. My tail wanted to wag involuntarily but it was clamped between my shaking back legs. I wanted the man to know I would not bite him. I didn't struggle, I let him throw me in the van next to my sister. At least we were still together.

In the dark I started to nudge Shimeka gently, breathing in deeply to smell if death had yet come. She was cold and wet, but still alive. I remembered when Mum died. I don't know where we all go when we die, but she became an empty shell. Shimeka was still there, I could smell her spirit.

Where were we heading? Would we be reunited with our long lost brothers and sisters?

No one had ever come back from the dog catcher to tell us what happens next.

I licked Shimeka's muzzle and reminded her that we were always the lucky ones, that everything would be okay, but I don't think she could hear me. She was very deep within herself, half way between life and death.

After what seemed like hours, the van doors were flung open and the bright light hurt my eyes. The winter sun shone on Shimeka like a celestial spotlight, but she still didn't move.

The dog catcher grabbed the dog with the pole, it was limp and unresponsive. He dragged the body out of the van and vanished. I curled into a ball in the back of my cage, hoping he wouldn't see me if I made myself small enough.

It didn't work, and when he came back I quickly felt the pole around my own neck. I dug my paws in, refusing to move. I had no idea what was waiting outside those doors, but something told me it wasn't good. My claws scratched against the floor and the metal of the crate as I fought my hardest to stay where I was. I growled and showed my teeth all in an attempt to get the dog catcher to let me go but nevertheless I was dragged by my neck out of the van flipping my body round as much as I could to try and free myself. On the floor was the body of the dog from the cage next to me. His chest rose slowly. He was still alive, just, but had been left there, discarded on the floor to die.

The dog catcher dragged me into a building full of small cages, each one with a wooden pallet as a floor. I could barely breath because the pole was so tight around my neck, making my growls and barks raspy and barely audible. He flung me into one of the tiny cages and left. Panicked, I scrambled to the far corner of the cage and curled up into a tiny ball, just as I had in the van. At that moment I would've chewed off my own back leg to be back out on the street. There, I knew what was going on. I knew how to survive and where was safe. Here I knew nothing, and I couldn't second guess anything.

As I nervously looked around the cage I quickly realised there was no water and nowhere to get water. Often, I had found that drinking in heightened states of stress had calmed me down. Evidently that wasn't an option here. Then, as my eyes darted around the room for any form of life I saw it. The pallet of the cage next to me was stained red from blood. The stain led to a dog lying on the floor, but not all of a dog. The body had been mauled and parts of the dog" insides were outside. Then I saw the dog's cage-mate, it's mouth was stained red and his eyes were crazed. It was obvious that this poor dog had been driven to extremes to survive and was as much a victim as the dog laying there half eaten.

I tucked my head into my chest and closed my eyes. I didn't want to see any more. As I lay there, eyes closed tight and pretending I was anywhere else, a noise brought me straight back to reality. It sounded like something being dragged along the floor. I lifted my head towards the sound to see a dog in one of the other cages. The noise came from him dragging his legs along the wooden pallet floor of the cage. The legs were obviously useless and sore from being constantly dragged along the floor, there were various bloodied marks where the legs had been cut by the rough pallet flooring. What kind of hell had I been brought into? I didn't want to see any more. I went back into my own world, head tucked into chest.

The next morning, I woke, not that I head really slept properly, to the cage next to me being opened and a dog being thrown in. She was so thin I could almost see straight through her. I had hoped yesterday had been a dream, or a nightmare, and I would wake up back under the car with Shimeka's head over my neck, but my pathetic alarm call brought me back to my hideous reality.

The dog turned, and our eyes met briefly. She spun around displaying her hind leg. It sickeningly stuck out at a ninety-degree angle from her body. It was a miracle she had lasted as long as she had out on the streets. I dropped my head back to the floor, unsure of what was going to happen next. Was I staying here? Was I going back to the streets? Or worse? What was happening?

The wooden slats of the floor dug into me as I lay there, pushing into my bones. It made a change from stones. I didn't know what else to do. My entire body was on edge, even more than it had been when we were living on the streets. At least out there I could pre-empt most outcomes. In here I was lost. I had no experiences to pull from. No prior exposure that would mean I could at least have a vague idea of what was to come, which may have reduced at least some of the stress. Instead I lay there trembling with fear and feeling my throat begin to sting from thirst. Outside I was used to constant hunger pains, but there was usually always somewhere to get water. In here there was nothing and my dry throat was beginning to hurt.

Whilst lost in my own thoughts of lakes, water fountains and puddles, a sudden clanging signalled the opening of the cage next to me. The dog, that was barely alive with hip bones and ribs more visible than fur, was dragged mercilessly out of the kennel. I watched as the dog, limp but breathing, was thrown into a large white chest at the other end of the room. The man then headed towards my cage. I immediately crawled as far back into my kennel as I could, trying to be as small and invisible as possible. Thankfully, he carried on walking. That dog was still alive when it went in to that chest, I could see its chest rise and fall. It was faint, but it was there.

Was that what was going to happen to me? All the dogs that were in the cages around me were ill or wounded in one way or another. Dogs on the streets never looked exactly healthy, but these looked particularly unwell. Something felt wrong. I could sense something in the atmosphere, an unease that I didn't like. In my tight ball I tried not to look around too much. I didn't want to be reminded of what now surrounded me. I closed my eyes.

Sleep was never going to come easy that night, not that it ever did. I had hunger pains, as I hadn't eaten for nearly two days by now. A small bowl with some water in it had been placed in my cage and I had drank most of it, but food had never appeared. There I lay, exhausted but too scared and anxious to sleep. My heavy eyes would drop closed and then an intense pang of hunger pain or a sudden noise would bring me back into the hell I now found myself in.

If it wasn't my pain that woke me, or the people making noise, it was a scream or whine from one of the other dogs that surrounded me. There had been many sleepless nights in my life to this point, as there had been pain, hunger and fear, but never had the fear or anxiety been so intense that I couldn't sleep at all. Never had the stress been so high that I couldn't stop trembling. I hated that place. I hated it. I was so alone, and I felt completely lost, with no idea what I would wake up to if I ever did manage to fall asleep. Would I wake to the pole around my neck again? Or would I wake up in that white freezer.

I soon learned that at night the cage room was a very different beast. After a certain time, the people stopped coming in and there was no light in the room. If possible, it felt colder than living on the streets I was shaking as much from that as I was from pain and fear. The sheer effort from the constant shaking and trembling only added to the tiredness that was gradually growing.

The shadows that moved around the room as other dogs moved around their crates, the creaks, squeaks and cries all made the room seem even scarier at night than it was during the day. It felt like lying under that car without the security of knowing what was outside and having Shimeka and the other dogs to get warmth and contact from. It was these times that I really realised I was completely and utterly alone. Part of me wanted to just fall asleep and if I didn't wake up did it really matter? But a bigger, stronger part of me instinctively wanted to survive, like there wasn't an alternative.

Then I felt something almost familiar at my side. There was a warmth that was seeping through my fur and onto my skin. It couldn't be. Shimeka? No, I saw and felt her die, it couldn't be her. I hoped it was, though. Maybe, by some wonderful miracle she had survived and had been brought here and we could get through it together. It took me a while to muster up the courage to see what was touching me through that mesh. I wanted to know, but at the same time I didn't want to see that it wasn't Shimeka.

Slowly, I turned my head. No, it wasn't Shimeka and I felt a sharp pang of sadness. Instead of seeing Shimeka, I saw the dog with the deformed leg pushed up against the cage, just like I was. She had squashed herself up so close to the mesh divider that her skin was touching mine and we could share some warmth. Just like I had done in the past, I could get some vague sort of comfort from the contact. She raised her head and our eyes met briefly. Hers were filled with a dark sadness. I wondered briefly what she saw in mine before we both put our heads back down, staying in contact through the mesh. I might not have had Shimeka back, but it was better than nothing.

Time passed in the cage room, but I barely moved. I hoped that remaining still and small would make me insignificant so the people that came and went would keep passing my cage. If they didn't come in to the cage, they couldn't take me out of it. Not only that, but I was so tired I wasn't sure that I could move even if I wanted to.

This was an exhaustion that was utterly overwhelming. Yes, I was totally tired, but my body wouldn't let me sleep. The contact from the dog in the adjoining cage was reassuring but I was still on a constant fight or flight edge, ready to respond at the drop of a hat to whatever threat may present itself. I hadn't been able to replenish any of my energy with food so my whole body was completely exhausted, as were most of those dogs that surrounded me. Those that were still alive.

The dog next to me remained still, but her body rose and fell methodically as she breathed. At least she had made it through the night. I didn't have much time to feel thankful for her presence, I was soon distracted. I was so hungry my stomach felt like it was tying itself in knots.

Lying in one space for so long meant I noticed details in my cage. The metal mesh that made up the walls was bent and mauled in many places where previous occupants had obviously chewed on it. I had assumed they were marks from escape attempts, but now I understood it may well have been dogs simply trying to stop their hunger from consuming them. Nearby where I lay there were teeth marks in the wooden pallet floor where a dog had done similar to try and appease hunger pains, to try and convince their body that they were eating something even if it was cold metal or splintering wood. On top of the desperate signs of hunger, there were layers upon layers of urine and faeces stains and the smell was intense. From the moment I had entered the room, I could smell more dogs than it was possible to fit in the room.

As morning light began to seep into the cage room I knew I had to eat something. I had to. The complete and utter desperation to eat was driving me mad, I couldn't stand it anymore and I had to do something about it, no matter what it was. But what? Then I felt the deformed leg dog move in her cage. I turned to see her just standing there, staring at me. For a brief minute I wondered what she was going to do, was she going to launch at me? Was she going to bark? Was she going to collapse? Instead she hobbled quietly to the other side of her cage, the part she had used as a toilet. She met my eye once more before she bent down and began to eat her own faeces. She stopped and raised her head to me, as if instructing me what to do.

So, I crawled tentatively from my position at the rear of the cage, fear had kept me there all night. The smell of urine stung my eyes as my movement disturbed it, my underbelly was stained yellow where I hadn't moved all night, but it didn't put me off my mission. I moved slowly forwards across the wooden floor to my goal which sat near the entrance to the cage; a pile of faeces from the night before.

Conflicted, I licked at the pile. It was equal parts disgusting and satisfying. Even just having the taste of something on my tongue made me want to delve in, regardless of what it was I was diving into. I took a bite and quickly swallowed it. It was ultimate relief and I quickly gobbled down what was left. Once it was all gone, including licking at the wooden floor for a minute to make sure I had got it all, I slowly made my way back to my spot. It hurt, but at least the hunger pangs were diminished. The deformed leg dog looked at me knowingly as she retook her position laying against the cage.

I lay back down and, feeling some form of relief, I closed my eyes. As before, I could feel the warmth from the deformed leg dogs' skin as we came into contact through the cage mesh and I was immediately transported back to the abandoned car only days before, Shimeka's head resting protectively on my neck. There was some stress release and some of my muscles seemed to relax just slightly, but I couldn't help but picture her cold body lying on the concrete as I was carried away.

I was rushed out of my thoughts when the door to the cage room banged and my eyes shot open, all the relief gone and stress flooding back in to replace it. I didn't move but my eyes darted quickly around the room as I shrank into a tighter ball, feeling the deformed leg dog's body do the same.

I fully expected to see the dog catcher with another victim, or one of the staff members with a pole coming to collect one of us and put us in the white chest. I couldn't see properly from my balled-up position but the next thing I hear isn't my cage door clanging open, or another dog screaming as they are dragged out of their cage. It's a soft, warm female voice. Compared to everything else I had heard in the previous days it was soothing and welcoming. The melodic words felt inviting and my ears pricked towards them.

I managed to lift my head slightly and risk a look towards the sound. There, outside the front of my cage was a woman squatting on the floor. She pointed something towards me which clicked and flashed. She smiled, which was rare in the cage room. None of the usual humans smiled at us. They barely looked at us. Her hand moved towards the cage and immediately my ears went back against my head. I didn't growl or bark, but I didn't move from the back of the cage either. Human contact had come to mean something painful and stressful to me and I definitely didn't want to move towards that hand. But there was something different about this person; something softer, less threatening than the other people I had been around. I stayed in my safe space as she moved away and did the same to other cages around the room. My eyes followed her, I was intrigued.

I don't know how long I stayed there on that wooden floor. I do know that I only managed to stay alive by eating my own faeces, driven by utter desperation to survive. An underlying, natural survival instinct that had kept me alive from a puppy and was still doing so now, whatever it took. Humans came and went with little interaction, passing us all by whether we were dead or alive. Eventually they would take a dead or dying dog out of a cage that was needed for another dog and put them in the white chest. Old dogs, young dogs and puppies all went into the chest. Sometimes I could see them moving as they were flung into it. They never came back out. It became a countdown to when it would be my turn.

Most of my time was spent lying in that same spot, skin touching the deformed leg dog It was the only source of comfort I had. We would stand and eat together, each knowing how wretched it felt, but understanding how necessary it was. I'm not sure if I would've made it as long in that dank hell-hole if I didn't have that contact, that relationship, to help me through. Just to have another being there going through the same thing, to be able to have some physical contact, as minimal as it was, gave me some encouragement, some sort of emotional lifeline to cling on to. I had no idea what was going to happen, but I did know that the dog next door with the ninety-degree angle leg would be there. It was the only constant I had, aside from fear.

The softly spoken human never returned. For a day or two after she left my ears would prick in hope every time the door to the cage-room opened, but it was never her. One day not long after the human squatted outside my cage, a man opened my kennel and plunged to catcher's pole in. I was too tired, too hungry and too dehydrated to fight. He dragged me by the neck from the cage. Despite my exhaustion, panic now began to set in. Deformed leg dog started to growl and bark. Her barks got louder as saliva flew from her mouth as she snarled at the kennel man who dragged me along the corridor. I suddenly realised I was headed towards the white chest.

I didn't know what that white chest was, but I did know that I didn't want to go in it. I tried to fling myself around, but I had so little energy it was pointless. I didn't want to go in that chest and I put everything I had into trying to free myself.

But we didn't go to the chest, we went out of the cage room into a smaller room. There was a distinct smell of rotting flesh and old blood. It was a smell I had come across before, and it rarely meant anything good was going to happen.

I was shoved roughly onto a dirty table, I tried to move and scramble off but suddenly hands appeared and held me down by my hips, legs and shoulders. I started to cry loudly but I couldn't thrash around or try to escape. The hands held me down tightly and I could feel my hip bones digging into the wooden table. My nose was so close to the stained wood that the smell of embedded blood and bodily fluids was over powering. My lip intermittently curled back as I growled in fear, but the hands never let up. No one noticed, or they noticed, and no one cared.

Suddenly the reason for my restraint seared through my body. Pain exploded through my abdomen as something sliced through my skin. I screamed out as a hot, burning agony encompassed me. The hands didn't let up as I screamed and struggled against the grip. All my exhaustion was gone and was taken over by a raw desire to live, and to escape the pain. Then the room started to go blurry and everything was black.

The next thing I remember was my eyes flickering open and as I began to wake up my first thought went to pain. It was instant and like fire in my stomach. Then came the barrage of thoughts. Was I still there? Was I still being held down? Immediate panic. I couldn't move which made me freak out even more. The hands were still there, as was the unbearable, searing pain. I could smell fresh blood and raw flesh and as I looked towards the smell I could see blood dripping from the edge of the table. My blood.

My eyes found another dog on a different table. The dog was young, maybe a year old at most and unlike most dogs in the cage room it wasn't more bone than flesh, but it did have something that made it fit in. This poor, pitiful dog's bottom jaw was hanging off as if it had been kicked like a football. The man next to the table filled a needle with a thick white liquid from a large tin and with an ear-piercing squeal from the dog stuck it into the dog's leg. The white liquid vanished into the dog, who was then put on the cold concrete floor and left.

As I stared at the dog it just lay there as the last breathe escaped its body. The hands that had held me down picked me up and the pain in my stomach felt like a blaze. I screamed the entire walk back to my cage where I was thrown back onto the wooden floor. I crawled slowly back to my spot in the back of the cage, careful to avoid letting my stomach touch the floor. I curled into a ball, protecting the painful area from the world. I licked at my wound in an attempt to relieve the pain, but it didn't work. As much as it calmed me a little, licking always did, the pain still radiated through me.

Then I felt something. It was warm, and wet. I looked to see the deformed leg dog licking at me through the mesh. As much as the insurmountable pain encompassed me, it felt good to have another dog there to offer some form of comfort. To know I wasn't completely alone alleviated at least a little of the fear and anxiety that flowed through me amidst the searing pain.

Light and dark passed. The pain remained, and I remained in the same position. I waited for my turn in the white chest. Then one day, once I had pretty much given up any hope of leaving the cage room again, another human I had never seen before came through the door. She held something in her hand as she walked slowly along the cages, holding it up to some of the dogs as she did. She got to my cage and stopped.

What was happening? Why was she here, at my cage? Was she taking me somewhere else? Would it be better or worse?

Her voice was soft, like the human that had been here previously. I looked to her but didn't move. Not only was I too exhausted from hunger and lack of sleep, I also felt relatively safe in there, even if it was disgusting. She soon left and began speaking to one of the kennel men. Maybe she wasn't taking me away from here after all, but at least I could stay in my corner of my cage. Nothing happened to me in there. It's out of there that bad things happened.

Then she returned. She pointed to me and left the building. I started to get nervous. Something was wrong. I could sense that something was going to happen, something instinctive made me uneasy. The man grabbed the pole and opened my cage door. 'No. No. Please, no.' Every time that pole had come near me I had been hurt, or scared, or both. I didn't want that again, but I was so physically drained I couldn't put up much of a fight. My head screamed for the man to go away, but my body couldn't respond.

I looked to the deformed leg dog who growled and barked as she had before, but she was completely helpless. There was more of a desperation to her barks now, rather than an anger. The man pulled me out of my cage but rather than going towards the back room I was dragged to the door that people always came in and out of. What was the other side of that door? Was it good? Was it bad? I looked back at my friend in her cage. Her eyes pleaded with me as her barks became more and more desperate. I didn't want to leave her in this place, every bit of me ached for her to come with me, to help her and protect her as she had tried to do for me. As quickly as we had met we were torn apart.

Through the door a blinding light immediately made me squint and try to turn away. Wait, I was outside. Finally, I was back outside. The cold, fresh air washed over me cleansing me of the grime and dirt that filled the heavy air in the cage room. This air was light and unpolluted. A huge relief washed over me but was quickly replaced by anxiety and fear as I went into the unknown once more.

Outside a mesh gate stood the woman who had just been in the cage room. Something about her demeanour calmed me a little. She opened a car door and I found myself being coaxed in, wincing at the pain that was still present in my abdomen. The car door shut and before I could really process anything we were moving away from the building.

There was another person in the car, a male, but I didn't really take much in. My mind was reeling as I stared out of the car that passed through familiar streets, in unfamiliar circumstances. Thoughts raced through my mind. Shimeka lying frozen behind the bin, the dog dying on the cold concrete floor in the dirty room at the kennel and then to the deformed leg dog. I could feel a dull ache of sadness as I remembered her dark eyes filled with desperation as I was dragged from the cage room. Was she OK? What were they going to do to her? Was someone going to come and drag her out to a car? Or was she going into the white chest?

Both humans talked and occasionally their words were directed at me, but I barely noticed. I just curled up on the seat and protected my wound. The pain was still excruciating, but I didn't want to show it. Now I was out of that cage I was determined to survive, so I wasn't willing to show any weakness. As much as my instinct told me this human was safe, I wasn't going to risk displaying any vulnerability. I had got out of the cage room and I wasn't going to give up just yet, no matter how tired or broken my body was.

The car came to a halt and I was gently encouraged out of the car. A lead was placed around my neck, which at least was more comfortable than the dog catchers pole, and I was led into a building that smelled of a myriad of different animals and chemicals. Straight away I was nervous, or more nervous than I already was. I tried to keep myself low to the ground without causing my abdomen more pain, which was already making me panic. The pain had gotten worse since it had happened, and I had begun feeling worse. I was hot, and I felt sick. I just wanted to curl up and sleep underneath a car or behind a bin where I was safe.

I was taken into a small room where another person was waiting for me. What were all these people doing? Why was I being taken into all of these different places? I was so exhausted I could barely stand, but that didn't stop me being terrified. I was lifted onto the table which made me squeal in pain and I just collapsed. At that point I had nothing left in me. As I lay there, there was silence as all the people in the room stared at my wound with their mouths wide open.

Chapter Two

MEANWHILE, ANOTHER STORY UNFOLDS

~ • ~

WHILE FLEUR TAKES in her new surroundings and hopes it is probably a good time to introduce Andrew and Wendy that they might be able to tell you their stories and how Fleur came into their lives. Andrew, being a gentleman, steps aside for Wendy to begin her tale.

A lot of people have asked how Andrew and I came together. This is really Fleur's story but it would make sense to provide some background. Well, our contact was supposed to be a blind date but neither of us liked surprises, so we had a pre-blind date, just to be sure.

We still both turned up early to scope the other out. We had several more pre-dates before our official one!

Andrew and I had both been married before. I was a nurse, he was a soldier. We both saw people die in our jobs, we both wanted to get on with living.

You could say we both came with baggage, but if so, our respective kids were definitely Louis Vuitton, baggage that was really worth having.

It was a whirlwind romance but why wait when you know it is right? And we did, right from the start.

We married and bought a house in Ropley, a beautiful little village in Hampshire. The five kids were all either 'his' or 'mine' – we weren't going to have any more. But if we got a dog, that could be ours. It would make our house a home. I guess I thought a dog would complete us. There was a snag though – Andrew was adamant, he didn't want a puppy.

I hadn't thought of anything other than a puppy, it seemed logical to me.

I grew up in Yorkshire and we had a beautiful Old English Sheepdog called Jessie. One of my earliest memories was being told to sit still and be quiet while I watched three of her puppies being born – it was magical.

I was an army wife at nineteen and the first thing we did together was to buy a Boxer puppy from a newspaper ad. Naively, we brought him unseen over the phone and decided – unoriginally – to call him Rocky. We instantly noticed he had an unusual lump on his nose. The breeder pretended to be surprised and said he must have just bumped it. Of course, the lump never went down. The vet removed it, but two years later the lump came back. This time it was malignant.

Rocky was a real handful and he was always escaping. He would go next door when he was bored, often ending up asleep on their bed. Thankfully the neighbour usually thought it was funny, until the day Rocky did it when he was very, very muddy. Poor Rocky died very young of cancer.

After Andrew and I were married all was very well but I definitely felt the need to nurture something. My kids were getting more independent. But Andrew, sadly, still didn't want a puppy.

When my first marriage had broken down there were a few difficult weeks during which I had to stay in the same house as my ex. I decided to take up running to get out of the house.

On one of my runs I met up with someone who had a Border Collie. We chatted and I discovered that she had a bad back so I offered to exercise her dog at times when she didn't feel that she could. It gave me something to do (my kids were then both away at boarding school) and spending time with that dog made me start to feel a bit happier.

Then, not long after we were married, Andrew and I looked after a friend's dog, a beautiful black and white Border Collie named Muppet. His owners were lucky to get him back. It was nearly a 'curtains drawn, hide behind the sofa' scenario. We instantly loved him.

We missed him when he returned to his rightful owners but life had to go on. I was in my final year of a nursing degree and I took a night job in a care home to pay some bills. Andrew and I were supporting a combined family of five and you don't join the army to get rich. I would work at night and study during the day.

Life was about to get more complicated when I spotted a poster on the staff noticeboard.

Meanwhile, Another Story Unfolds

Another carer had put up an advert for her litter of Border Collie puppies. I thought it was a sign, well it was literally! But a Border Collie litter? That shift was probably the longest I ever had.

As mentioned. Andrew had said that he didn't want a puppy, but after spending time with Muppet, had he changed his mind?

When I got home I rashly told the kids we were going to just see a colleague's litter of pups. I knew it was wrong, but with the kids all excited, it would mean Andrew would come and look, too – just to make sure we didn't bring one home, of course.

It is at this point that Andrew must be allowed to step in and reveal his side of the story so far.

Wendy is right, I didn't want a puppy. But that didn't mean I didn't want a dog, quite the opposite.

To give some idea of how I have always viewed dogs it is worth mentioning that I had joined the army at the age of seventeen and, while in basic training, one perk soldiers were allowed was permission to display a photograph on the inside of their locker door. Most people had pictures of their girlfriends, but I had a photo of my dog Josey, a picture that has stayed with me to this day.

I was serving in Germany when Josey succumbed to a tumour. I was completely devastated. Josey was the canine love of my young life. She taught me everything. One of my first times walking Josey alone she had pulled on the lead. I wasn't holding it properly and she ran off.

Panic kicked in. There was danger ahead. Somehow, I managed to stand on the lead to stop her. I can still hear that yelp when her head was yanked backwards. It tore through me like a knife through a boat sail. I cuddled her close, crying hard because I couldn't stand that I had hurt her.

A life lesson learned that day.

So, hopefully that gives some idea of my great love and appreciation for dogs since childhood. Even as a kid, I was aware of the class divide between pedigree and crossbreed. Within my friendship group Josey was the only cross. There was a Border Collie called Ben and a Golden Retriever called Wanda.

The other boys were quick to point out Josey's defective curly tail and mixed heritage. Obviously, Josey couldn't give a crap what they thought. But that didn't stop me earnestly consoling her that it didn't matter what type of dog she was, I still loved her.

Josey did everything a boy could want. She played fetch and football. Her dribbling skills could have rivalled Beckham or Rooney. Josey was the most amazing, constant companion – but, I wasn't her first love. She doted on my father.

Dad was a long-distance lorry driver. He would leave the house around four in the morning and some nights he wouldn't come home at all, he'd sleep in his lorry.

If Josey and I were out when Dad arrived home, Dad would let out a whistle. No matter where we were, Josey would tear back home, leaving me choking on her dust.

She would literally hug my dad by climbing onto his lap and nuzzling her head deep into his shoulder. If he came home with toffees, she always got one (which may explain the hugs).

Josie gave my hardworking Dad a release, walking her was a way of getting away from everything and clearing his head. That was my Dad's vice. That, and smoking.

My Dad could smoke up to forty cigarettes a day, and not just any cigarettes, unfiltered Capstans.

After a while in the army I was lucky enough to become a dog handler, but I still missed having a real companion rather than a workmate. I wanted a Josey. I knew the instability of my military life meant I couldn't yet have a 'civilian' dog. I'm a realist. With me being away so often, it wouldn't have been me doing the caring for any dog I had. I would just have been the bloke who comes hoe now and then.

At long last, I was just two years from the end of my army service and life was starting to take proper shape. The life Wendy and I had now built together meant I had a real home at last. I was definitely warming to getting a dog. Not a puppy though. A dog.

I must mention at this stage that I hate flying and hate it with a passion. I know that might sound irrational and have nothing to do with Fleur's story but there is a connection. You see, to help me get through a tense flight, I did something I don't normally do. I looked for a book to read.

I scoured the bookshelves, not expecting to find anything to distract me but then 'One Dog at a Time' by Pen Farthing jumped out at me.

He was a soldier who had served in Afghanistan. I, too, was very familiar with Helmund.

Farthing told the true story of how he had adopted stray dogs when he was serving overseas. He'd set up the charity Nowzad to help bring more of these adopted dogs home and opened the first animal shelter in Afghanistan.

It was a very emotional read for me.

The horror and pain he wrote about were stories that I could really relate to. I had had my own experiences. I was hooked.

Later, while stationed at the British embassy in Kabul, I would visit the Nowzad kennels and meet Pen.

Visits to the kennels provided much-needed stress relief. Rolling around on the grass with an Afghan pup is very theraputic for even the hardest of soldiers.

If I couldn't have a rescue, I didn't want a dog. But no one seemed to want to rehome a dog to a soldier. The rejection began to grind me down. I had been trusted to serve in conflict zones and war, to handle service dogs in some of the most hostile environments, yet I was being pre-judged as irresponsible and incapable.

The final straw was when I saw there was a Border Collie in desperate need of a home – a dog at imminent risk of being put to sleep. I enquired but we still received a cold generic reply, "we do not re-home to soldiers."

With that, I put the barricades up.

Those barricades were still up when Wendy arranged for us to look at those Border Collie puppies. As far as I was concerned, we could look, but we were definitely not bringing one home. I tried to distance myself. We were not getting a puppy – absolutely not.

I tried not to really look at them as I knew that would be the danger. But in the sea of cute brown collie noses, a little black one stood out and I was lost. As Wendy knew I would be.

It was like the famous arm clutching the sword of Excalibur. If a sunbeam could have shone to accentuate him, it would have.

We called him Nero. Sue, the breeder, was much more understanding than the rescue centres had been. But if our circumstances changed, the pup must be returned to her.

In my final year in the Army, I was working close to home at a Longmoor training camp and I could take young Nero to work with me. He would bark for all of the 40 minute drive each way.

People were always making excuses to come into my office to see Nero. There was another dog at work who was not so friendly, a Jack

Russell who had issues. One day he gave Nero a proper beating.

After that Nero was a very sad dog, I felt I had let him down. I blamed myself, I should have made sure he was always safe.

Wendy takes up the story again.

When Nero was about a year old everything changed. Andrew brought him home as usual, he ate his dinner and looked contented.

Then suddenly he started thrashing and crashing around – out of control, I thought we were watching him die.

Andrew says he will always remember seeing Nero in such trouble.

Poor Nero's tail went completely rigid. He seemed to be holding his breath. Wendy was in pieces. I was terrified he was going to injure himself as he thrashed about on the stone floor. I lay my arm under him to try to lessen the heavy blows he was taking to his head.

At last Nero went limp. The glaze in his eyes cleared – he was back with us again.

I was glad of my army training which meant that I seemed able to remain calm in very stressful situations. As I laid down next to Nero, comforting him, I asked Wendy to turn off the lights and call the vet.

We eventually discovered that Nero had epilepsy and would need medication for the rest of his life. Our first dog might not have been a rescue, but he still needed our life-long special care.

Wendy explains what happened next.

When Andrew left the army, we were ready to try again at rescuing. We headed for Valgray's Border Collie and Animal Rescue as we had spotted Marti, and in theory she appeared to tick all of our boxes.

Marti was ten and had come from Ireland. Val, who ran the rescue, thought she was a perfect fit, too. So much so, she let us take her home immediately, I think Val was impressed by how we'd cared for Nero.

We had friends around for dinner that first night, and elderly Marti nimbly leapt onto the dining table and helped herself to the garlic bread. We discovered she was usually very nervous and wasn't in any way house trained.

Those first six months were very, very hard. Some dark days I played through the conversation in my head telling Andrew how we needed to take her back to Valgray's.

She was constantly scavenging for food – she once opened the freezer and had a chew on everything in there.

I was convinced she would die, surely no dog could consume a frozen smorgasbord without dire consequences. There were consequences of course – all over the carpet, and eye-watering wind. But 48 hours later Marti was fine.

Maybe she finally realised she was safe, she had obviously come from a place where she had to fight to survive. As our bond grew stronger, she became a princess.

But just as we were counting our blessings, Marti had a stroke.

It was as if someone out there knew we could care for broken dogs.

Marti had difficulty with steps and stairs after that, but we were determined to give her all of the love she deserved. Two weeks later, Marti had a second stroke. This time the vet tests also revealed that Marti had early onset dementia.

There was more bad news.

Marti had mammary tumours. The risks were too great to operate, but when they

started to grow, and she repeatedly licked them, which is a sign of pain, we had to do something.

The vet used a local anaesthetic and she survived the surgery, but her dementia was definitely getting worse. During this period, Andrew and I discussed euthanasia.

Fortunately, we found we both had strong and similar feelings. If a dog was able to walk, eat and drink and free from pain then euthanasia was a last resort.

We knew that Marti wouldn't be with us forever.

Both of our dogs had provided us with unexpected challenges, we didn't know, but our biggest challenge was still to come.

Chapter Three

THE RESCUE THAT HAD TO HAPPEN

~ • ~

EVERY SINGLE DOG has its own tale to tell, many are tales of happiness of course but sadly there are many other tales which are far from happy. Humans can only look and read the situation. Those who are sensitive will also feel at least some of what a dog is enduring.

Andrew continues Fleur's story and flings open the doors on the best and worst of human 'caring'.

When you have an interest in animals and perhaps dogs especially, you find yourself reading all kinds of things and watching documemtaries, news stories and so on because you are attracted to something that matters to you. That is how Wendy and I were.

I had heard that the public animal shelters in Bucharest were a thing of nightmares for animal lovers These places are run as businesses and money-making schemes, so costs are kept to a minimum regardless of the impact this has on animal welfare. Animals are put to sleep via an injection of paint, and castration or spay wounds are stitched together with string. For us dog loving Brits this kind of attitude is incomprehensible, but in Bucharest it's about money and if they can save money by cutting corners they will, regardless of welfare. These dogs come with a price tag, even to the point that dog wardens will snatch domestic dogs so that they can reap the monetary benefits.

At this point, I must say that I had little or no prior knowledge of Romania and probably couldn't even have told you that the capital was

Bucharest, and I had no idea Dracula came from Romania. So initially I had no idea what the dog situation was in Romania, or that there even was one. It did not take long to discover that it was mostly a bad situation.

There is an argument, maybe it's a poor assumption, but it's one that would explain a number of issues within the public shelters, that their funding comes from the government and much like most other countries, it isn't sufficient to do the job properly. If you then take a portion of this funding to pay people's wages, maybe more than you should, there is less that can be spent on the animals' welfare, food and so on. This, of course, has a negative knock-on effect when it comes to health and hygiene. The public shelters hold a tremendous number of dogs so if you are taking funds away from their care, the effects are sure to be pretty grim.

Are they employing the right people? We are fortunate in the UK and other Western countries that we have a wealth of people who do strongly believe in animal welfare. Our culture imprints on us early on that animals are to be cared for, not used, at least not to the extent they are in other countries, with the depleted levels of welfare that come with it.

So, if there are people employed in Bucharest to work in these animal shelters, the question must be asked – are they appropriate people to work there? Are they just folk that are lucky enough to get employed, but don't give a monkeys about the care of the dogs as long as they get paid? Does this mean that they are happy to cut any corners they can? Not only that, but it appears that the number of staff employed is insufficient to care for the number of dogs under their care.

The dogs in this situation are purely a commodity used to make money. As an individual it makes your blood boil because even if you know it's going on, as an individual how do you make a difference? How do you challenge an entire business in which the majority of people involved are there purely to make a profit? How do you fight an entire state and local/national governance who are happy for this kind of abuse to occur? Thankfully, there is the minority of wonderful people involved in stray dog welfare in Romania who do care, and those are the ones who have made this story possible.

So, how did we get involved? Well, we had become dog rescue people ourselves in our own small way and did our best to give our dogs a life change that meant that they had at least some years of peace and happiness.

Little did we know it then but our next dog was living in dreadful conditions in a supposed shelter in Romania but indeed, she was. In fact she was sleeping on a wooden pallet in dirty conditions, not knowing what was coming, where she was or if she would even get fed. We can only imagine what this dog, soon to be known as Fleur, was going through whilst we, and our two dogs, were sat at home in a warm and caring environment.

Thankfully for Fleur, the first of many guardian angels to grace her life was about to start a chain of events that would change all of our lives.

One of those in that minority of caring people, Eugenia Tudose, lives in a small apartment in Bucharest with her mother. She is a completely selfless soul who, outside of her full-time work as a teacher of children with special needs in Bucharest, visits shelters all over the area taking pictures of the dogs in need and posting them to social media to try and find them new homes.

With this as her canvas and the untold misery and pain the dog had suffered getting there in the first place, as well as the potential threat of who knows what during what may be their final days, Eugenia began her work. As on many other occasions she was trying to get the best photograph possible of a dog that had both gone through hell and was then currently still in a living hell. Eugenia is the original saviour of Fleur, and because of her picture Fleur is the dog she is today.

It was one of these pictures that grabbed the attention of Sabine Hintegger. Sabine is one of those amazing and all too rare people who take dogs from death's door and try to offer them a second chance. Since 2014, Sabine, along with two other individuals, has worked hard to try and find homes for dogs in death camps such as Galati, Bragadiru and Mihailesti as well as taking dogs off the streets to try and find them loving homes. It was Mihailesti that Fleur was discovered.

Fleur was one of these 'lucky' dogs that grabbed Sabine's attention. She immediately spoke to the pension where she fostered her dogs, owned by Ramona Apostol and Radu Serban. The pension, called Pets and Friends, is what we would call a rescue kennels. Ramona started it after spending time volunteering for a Non-Government Organisation campaigning to get sponsors for dogs in Spain. The NGO had no shelters, or pensions, so dogs were distributed all over Bucharest in clinics and all kinds of other pensions. So, Ramona had an idea to make her own pension. This way she could keep a closer eye on all the dogs in her care.

She and Radu took out a loan and then a second loan and spent three years developing and building their pension. It was a complete labour of love, and a huge risk both financially and emotionally. Ramona and Radu built the pension themselves from scratch, but they got there in the end and later were able to move to bigger premises. They now have a staff of seven and care for up to sixty dogs, including a number of disabled dogs that utilise wheels to mobilise themselves.

This was one of the few places that Sabine trusted to care for the dogs she saved, and her trust was well placed. Radu and Ramona made a point of taking the sickest or the most terrified dogs in the shelters, those that have the least likelihood of passing through and into a new home. Their aim was to give those unfortunate dogs a last chance of finding a forever home.

The dedication of both Ramona and Radu, true canine angels, is unprecedented, so much so, that when I visited them to find out more about where Fleur came from, Radu and Ramona collected me from the airport and when I opened the boot to deposit my bag, I was met by the fluffiest little ball of black fur I had ever seen. And then I was met by the most horrendous stink I had ever smelt. It was just as well this little guy was on his way to the vets, as he had oral hygiene issues as well as a swollen tongue and possible jaw structural problems. Even though they were taking time out to pick me up from the airport, Radu and Ramona were still helping dogs in need. No matter how much he stank out the car for their guest.

This little guy may have been saved, but unfortunately for Fleur, the horror she was to go through was just beginning. Before she could be removed from the dog death camp Fleur had to be spayed. In the UK this is one of the most straight forward, uncomplicated and low risk procedures there is. In Romania, the case can be very different due to lack of compassion, poor sanitation and as we said before the cruely of cutting corners simply to keep profit margins high. As we would soon know first-hand, nothing in Fleur's life ever seemed to go the way it was supposed to.

These utterly selfless, completely altruistic individuals, Sabine, Eugenia, Ramona and Radu, are the greatest reason that Fleur and so many other dogs are saved from an end that is unimaginable to us dog lovers. They deserve much more recognition than they get, not that they would agree. According to the Dalai Lama, the root of happiness is altruism – the wish to be of service to others. If this is true, Ramona, Radu, Sabine and Eugenia must be four of the happiest people I have ever met.

And so, on October 22nd 2014 Ramona, armed with a description from a photograph, went to collect the newly spayed Fleur. A tiny, dirty predominantly white dog scrunched up on a pallet when Ramona had arrived. This poor dog had been the victim of a barbaric spay operation, the extent of which would soon present itself. It was a pitiful sight, one that would tear at the heart of any dog lover. Ramona immediately took Fleur to a veterinary practice as it was obvious she was in need of veterinary care. It was here that Ramona took more pictures of Fleur, and it was these that ended up on the Valgrays Rescue Facebook page.

Fleur must have been totally bewildered by another change in her life although she was too ill and feeble to understand what was happening to her. She probably felt too low to even care as she would probably explain.

I knew something wasn't right when I was taken from the cage room. I knew I felt different than ever before. I felt more exhausted than I ever had before, but I also felt wrong. I felt drained and sick, but I had no idea what was happening to me. I knew my abdomen was in intense pain and that there was a smell that every now and then I got a whiff of, but I didn't know what it meant and that scared me. Not only that, but I had no dog to lean on or gain support from. I was on my own surrounded by people I didn't know in an environment I didn't understand. What I wouldn't have given for Shimeka's head across my neck, or the deformed dog's skin against mine through the mesh.

In those first days I just wanted to get out. I wanted to be away from all of this, however that may come about, and be somewhere where I could be alone. As far as I was concerned, if I could get back onto the street I could find somewhere I could be safe. The human that picked me up left me at the new place that smelled of chemicals and I was put into a crate in a much smaller and cleaner cage room than the one I had just been dragged from. By this point I had given up trying to warn humans to stay away. It never worked so I jumped straight to trying to bite. I was in pain, I wasn't feeling right, and I was terrified so the last thing I wanted was people grabbing at me. I had no desire to bite people, I didn't want to bite, but I had no other option. I couldn't run away because I was shut in a small room or in a crate, none of my warning behaviours worked so fight was my only recourse.

And yet, despite the warnings, they still carried on touching me and stabbing me. I hadn't been there long when I was taken into a room that reminded of the place where I experienced the worst pain of my life and where I got my wound. I immediately panicked. A human stabbed something into my leg and very soon I was really sleepy, and everything went black.

When I opened my eyes again I was in my cage on a warm blanket. There was fresh water in the weird silver thing on the floor. That had freaked me out a bit on the first day I was there, but I soon realised it was fine. It just held water, like a puddle. But what hit me first when I woke up in the warm cage was that my abdomen no longer hurt as much. I still didn't feel right, but the pain was less. I looked down and there was still a wound but everything that had been outside was gone and the wound looked clean.

I lay in my kennel, still so tired. I still felt sick, but I did feel more comfortable than I had felt for some time. Then someone else I didn't recognise approached the kennel. No, please just go away. I didn't want anybody near me. I just wanted to be left alone to let whatever might happen, just happen. Whenever someone came near me something bad happened and I couldn't take anything else happening right then. I was barely registering what was around me as it was.

The person opened my cage door. I curled back into as small a ball as I could, automatically protecting my wound and pulling my ears close to my head. Go away, go away, I'm invisible, go away. Then I smelt something. Something meaty and warm. The person held out something brown and sloppy. It smelt delicious, my nose twitched, and I could feel myself begin to salivate but I couldn't move. If I moved I knew something bad would happen, it always did. My hunger was so intense, having barely eaten anything but my own faeces for weeks, but fear and apprehension held me back. A self-survival instinct that overrode my hunger to ensure I didn't put myself into danger.

I turned myself away and closed my eyes. I felt safe enough to let myself sleep, even if I didn't want to leave my safe cage. In there no one could get at me, and if they opened the door I knew I would wake up and could try to fight them off.

I drifted in and out of sleep but never really slept properly. There were

The rescue that had to happen

too many noises, too many comings and goings and I was still on edge, ready to fight or respond to whatever threat appeared and as far as I was concerned pretty much everything was a threat. The one huge benefit was I was getting food. The shiny bowl thing would appear twice a day and I would be able to eat, so the hunger pains were reducing.

Then the bowl would come, but the person that brought it would stay. They would take some of the food and hold it out to me, as they had when I first arrived and, as I had when I first arrived, I remained at the back of the cage, refusing to move forwards. Hands equalled pain, no matter how good the smell was from what they held.

When I didn't move the hand would throw the food towards me. Initially this would make me flinch as I fully expected the hand to strike me or throw something at me that would hurt. But then I got to eat something. Then the hand would throw some more food towards me, and I got to eat. I still steadfastly wouldn't move from my spot, but I uncurled slightly and moved my head forwards to grab the food. Again, the hand threw food, and I leant forward to grab it.

Later that day, the hand came back with more food. This time, I felt a little pang of excitement, it was small, but it was there. As the door opened the fear rose again, but a tiny part of me expected food. And, as before, the hand would hold out food to me. Nope. I wasn't ready to move out of my spot, but I raised my ears a little and leaned my head forwards ready, anticipating the meaty morsel. Just like it had before, food came. The hand threw the food towards me and I leant forwards to get it. Oh, it tasted good. So much better than what I had been feasting on in recent weeks.

The hand would keep coming back and each time it would provide food. Then the food started to get a bit further away. The hand wouldn't throw it as far into the cage. I wanted that food, I really did, but what if I moved forward and the catcher's pole came around my neck and I was dragged out of my safe cage again and back to the dirty cage room, or back onto the cold streets?

That food was so good though. I could smell it. I could almost feel it in my mouth, I could almost taste it. I didn't want those hunger pains to come back again, I was still feeling bad enough without those coming back. So slowly, carefully, I edged my head forward. But I couldn't quite reach without moving my whole body forward slightly. I really didn't want to give up my safe space. I didn't want to move from the back of the cage. If I could feel the cage bars against my skin, I felt safe. The smell met my nose again. It really did smell good. I moved further forward but my skin left the cage bars and I shot back. No. I needed to stay attached to the back of the crate.

A finger from the hand pushed the food forward a little. I couldn't resist, I shot forwards and pulled the meat back to my safe space. It tasted so good, and nothing bad had happened. I hadn't been hurt, the pole wasn't around my neck and I was still in my cage. I looked back up and another piece of food landed in the same spot. I had to move to get it. Slowly I did. I stayed low to the floor, ready to fight or dart back to the back of the cage, but I got to the food and enjoyed every bite, whilst still being very aware of any movement around me. As I was chewing, another piece landed. I ate that without moving back to my safe space. Then another. And another. Soon the silver thing was empty, and the hand closed the crate door and left. I moved back to my usual spot. I was safe. I wasn't injured or scared (more than I already was, at least). Maybe the hand didn't automatically mean something painful or scary was going to happen.

The next time the hand appeared, I moved forward automatically. I knew what was coming this time. However, this time the food didn't land in front of me. It stayed in the hand which reached into the cage. This I wasn't sure of, I had no experience to draw from like I did with food on the cage floor. I knew if the food landed on the floor, it was safe to eat it. But doing that meant I didn't have to go near the hand, specifically not within grasping distance. Taking the food from the hand opened up other opportunities for pain, hurt, fear and stress. I moved hesitantly forward but stopped. This didn't feel safe.

The hand dropped the food but remained near it. It didn't pull back to allow me to eat like it had before. I inched forward slowly, not taking my eyes from the hand which remained still. I took the food and backed away a little to eat it. Once again, nothing happened. I was fine. The hand held the food out again and I gently took the food from the hand and retreated quickly to the back of the cage to finish it. The hand didn't follow me, it hadn't grabbed out for me as had happened so many times in the past. The hand stretched out again and I took the food from it. Maybe hands didn't always mean that I would get hurt, or dragged, or thrown. Maybe hands

The rescue that had to happen

and people could bring things that were nice, and tasty.

I lay in my cage that night and for the first time in a long time I was warm, I wasn't starving and although I was in pain and felt weird and sick, I wasn't completely terrified. I wondered how the deformed dog was. She wouldn't be warm, she would definitely be starving, and she would undoubtedly be terrified. Maybe another dog had gone into my kennel and they had bonded as we had. I hoped so. I missed feeling her warmth next to my fur as I lay there. There were no dogs in cages surrounding me in the clean cage room. Just me.

The next day when the hand and the human came to my kennel I didn't feel quite as scared as usual, expecting to be given more food. But I wasn't, instead when I moved forward expectantly a lead was placed around my neck and I was taken out of the room. No. No, I didn't want to go anywhere. I felt the safest I had felt in weeks, months, and now it was being torn away from me and I was being taken somewhere else I had no idea about or experience of. I initially panicked that I was going back to the streets, or worse the dirty cage room. Despite my internal panic I was too weak to put up a fight. I was stumbling as I walked I was so weak. I ended up in another room, in another cage.

This room was smaller and with much fewer cages. It smelled heavily of chemicals and the humans wore different clothes in this room. They put them on when they came in and took them off when they left. I was angry with myself as I found a spot at the back of this new cage. I had let my guard down and trusted the people who appeared to be making me feel better only to be moved into yet another new place with no idea what was happening.

I crawled back to the back of my cage and tried to make myself as small as I could. I had learned my lesson not to trust so easily, because contact with humans only ever led to one thing and it wasn't pleasurable. So, in that new room all alone as far as I was concerned, I stayed at the back of my cage. When the hand next returned with food there was no way I was moving from my spot. Despite the hand throwing food down, even close to my spot, I refused to move. I ate once the human had left the room and not before. I wasn't making the same mistake twice.

It was warm, and I felt relatively safe as long as I was inside the cage and the pain had diminished, although I still felt horrible. Much as I had in the dirty cage room, I resigned myself to the fact that this was my life now. Or was it? I had no idea, but it was easier just to lie down and let it happen. I didn't have the strength to do much else. I didn't really care very much anyway.

While Fleur was experiencing these things there were other events going on in the Morris household and there was a very significant date, as Wendy recalled.

October 22nd 2014 was a significant date in our household, as well as for Fleur over in Romania. It was a Wednesday evening, much like any other Wednesday night in the Morris household. Both myself and Andrew had returned from work. I had just finished my Nurse Prescribing course, which had freed up my evenings from researching and reading articles for my course and had allowed me time to reconnect with social media.

The nights had begun to draw in and the leaves were beginning to change as we took Nero and Marti out on their evening walks. This night was no different as we returned home from a typical walk. We settled down for the evening, me on the sofa while, as usual, Andrew chose to sit on the floor with the dogs. He groomed Nero as Marti sat next to them.

I spend a lot of my time apologising to guests for Andrew choosing to sit on the floor rather than at a more sociable level, or at least eye level with friends and family. The fact of the matter is, Andrew feels more comfortable on the floor. He feels closer to the world that he prefers, that world being inhabited by Nero and Marti. He will sit in the meadow for hours cuddling the dogs if the weather allows, and he can also disappear for hours only to be found lying on the recreation ground with the dog. Maybe it's something about safety, or experienced comfortability.

So, there I sat, behind Andrew and the dogs browsing Facebook groups trying to find the perfect four paws to add to our current menagerie of two dogs and ninja cat. As I browsed through the Valgrays Facebook page a picture caught my attention. A small white dog curled up into the tightest ball I've ever seen underneath a plastic chair. This ball of fur was obviously terrified as she faced away towards the wall, lying on a cold tiled floor. It was Fleur.

Something about this picture drew me in. There was something there that I connected to. Something that cried out to me and I knew I needed to try and help this poor little dog. I delved further into social media to see if I could dig up anything else. I found more images of her lying in the back of the car, dirty and lying on a plastic sheet.

Everything within me wanted to help this little girl. To bring her home and cuddle her, make sure she was safe and cared for. To give her that warm forever-after home that she deserved. It was instant attraction. Love at first sight.

And then came the shock. A sharp intake of breath at the image on the screen. I stared at a photo of Fleur, small and frail, with her intestines on the outside. It was horrific, I could hardly believe what I was seeing. I had to turn away and I went back to the other pictures, but I couldn't shake that image, that hideous, unforgettable image of a poor, defenceless dog that had been butchered by people who were supposed to care for her.

I handed the computer to Andrew and quietly said, "I want this baby…"

Andrew's response was almost instant when he saw the image.

"Do it!"

Chapter Four

IT WAS NOT THAT SIMPLE

~ • ~

ANDREW AND WENDY were instantly resolved that they had to do something for that little dog that was not even in their own country. The strength of that resolve becomes apparent as the story unfolds. They did not take their time to consider the matter, They instantly sprung into action as Wendy recalled.

I immediately messaged Val at Valgrays telling her that both myself and Andrew were hoping and praying that Fleur pulled through and, if she did, that we would like to be considered to give her a happily-ever-after home. Having got Marti from Valgrays, who had turned into such an adorable princess and a successful adoption and knowing that every day we had with her was a blessing, we wanted to be able to offer that to another dog in need, and if ever a dog was in need of a safe home, it was Fleur.

The response from Val was immediate, and it marked the start of a journey that we had no idea we were about to take. Val seemed happy for us to take on Fleur, I was surprised that nobody else had shown an interest. This was very quickly replaced with excitement. I did think that it was a quick yes, but Andrew pointed out that Val knew we were good owners because of our experience with Marti.

Then suddenly reality hit. We were going to have three dogs! Three! How much harder could this be than two? Three dogs meant no more holidays abroad, which I could live with. We could always holiday in the UK with the dogs. Marti was hard work when we got her, it couldn't be any more difficult than that, right? We had friends with four dogs and they managed. Michelle had three dogs and managed. It would be fine. Right?

In the meantime, I was happy and excited and was consistently showing off the picture of my new dog to anyone that would look like it was a picture of my new grandchild. Look at my new baby girl, isn't she pretty whilst I flaunted a picture of a dirty, scared dog you could hardly see. They must've thought I was mad. My parents certainly did. They made it clear they thought we were making a poor life choice, but I knew I could make her happy and keep her safe.

Val stated it was now essentially a waiting game to see if Fleur would make it. Everybody had fingers, toes and paws crossed that this beautiful little girl would have the strength to make it.

Waiting for news became a daily task. There soon became a daily routine of checking Facebook pages, messenger and the relief that came from there being no updates. No news was good news. At least that was my thought process. It progressed to the point that I was checking twice a day, morning and evening, and then I began to check at lunch times, and soon I was checking before bed and waking up at night to check.

When we heard Fleur had contracted an infection following her spay, I genuinely believed that that was it. She was ill and weak. I honestly thought she wasn't going to make it. That we would never get to meet Fleur and that the next message we would get would be that she passed away in her sleep, or that she had been put to sleep.

Fleur's eyes were red and swollen where the infection had taken hold. Andrew kept reiterating to me that we shouldn't be surprised if Fleur didn't make it. He saw a dullness in her eyes that he said often comes with problems, even potentially blindness.

We waited with baited breath for news, and it didn't take long. Sadly it was both good and bad news. Two days after our original message Val replied to tell us that Fleur was holding her own, however the journey to the UK may not be possible. Val explained that there was a potential home for Fleur in Germany which would obviously be a much easier journey for Fleur to endure. So, for the sake of Fleur's health and wellbeing Valgrays had stepped down, and in turn so had we.

I was devastated at the news that we weren't getting Fleur. Over the previous weeks, as days had passed I had felt my bond with Fleur grow. All I wanted was to bring my girl home, and now I found out she was no longer my girl. Social media had taken over my life, checking and

It was not that simple

spending hours looking for updates, and now I felt as if my heart had been ripped out. After all that time and effort, I felt as if I was grieving for a dog I had never met. And what should I tell everyone? Will they think we pulled out of saving her? Nothing could be further from the truth.

We were deeply disappointed, but we understood the decision. Andrew and I discussed it and he pointed out it may be for the best given Fleur's health, given how much closer Germany is to Romania than Hampshire in England. And hopefully we could still keep up to date with Fleur's progress via the social media updates.

Still upset, our mission to find the newest Morris fur-baby continued. Not only was the image of Fleur ingrained on my brain, but our needs were quite specific both on terms of Marti's health needs and Nero's aversion to younger dogs. Nothing in this story was ever straight forward.

Val kept in contact, offering us a number of the beautiful dogs she had in her care at Valgrays, but I just couldn't shake off that image of Fleur curled up under the chair. What could happen to a dog to make them so scared that they curl up under a chair when they should be out playing, enjoying life, running in grass, barking at birds and chasing squirrels?

Then the image of Fleur sitting on the plastic sheet on the back seat of Ramona's car would come into my head. Seeing a dog so terrified and abused at the hands of people that she should've been able to trust absolutely broke my heart. She looked so sad, so depressed and scared with her tail buried under body and her ears back against her head. This reminded me so much of Marti. She too came from a shelter and had survived living off other dogs' faeces. I had seen her flourish from a timid, scared dog with those dark, lifeless eyes into a princess who occasionally barked with glee. She grew into a happy, thankful, loving bouncing dog and I knew that Fleur could be the same. I wanted to give her that, and now I couldn't and that broke my heart. I told Val that if the situation with Fleur changed our offer would still stand.

The offers of other dogs continued to come in, but we had to turn them down. Due to Nero's epilepsy we couldn't re-home a dog under two, he just couldn't cope with puppies bouncing in his face. Whilst Marti may have run circles around him, she never got in his face, so it worked. Val would offer us the opportunity to foster various dogs and my immediate response had to be, "Sorry, no. Too young."

I also knew that if we fostered a dog we would form a bond and not be able to give it back. I didn't even show Andrew half of the messages as I knew they would be unsuitable. I knew Fleur would be suitable, she was older and would fit into our family and as that had fallen through I had closed the door on bringing another dog into the family. I had set my heart on Fleur and I still thought that if it was meant to be, it would be. Maybe Germany would fall through, and she would come into rescue again. I couldn't replace her with another dog, and that's what it felt like I was doing.

It was winter now and we decided to wait until Spring to find another dog. We knew we would want to bring another dog into the house, but Fleur had taken over so much without even being here we needed time to recalibrate.

And then came the message we had been waiting for. Val messaged me to say that Valgrays had now been chosen over Germany and it was all back on. Fleur had been reserved to us. The road to Fleur had already felt like a bumpy one, and it was soon to turn into a roller coaster. And little did we know that Val's words, "they had chosen Valgrays over Germany" had much more depth to it than any of us were aware.

Andrew, of course, was equally sharing this roller-coaster ride to adopt the little dog.

I have had a mobile phone for many, many years and have also kept the same telephone number, though if you put a gun to my head and asked me to recite my phone number in order to live, I'd be a dead man. Absolutely no idea. But isn't the world of social media a revelation? The ability to connect with people the world over at the touch of a button, and with the growth of smart phones we can do this anywhere we are, assuming you have signal, of course.

This is exactly the reason why I was so late to the party in regard to social media. I spent the majority of my adult life in a world where this kind of communication wasn't feasible. Working in the army, serving in active duty means spending a lot of time at work so Tweeting, Insta-ing or Whatsapping just isn't as straight forward as it is in the civilian world.

I only really started using social media once our journey with Fleur began and I had absolutely no idea about posting or any concerns regarding privacy or privacy settings so everything that was posted onto Fleur's FaceBook page was public and quite frankly, had I not been married and wanted to run off to another country and live a much seedier lifestyle all

I had to do was look through the posts on her page. Anyone and everyone was posting their wares on there, so that was quickly changed.

Of course, it comes with its issues. A common one being the ease of confusion and misunderstanding. This in particular happens with people posting their opinions and you then getting involved with a counter argument. This can sap hours from your life, hours. It takes practice to be able to distance yourself and train yourself not to respond, especially when it is something you are passionate about. I'm jumping ahead, and thankfully, in terms of my experience, there haven't been too many weird and wonderful occurrences, however social media was to cause an issue that we weren't to find out about until later.

This was the next bump in the road to Fleur. It was not one we encountered, but Val and Ramona did. Apparently, as we now understand it, whilst we were happily sat at home waiting for Fleur to recover enough to come over to the UK there was a whole conversation occurring via social media about how Sabine had assumed Fleur was going to Germany, and no one had told her about Fleur going to the UK.

This caused confusion and both sides had to navigate their way through this two-dimensional communication. As far as Sabine was concerned Fleur was her dog, coming to her in Germany and, understandably, she didn't want to give her up. On the flip side, Val assumed Fleur was coming to her. In the middle was Ramona and two other people to try and mediate.

It took two nights, but eventually everything was straightened out. The upshot being, Fleur nearly didn't get to come to us at all. As would prove to be the case, getting Fleur into our home was to be met by constant setbacks and hurdles. She nearly went to Germany, and this story would be over before it really even started. However, much like us at this time, Fleur had no idea this was going on.

Once Ramona had removed Fleur from the public shelter, she had been taken immediately to a vet where she received the treatment she needed. It's difficult to imagine how Fleur must've felt at this time. How can we really ever know what an animal that cannot communicate through words is ever thinking? I sometimes wonder if a dog knows what death actually is, or how close they are to it at certain points in her life. There was no way Fleur could know she was being saved.

During that first trip in the car Fleur must've been terrified, as well as probably constantly hoping for an escape route having been confined to a cage for so long. We naturally humanise other animals' actions and thoughts, which is what I do when I think of Fleur in that car. I would be looking to survive, I would be looking to escape.

I remember looking at those first photographs of Fleur in the shelter and all I could see was a dog saying; "kill me." Those sad eyes that just said; "If this is what life is, take it away from me now please." We always talk about Fleur as a fighter but at that time, in that shelter Fleur had no fight left at all. When these dogs are taken from those shelters the person rescuing them doesn't go in gently and take the dog out, whispering that everything will be OK and reassuring the dog. The rescuer waits outside whilst somebody else goes in and gets the dog on the end of a catching pole which goes around the next and the dog is dragged out and pushed into a crate.

Given how Fleur's eyes were in those photographs, to then be dragged out of the kennel by her neck and pushed into a crate must have been horrific. Maybe she had just completely shut down by this point and was away in her own bubble. That would probably be the kindest and most humane option, but unfortunately, I doubt it. Add to that the physical pain she must have been in, given what we were about to find out and it brings to mind watching people at the Tower of London being tortured. Right now, being dragged from her kennel, Fleur was being tortured and I cannot bear that thought.

She was then handed to Ramona, but she still had no idea that she was safe. Once under the control of Ramona she was taken to the vets and this was where she was under the care of Alina Stan at MediVet. I have already mentioned the guardian angels that graced Fleur's life, especially in those early months, and Alina is most definitely in that category. Without her, Fleur wouldn't be here today.

Alina has her own shelter where she rescues dogs, as well as managing the veterinary clinic. Every day of her life she is involved in saving animals and improving both their health and welfare, and she was instrumental in ensuring Fleur survived those first weeks after leaving the public shelter in that abhorrent condition.

Fleur arrived at the clinic a tiny white bag of bones, terrified of everything around her. Fleur was seeing a whole new world for the first time. No one really knows what happened to Fleur prior to her entrance into the public shelter but the assumption is that she was a street dog and as such would have had no experience of veterinary treatment or procedures. Everything with which she now came into contact was new and it terrified her. Every new sound, every new movement was met with terror.

Fleur spent the next few days in the treatment room. Heaven only knows how scared and anxious she must have been, locked in a strange, away from a life on the streets that she at least knew and understood into a world of change and interference.

There is a natural assumption that taking a dog off the street and giving them shelter is improving their welfare, but what is often overlooked is that that dog is being torn from a world that is potentially all they have ever known. From an outside perspective they are being saved, but for all we know that is a life they are content with. It's a comfort zone.

Dogs have been born in the wild for as long as there have been dogs, so if a dog is born in the wild, or as a street dog, then I have no doubt that that is the life they are comfortable with. Whether they enjoy that life or not is a different question. However, taking a dog from that situation and putting it into a situation that is possibly worse is an ethical conundrum.

Yet, what we can do, and should strive to do, is to take these dogs from an unsavoury environment where they may have stones thrown at them, be beaten with sticks and have people trying to run them over and get them into homes where they can thrive.

The potential issue then is these dogs going into homes where they are not taught or shown how to adapt and are unsuitable for dogs coming from this environment. Homes where they are not given what they need to re-calibrate to this new life. In these situations, maybe a life on the streets where they have an escape and they have knowledge of what is going on is better? There are arguments on both sides of course, arguments that I understand and could argue for from both sides.

Whatever the case for Fleur, the reality was she had been taken, put into a rescue centre, subjected to horrendous living conditions and was now in a veterinary clinic due to the actions of humans. For every angel such as Sabine, there is a devil waiting to counteract their kindness.

It was during this stay in the treatment room that Fleur was hit with yet another blow. She tested positive for distemper. In hindsight Fleur had probably contracted distemper after her horrendous spay operation, and it explained the illness that I saw in her eyes in those initial photographs where I knew something was wrong. With her intestines outside a semi open wound and surrounded by urine from dogs that were probably carrying distemper what chance did she have?. Given how poor Fleur's health was already, this was the last thing she needed.

She was moved to the section for infectious dogs which was, of course, yet another new and intimidating environment for a dog that was already terrified. There was no way for anyone to explain to her that it was for the best, that it would be worth it in the end when she was better and in a new home. And Fleur couldn't explain how she felt. If social media caused confusion in communication, it was nothing compared to the communication between human and Fleur.

She did have one ace up her sleeve, when it came to communication. According to Alina, she bit a number of times during those first days. She was terrified and was being subjected to a myriad of new experiences, many that caused pain such as injections and the application of an IV drip. It's hardly surprising that her response was to bite.

Dogs, along with all animals, have a natural set of responses to situations that they deem to be threatening or aversive stimuli that evoke a fear or anxiety-based response. It's the fight or flight response. Now imagine a dog used to open spaces and the ability to run or hide placed into a confined room with no escape options. This was Fleur. Her flight option had been eliminated, so she used fight.

The staff at the veterinary clinic began hand feeding her, a bid to improve her trust in us and change her perceptions of the staff from negative to a positive. As the days passed Fleur began to take the food and she became more comfortable with the staff – the power of food.

From one of the early pictures I had noticed bleakness, dullness to Fleur's eyes that I felt beheld an underlying problem and when Wendy read the update on the Valgrays Facebook about Fleur's distemper, my fears were upheld. We both read the update with trepidation. We knew distemper was deadly. In the UK if a dog contracts the disease they are put to sleep, there is no other option, but we had no idea what it entailed, having never encountered it before.

For Fleur, contracting distemper was a particular risk because she was immuno-compromised. In ordinary circumstances Fleur would have a fifty percent chance of survival in Romania if she was treated, according to Alina. However, because of her spay and then abdominal surgery Fleur was in a compromised position and her chances of survival were diminished. Of course, the fact she was being treated at all upped her chances of survival from zero to fifty percent, thanks to Alina and Medivet.

Distemper is related to measles in humans, and in Romania they used the same medicine used for humans but adjusted to use with dogs so that it weakens the virus. A treatment was developed that includes high immune stimulation along with a lot of vitamins. There is a hyper-immune serum that can be used and human immune system stimulants, as well as a range of antibiotics. This treatment is long and complicated, but it seems to be successful in seventy percent of dogs treated.

Fleur's treatment was difficult, because of her past. It was obvious to the veterinary staff that Fleur was not domesticated. She had no idea what a food bowl was and was terrified of everything. During her time in the clinic she stayed in a crate, which seemed to suit Fleur. It was a small place where she could feel secure, potentially a reminder of a secure place she had whilst on the streets. Alina told us in those early days Fleur would have crawled under the ground if it was possible, such was her fear and anxiety about her new surroundings.

Fleur stayed at the clinic for three or four weeks before being released to Ramona, so that she had space to exercise and mobilise herself. Of course, back in Hampshire we had no way of seeing how Fleur was doing, other than relying on the updates via the Valgrays Facebook page and messages from Val.

Wendy was very keen to follow the Facebook posts from both Alina and Ramona and on a number of occasions she would say, "Oh, look at this picture of Fleur, isn't she doing well?" I would look at the photo and think, "Are we looking at the same dog?" There would be a number of comments about how she looked well and as if she was improving and I would look at the picture and think I was looking at a dead dog. This was a dog that was on her way out. Especially when looking into the right eye and taking in the pigmentation and colouring, all I could think was, "Oh my days, this dog has got just days to live."

We had always said that we would provide support for Fleur to make it to the UK and when she got here would give her all the support she needed but I honestly did not expect her to survive the medical procedures she was going through. Every time I looked into her eyes in the pictures that were being shared I just couldn't see how she could pull through.

I had remained objective in my understanding that there was every chance Fleur may not make it to us, especially after seeing the pictures of her, but hearing of her contracting distemper made us both realise that actually, maybe Fleur really wouldn't make it to the UK and we would have to start looking all over again, knowing how close we were to changing this poor dog's life. But Fleur is a fighter, we just didn't know at that time how much of a fighter she was, perhaps she didn't know herself.

Chapter Five

WILL FLEUR MAKE IT?

~ • ~

WHEN WENDY HEARD the word 'distemper' she admits that it came as a shock and a huge disappointment. She felt even more that she wanted to be there for Fleur but also felt quite helpless.

Of course, the first thing I did when I read about Fleur's distemper was to utilise Google. I needed to understand more about distemper and what it entailed. Up until this point distemper was a word with no substance, how bad could it be? I soon faced the harsh reality –

'Distemper is a viral disease which affects the gastrointestinal respiratory and central nervous system'.

Oh.

'The canine distemper virus causes the disease. It is highly contagious and is often fatal'.

My first concern was how contagious it would be to Marti and Nero, it had never occurred to me that humans could catch it until someone asked me if we could. And the answer was yes, we could but if they have had the measles vaccine they were also vaccinated against CDV and we were all up to date with our immunisations.

My main concern, however, was our grandchildren. I knew routine cleaning would minimise any threat of contamination. I'm a nurse, so I swear by Dettol and clean my carpets with it every day, and my wooden floors daily. On top of that, I knew that they wouldn't allow a dog with an infectious disease to travel, so I was happy to wait as long as it took for her to be well enough to travel.

Despite this, the internet is a minefield of misinformation, and the worst place to go to if you are trying not to raise your anxiety levels. This was no different and my dreams of rescuing Fleur were becoming less and less of a possibility. That was until we received a message from Val on the November 8th.

'Hi Wendy,
Fleur is holding her own and it looks like we will be getting her mid-December. How are you fixed for this? She is going back into private foster so all being well she will be able to travel. We are now sorting out her passport etc.'

How was I fixed? Was this a trick question? Having resigned ourselves to the possibility that Fleur may never be coming to share Morris Manor with Nero and Marti, this was music to my ears, or eyes, as I was reading it on a screen. I couldn't wait to get her home and give her all the TLC she deserved.

This felt like the perfect Christmas present. All I wanted was to have Fleur home with us, so we could have a true family Christmas. We both took time off in December so that we could settle Fleur in and bond with her. We had been waiting for her since October, and as it had been so on and off we breathed a huge sigh of relief that it was actually happening. We had the time and patience to ensure Fleur could adapt to our home, to Marti and to Nero. It felt good. It felt right.

It was at this juncture that we found out something else; something that would change the course of our journey. Fleur's story was being followed and documented by the magazine Dogs Today. Val had only been told that week that the monthly dog magazine would be following Fleur's story from the shelter through until she was in her new home. Her story had been picked from a number of others to be featured.

We were more interested in getting Fleur home and making sure she was healthy enough to come home so Dogs Today actually had a story to write, and we were more focused on Fleur's introduction to our home. I had never read Dogs Today or Dogs Monthly and had always relied on

Andrew for dog knowledge, so I had little idea how much difference the following from the Dogs Today magazine would make.

We were both starting from the beginning with Fleur, a jump into the unknown. Fleur was starting a new chapter in her life, going from street dog to part of an existing household and it was our job to ensure that new chapter started as smoothly as possible.

Little did we know that elsewhere in the world of the internet Dogs Today Editor Beverley Cuddy had seen pictures of Fleur on the newsfeed on her Facebook page. Everything always comes back to Facebook From here, Beverley shared the story on the Dogs Today Facebook page The photographs of Fleur sad and depressed in Romania had broken Beverley's heart, much as they had done with us, and she felt compelled to share the story.

. Through Beverley, Fleur had become a poster dog for all the dogs that suffer in Romania. For all of the dogs that are injected with paint because it's cheaper than the medical alternative, and all of the dogs whose water and food are withheld in the days leading up to their euthanasia because it's seen as a waste of money. The public had begun to follow the story, and much like Beverley, they were checking for updates daily, and this is when Beverley decided to write up Fleur's journey.

Our focus wasn't on Dogs Today but on getting Fleur home but anything that aided that was fine by us. And so, Fleur was due to be with us in a few weeks, her story would be featured in a national magazine and from a rough start, and a battle for her life, she would settle into a content and secure future in Hampshire. When is life ever that straight forward?

Christmas came and went, and the New Year passed us by without an extra four paws in our home. Both Marti and Nero got more bear hugs during December. They got more cuddles and kisses and instances of telling them they were the best. My bond with Marti grew stronger. I would look at her with so much love and pride that she had become my princess. I was always so grateful for the time we had together, and she made me smile so much.

I knew our time was limited and I put so much love into Marti so that if Fleur was the first to die, I wouldn't feel as bad. By funnelling my emotions into loving Marti, I avoided thinking about the potential passing of Fleur. I hadn't experienced losing a pet yet, and as I couldn't physically love Fleur, I put that into Marti and Nero. By walking their favourite walks and generally spending time with them I could distract myself from thoughts of Fleur.

And, my goodness, some of those walks with Marti and Nero could offer great distraction. One very cold October day, I woke early and arranged with a friend to walk Nero and Marti in the nearby old dell woods. The walk took about an hour and a half, which was enough time to get home, shower, and get to work. At one point I did question if this was an appropriate walk, given the heavy winds and falling trees.

Nevertheless, we ended up in the woods. Both dogs were off lead, so they could run around freely and chase squirrels, deer or whatever other scent their sensitive noses picked up. It was always wonderful to see them enjoy their environment, to explore and be free, especially for Marti who had come from such a distressing background.

This was a daily routine and the dogs never went out of eyesight and always came back when called. But for whatever reason, today was special. Today was different. Maybe it was the winds blowing a buffet of scents across the path, but Nero was off.

Marti followed, as per, but she came back when called. Nero, however, did not. He vanished into the woods following a particularly enthralling scent. Thankfully I was with Paula, so we had four eyes and four legs to utilise. I stayed still and called out for Nero, in case Nero returned to the point of vanishing, whilst Paula head off into the woods.

I called and called but nothing. Paula returned from her woodland tour but no Nero. Time was beginning to press on and I was getting increasingly agitated. Andrew was away, I hadn't brought my mobile phone, so I couldn't call him. I was crying and emotional. Where was my boy? What if something had happened to him? What if he had found his way to a road? I didn't know what to do and I had all these terrible thoughts running through my head, so we ran home.

By the time we got home Nero had been missing for two hours. Anything could have happened in that time. Andrew was going to be so upset. How could I tell him I had lost his dog? The bond between them was so strong. I checked my phone and – thank goodness – there was a message. Maybe someone had found him and got my number from his tag. He was safe.

Alas, no. It was the dog warden leaving me a snotty message. He had found my dog and I had thirty minutes to collect him, or he was going to the pound. What?! Nero would not cope with the pound and my husband would not cope with his dog going to the pound.

The thirty-minute window had already lapsed, so I quickly called the number, my hackles already up. I tried to explain that I had been looking desperately for Nero, which is why it took me so long to respond to his message. Thankfully, he agreed to wait for us in Four Marks. I had fifteen minutes to collect him. It was all systems go as I made my way as quickly as I could to the meeting point.

There, in broad daylight was the dog warden's van, back door open, displaying the cages. In one of those cages was Nero, staring out at me. The tears came quickly as I saw him sat in that cage, it was like seeing a loved one in a prison cell.

I flooded the dog warden with apologies as tears streamed down my face and he took pity on me. He gave me the paper work to sign to release Nero, along with a ten minute lecture on how to look after my dog. As I put Nero into my car, I plucked up the courage to ask the dog warden where he found Nero.

As it turns out, Nero had had a great time whilst I was going out of my mind. After chasing whatever the scent was, he had chased a deer and then found himself five miles away in the local primary school. By some stroke of luck, a neighbour's child recognised Nero and fed him sweets through the gate whilst talking to him. This had in turn led to Nero barking at the school gate to elicit more goodies. A teacher heard the noise and Nero ended up in their office being fed crisps and biscuits by students to keep him quiet whilst they called me, to no avail, and then the dog warden.

So, despite running away and sending me into a mental breakdown, Nero had had a month's worth of treats and attention in one afternoon. Andrew returned home, and I recounted the day's events to him. The next day he went to the school with some 'thank you sweets'.

As we had for the entirety of December, we were waiting for the ping of a message that would hold the information for which we were so eagerly waiting. When would our Fleur be coming home? On the 5th January 2015 I started a new job, which in hindsight may well have been kismet. The new job meant my working hours were reduced so I had more free time, and on December 8th we got a message from Val:

'Hi Wendy,

Just to update you all is going very well with Fleur. She will be arriving in the UK on the 24th January, so looking at you taking her pretty much ASAP so that she doesn't get settled here. You will be getting the press following her story'

We had completely forgotten that Dogs Today were publishing Fleur's story. Life, as it usually does, got in the way and our focus had remained on Fleur and our current household. Andrew contacted Dogs Today and requested a copy of the magazine, and to set up a subscription for future issues (which continues to this day).

That first article was on one of the back pages, titled 'Rescue Mission'.

Rescue Mission

Valgray's Border Collie and Animal Rescue is a small charity based in Surrey that works hard to rescue and re-home as many homeless dogs as possible. It was dedicated to helping Romanian shelter dogs in desperate need.

As part of our in-depth look at rescue world, we will be following a homeless dog's journey to finding a forever home. Our first case is Fleur, a Romanian street dog, who is being cared for by Valgray's Border Collie and Animal Rescue.

Last October, Valgray's was asked to help the plight of a little dog named Fleur, a Romanian stray caught by dog catchers, dragged along on poles and thrown in to the Mihailesti Shelter in Bucharest. After being barbarically spayed, she was left at the shelter to live on a pallet. Pictures sent to Valgray's showed she needed urgent medical attention, as her intestines were hanging out!

Val Philips, founder of Valgray's, instructed her contacts in Romania to get Fleur out of the shelter as soon as possible, and she was rushed to the vets immediately after her release.

"We were horrified at the state she was in," recalls Val. "She had a very high temperature and was totally terrified of everyone to the point that she would fight and bite as if her life depended on it".

Fleur's stomach was operated on and she underwent a number of tests, one of them being for distemper, which thankfully came back negative.

Once in the care of helper Ramona Apostol, this furry little fighter seemed brighter. She started to eat and taking an interest in her surroundings. However, just when it was thought she was making headway and plans were being made to bring her back to the UK. Fleur's health suddenly went downhill.

She was put on a drip at the vets and given antibiotics to reduce her temperature, but then came the worst possible news: she had tested positive for distemper, a serious viral illness affecting the respiratory gastrointestinal and central nervous systems.

Val explains, "We were asked if she still wanted to help Fleur but giving up now was not an option. Even if it meant me going to sing on street corners, we were going to support this wonderful dog who just needed a chance.

"I know many people will question why we help these dogs when so many in the UK are in need, but in this country we have lots of rescues and generally good veterinary care – we do not throw dogs into pounds and let them starve to death. "I have been on both sides of rescue, being a vet nurse for number of years and also running Valgrays since the 70's and I think I have seen most cases of cruelty possible, but when you go to these other countries that do not care about the welfare of animals, then that is another story, and if we can help a few, we will, it gives us such pleasure to see a rehab dog come back to life and these Rommie dogs are so grateful".

The article ended with a stop press:

As we go to press, Fleur is still fighting for her life. This little dog so wants to live, and we are all praying for her recovery. (Fighting infection from the barbaric spay).

Reading through this article and looking at the accompanying photos was harrowing. Of course, we already knew the story, and had seen the images. Val had been fantastic at keeping us up to date with Fleur's progress whilst she was in Romania and we were certain we understood what we were taking on, yet to see 'our' rescue dogs story in print in a national magazine and to see her plight certainly gave us a wake-up call. Not that we really needed one.

In her short life Fleur had diced with death on at least two occasions, as far as we were aware. This didn't include the time she spent pre-shelter, which we have no idea about but can only assume and imagine what happened to her. Then came her traumatic and cruel capture before spending an unknown amount of time in the horrendous public shelter.

Now she had a glimmer of hope. An opportunity of security and love, and that opportunity lay with us. D Day was nearly upon us… No pressure!

Andrew, of course, was sharing that pressure and constantly on the watch for the latest bulletin although he was aware that life had to go on in the meantime.

Once released to Pets and Friends with Ramona, Fleur was able to have more freedom. She could spend time with other dogs and the freedom allowed her personality to come out more than it had before.

During her time at the vets, and whilst we were waiting for Fleur to be well enough to be booked onto the transport to the UK I didn't actually spend much time thinking about it, to be honest. I had already set my mind to the fact Fleur wouldn't be coming in to the country, that she would die in Romania, so it wasn't really a difficult time for me. It's not that I didn't care, of course I did, and it probably irritated Wendy how pessimistic I was being, but I was aware of all of the factors that could prevent Fleur from coming to the UK and into our home, the main one being she had to get from a country in Eastern Europe to the UK.

At this point I had no idea how prevalent it was for dogs to be transported like this, I had a naivety into the whole plight of dogs in Romania, and with very little research into it at the time I saw it as a one off long shot.

I knew that if she did arrive, things would change. I told Nero and Marti to suck it up because soon there was going to be a whirlwind of upset crossing the threshold and boy, were things going to change but my over-riding thought was that it would never happen. My biggest concern at this time was Wendy and how she would react if Fleur didn't make it to the UK. She had already bonded with Fleur and her story, whereas I hadn't. Of course, it would be sad and disappointing to hear of the passing of any dog, but I didn't have the attachment that Wendy already had. I honestly don't believe there was a time, regardless of how poor Fleur's prognosis was or how heart-breaking the pictures were that came through of Fleur, that she didn't believe that Fleur would be coming into our home. She had utter, and complete faith in this dog's ability to survive, and if that little girl didn't come to us, she would be devastated.

To explain, it was not that I wasn't as set on rescuing Fleur as Wendy was. Of course I wanted to help as much as I could. I think I was just more pragmatic about it in that I would happily provide any financial support needed to help Fleur, but I still didn't believe she would make it to us in the UK. Wendy was adamant that Fleur was a survivor and put much more belief into the power of prayer and keeping our fingers crossed where as I was much more practical in my thought process. I was a nagging wood pecker knocking lightly but persistently at her bubble of excited confidence.

The updates we received during her time in the vets were accompanied by pictures, and it was the pictures rather than the words that conveyed the real message for me. Seeing Fleur lying under the yellow blanket didn't fill me with confidence at all, despite the words accompanying the picture telling me she was alive and fighting. It didn't look like she was fighting to me.

One picture in particular I remember seeing and I focused on Fleur's eyes. They were mucusy and swollen and I looked deep into those eyes (medically rather than wistfully) and there was such a dullness there, as I had noticed before. It was this specific photo, a close up of Fleur's face, that made me genuinely believe that Fleur didn't have the physical strength to make it to the UK.

Now, in hindsight this probably wasn't the best thing to share with Wendy but for whatever reason I did and typically it would always be at the end of the day when we had gone to bed. This is the worst time for us to start a deep and meaningful conversation but because we both have busy lives this is when it tends to happen. Unfortunately, Wendy is not a night owl. She goes to bed early whereas I am more of a stay-up-late night person. Wendy will head to bed at nine or ten o clock and go straight to sleep. I, on the other hand am usually up until well after midnight on the computer doing things I am involved in outside of work.

When I do go to bed, I have an annoying (if you're Wendy that is) habit of waking her up to talk to her. On this particular occasion Wendy was actually awake, checking her social media and we saw the close-up picture of Fleur together. Without really stopping to think about it I voiced my thoughts and that was a big mistake as it really did affect Wendy who, naturally, quickly became upset.

She angrily challenged me and questioned me about if I was really up for rehoming Fleur. My response was that yes, I was, once she got here. Maybe it was some form of emotional safety net for me or a way of providing self-preservation until it was safe to bond with her at a time when I had control over what happened to her. At this point, in my mind, it was simply too risky and there were too many cogs that had to be in motion to get Fleur to us that were totally out of our control. I just thought that it was too big a feat to succeed. Should I have voiced all of that to Wendy? Probably not.

As Val had done during the time Fleur was heading to Germany, she kept offering other dogs on the chance that Fleur wouldn't make it to the UK. From her perspective she had a couple willing to adopt a dog, and should this dog not make it to them, she had a number of other dogs that needed homes or foster, quite rightly. Wendy had made it abundantly clear that we were adopting Fleur and Fleur only and I supported her on that one hundred percent.

Thankfully both Ramona and Radu were excellent at keeping those that are interested in dogs in their care updated, and Fleur had a significant amount of interest. As a charity it's in their interests to keep updates and information on their dogs and kennels public, as they rely on the public and on donations to be able to do the outstanding work that they do. This meant that we had a good insight into how she was doing and how well she was recovering.

Initially, back with Ramona in Romania, Fleur spent time with two dogs. The thinking was that spending time with other dogs would help ease her recovery, she could play and socialise which would help ease her fears and anxiety. However, Fleur is independent. She needed her own space. She needed her own blanket in her own corner. If anybody tried to take that blanket or invade her space, they got the teeth.

Having now come to know Fleur, looking back on it, it must have been a difficult situation for her to deal with; going into another new environment with dogs she didn't know. For Fleur to be comfortable in an environment or a situation, she needs to really trust it and during this period she simply wasn't afforded the time to be able to develop that trust. Fleur was having her worst day every single day. Everything in these environments was new to Fleur, she had no idea about opening and closing doors, the sounds the crate made, taps running. All of these things that we take for granted with our own dogs, because they have grown up around them, were terrifying for Fleur.

The teeth reaction is hardly surprising when you consider the experiences and situations (or lack of) Fleur must have been exposed to. Living on the streets of Romania Fleur must have had to protect anything that she valued, be it space, food, a blanket. A dogs' natural reaction is to protect its resources when they are under threat. Now, in a new environment, those threats are still there, from Fleur's perspective, so her reactions are those that she has learned.

On top of that she was going through an intense and almost constant mental and emotional ordeal, with no idea as to why. Even today, if Fleur goes into a situation that she isn't sure of her eyes immediately find either myself or Wendy and they stay there. Her tail goes up and wags, but if you don't reassure her very quickly that tail drops. New situations can be difficult for her now, but at least she has her security – us. Imagine how horrendous she must have felt being in an already heightened state of fear and anxiety but without any form of buoy to cling on to. How she didn't sink in the sea of her own fear is an absolute testament to her strength and determination.

Fleur isn't a shy dog, and Ramona saw this when she was at Pets and Friends, but she does like her own space. Every now and then Ramona would see a wagging tail. Fleur would watch what went on around her, but she preferred her own space and that was fine. Ramona left her to be herself in her own space. There was no reason to force her to be the dog she wasn't. If she wanted to play, she played, if she didn't want to play, she didn't.

During her time at Pets and Friends, Ramona noticed something special about Fleur. Of course, she loves all her dogs, but those that are withdrawn, those that are quieter and that need a little more attention come closer to your heart. This was a notion that both Wendy and I would experience first-hand in the coming months. There was a vulnerability to Fleur that really spoke to her caring soul, but also Fleur, still to this day, gives off a perception of being wily and smart but when you scratch away at that there is a real frailty to Fleur and Ramona could sense that.

Aside from that, Fleur displayed such a strong fighting spirit, such a raw, gritty insistence to cling on to life, that it was, and still is, impossible not to fall for her and her story. More than once whilst in Romania Fleur came to the brink of death but she fought back. It's hard not to be drawn to such a strong spirit.

Let's face it, we were drawn to it from hundreds of miles away without even meeting her. During this time Wendy found the waiting excruciating, and as a husband, that wasn't pleasant to watch. To watch someone, you love and care about so saddened by something you have absolutely no control over was difficult, but we didn't really have many conversations about it. I think Wendy may have almost backed up on having conversations with me about Fleur because she knew if I was provoked to talk about it, generally I would throw up my typically pessimistic response. I would say 'if' she got to us and Wendy would always say 'when' but underneath all of that we knew that when/if Fleur arrived we would be fine. That confidence in ourselves is what kept us going, and what helped keep Wendy going.

Having Nero around at this point was helpful in that he provided us with a constant. No matter what was going on with Nero, whether he was ill, jubilant, young, old he would always eat, toilet and sleep through the night. These were constants in both his life and our life and they acted as an anchor. They kept us grounded and they not only distracted us but also reminded us that life goes on. We had responsibilities and other dogs that needed our love and care.

Marti, however, was completely different. She was one of life's victims and she had the eyes of a dead dog walking and was the epitome of a sad dog. When she arrived with us she was in such a state that I think that if she had had the option of simply laying down and not ever getting back up again she would have taken that option. Of course, she didn't know what was around the corner, and we knew that every day she managed to hold on, her life would get better because we would make sure it did. She improved, but, if anything ever happened in her life that was out of the ordinary it would completely turn her inside out. It was as if she felt death would be instant when there was a clap of thunder, or one of us dropped a spoon or shut a door louder than usual.

So here we had two very, very different dogs that provided us with a very, very different distraction and everyday tasks that would take us away from what was happening with Fleur. They filled our day with constant care and in return they gave us constant care.

Over in Romania, Ramona and Radu had spent a lot of time working with Fleur, helping to build the poor dogs confidence so that she was prepared for her new life. Both Radu and Ramona built a bond with Fleur during her time with them, and understandably when the time came to say good bye it was difficult and emotional. For Ramona, who had formed a strong bond with Fleur, there were nerves on Fleur's exit from Pets and Friends, neither Ramona nor Radu knew me nor Wendy, and given Fleur's special circumstances they wanted her to go to the right home. It was the least she deserved. As the time for Fleur to head to the UK came closer, the pressure and tension began to build.

As had been the case up until this point we were regularly updated with pictures and videos that that Ramona or Radu would post. One video in particular stands out. It gave me a very clear indication of what kind of dog Fleur was, personality wise. It sounds mad because in the video Fleur was visible for a second, second and a half at most.

It was Christmas at Ramona's and Ramona was outside with the dogs. She handed them treats and all of the dogs were going doolally. The video panned around the compound and it caught Fleur maybe twenty yards off from the other dogs. She held her ears back and she had that vulnerability about her, but it was an aloof vulnerability. She looked as if she was in control of where she was, she appeared to want to be that distant from the other dogs. Yet, something in her shouted out to me that there was this little part of her that actually wanted to join the other dogs, that she didn't completely want to be that far away, but she just couldn't muster the confidence in the situation to let herself join in. That was one video that permeated my pessimism and my detraction from the situation to really pull at my heart strings. I wanted to reach in and drag her over to the UK where she could be safe.

Chapter Six

THE JOURNEY TO...WHERE?

~ • ~

WHILE THE MESSAGES and photographs were going viral the one person who still did not know what was going on was Fleur herself. She had no idea of the future and simply lived day by day, hour by hour and even minute by minute.

    I had been in the quiet cage room for so long that it had felt like maybe I was never leaving. Every day I sat in my cage as people put on the weird clothes and came to see me. They brought me food and sometimes I would have to get out of the cage while they prodded and pocked me. What I remember most are constant feelings of pain and fear. They never left, but they were almost familiar friends by this point. My life had been so engulfed by those feelings that I couldn't imagine them not being there.

    I always had a slight jolt of panic when someone entered the room, especially in those first few days. I fully expected to be dragged out and taken somewhere new. I wondered if that's what would happen from now on. I would just be constantly moved around, constantly passed from pillar to post without any idea of what was to come next. Gradually as people came and went I began to feel a little more comfortable in that cage. I started to feel less ill and thankfully the food kept coming. I actually started to feel a little stronger as the days passed.

    One day, as usual, one of the humans came into the room towards the cage. I saw they were holding a lead but assumed I was just going out for a toilet break as had become part of my routine. As we walked out of the room I automatically headed for the door to the garden, but I was lead a different way. I immediately tensed a little. As soon as something out of routine happened, I knew something was coming. I knew something out of the ordinary waited for me and my stomach sank. I didn't want to go somewhere else again. I had had enough of going to new places.

We walked into the same place where I had come in all those weeks ago and there, waiting was the woman that brought me here. She was taking me back to the dirty cage room. That's what I associated her with so that was what I assumed she would do. She brought me from there, so she was taking me back there. At this point I just went with it. Ears down, tail beneath my legs and head held low I plodded out into the bright sunshine and whatever fate awaited me.

They lifted me into the back of the car, and I let out a squeal of pain. My abdomen was still sensitive and try as I might to hide it, when it was squeezed the pain was too intense for me not to react. So, here I was again. On the back seat of the car with absolutely no clue where I was headed. My life seemed to have gone from the relative stability of the streets to a whirlwind of cages, people and unexplained pain. I spent most of my time on a knife edge between fear and exhaustion, never being able to completely relax and rest.

As before, we travelled along some familiar streets. I watched out of the window as we passed other street dogs I didn't recognise, laying by cars or wandering the streets scavenging for food. I felt a little pang of jealousy. I lay back down on the seat and curled into my now customary small ball.

We seemed to be in the car for some time, much longer than the previous journey from the dirty cage room to the chemical smelling building. Once the car came to a halt I released myself from the tight ball a little. It wasn't the dirty cage room, that was for sure. I heard dogs barking, but they didn't sound stressed or pained like the barks that I had heard in the dirty cage room. These sounded more excited, more alive.

The lady opened the car door and encouraged me out. I wasn't dragged out like I had been in the dirty cage room. In fact, since I left the dirty cage room my neck hadn't been as sore. I was still coughing and sometimes I was sick, but I hadn't been dragged around by the neck since the day I left. At the place that smelled like chemicals I was encouraged by the humans with the lead, but I was never dragged. I was allowed to go at my own pace and make my own choice, which helped to ease the anxiety a bit. It was the same here in the car. The lead was put around my neck but

The journey to...where?

there was no pulling or dragging. I was allowed to leave the car when I was ready. I didn't want people touching me, I was still scared by hands coming near me and I snapped at a number of people who had tried. I wasn't ready for that. In my head, hands still brought pain.

Once out of the car I was led into a room that had a number of dogs in it, but these dogs weren't laying down, starving, emaciated and essentially dying. These dogs were thriving. Many of them had health issues such as deformities or injuries, but they seemed happy.

I was given a cage of my own, as I had been in every other room I had been taken to, and in it there was fresh water and a warm blanket. It felt welcoming, but so had the two previously and they hadn't lasted long so I didn't hold out much hope for this one becoming home either. Home isn't really anything I had a real concept for anyway, it wasn't something I had experienced or had ever had any real desire for. Up until this point life had been purely survival. It had been driven by an underlying, animalistic need to keep going, to stay alive.

From six weeks old I had been alone. I was born in a shed at the bottom of someone's garden. My mother had been a street dog and when she found out she was having us she made a nest in a disused shed full of cobwebs and unused garden tools. We managed to hide there for a month and a half before our cries alerted the human that lived in the house to us. Mother tried to keep us quiet but the need for food was too much and none of us could help crying. We needed food and Mother was too frail herself to provide it.

The humans found us and beat my mum to death. My siblings were all packed into a carrier bag and taken away. I never knew where, and never saw any of them again. I hid behind a pile of rusted gardening tools, only crawling out hours later when I was sure they were gone. That shed was probably the closest thing I had ever had to a home, with my family. With Shimeka we moved a lot, rarely sleeping in the same place for more than a week and the dirty cage room and chemical smelling cage room that came later definitely weren't homes.

I crawled into my cage and once again found my spot at the back, with my skin touching the wire mesh. Something out of the ordinary happened then. The cage door was left open. The human left, and food was left with me, but the cage door was left open. I stayed in my spot, fear pinning me to that wire mesh, but my eyes kept flitting to that open door. I snuggled my head into the blanket. Up until going into the chemical smelling cage room I had never had a blanket before. They reminded me of snuggling up to my mother and litter mates as a pup, and then feeling Shimeka's warmth as she nuzzled me at night.

My cage was inside a much, much larger cage. It wascertainly bigger than the chemical smelling cage room. As I looked out through the mesh I realised there were two other dogs in there. They approached my cage with their tales up and hackles down. They didn't seem threatening, but these were dogs I didn't know coming into my space. I didn't know them, and dogs I didn't know usually turned out to be a threat, be it physically or trying to take something from me. My thoughts immediately went to my blanket. It was the only thing of comfort I had, and I wasn't going to give it up. As the dogs came nearer I snarled, showing as much of my sharp teeth as possible. My hackles went up and I made myself look as menacing as possible to try and scare them off, so I didn't have to fight.

It worked, and they kept their distance, though they kept looking over at me. It wasn't that I didn't like other dogs, or that I had any particular aversion to being around them. It was simply that I trusted myself and I knew I was safe in my own company. Although I had spent time with other dogs out on the streets the only one I had ever bonded with was Shimeka. I bonded with the deformed leg dog in a different way. We bonded through a necessity to be able to cope with the situation we were put in. Had we been out on the streets our relationship may have been very different.

All other dogs, often including those in the groups I stayed with, were a threat and often fights broke out within groups over food, or water, or shelter. If I stayed on my own I could avoid all that. So that's what I did. On that first night in the big cage room I stayed in my own spot. I made sure the dogs and the humans knew not to come near me and I had my safe place.

The female human came back later that day and put down shiny bowls. The other dogs flew at theirs like it was their last meal. I guess to them, if their journeys had been anything like mine, they may well have believed that it could be. My food was placed close to me. I was more hesitant than the others. The female continued to watch close by, which meant to me if I want to the food, the lead would be round my neck and I would be out of that door and off to somewhere else. I stayed in my spot, not wanting to make the mistakes I had made before. Eventually she left, and I could eat the food in peace, my eyes darting to the other dogs regularly to make sure they were keeping their distance.

So, once again here I was. New place, new cage, absolutely no idea what was going on. I was starting to feel better, but still not completely right. I don't think I had had a proper sleep for months, and definitely not since before going to the dirty cage room. That continued in the big cage room. I dozed every now and then, but I was always alert, especially that first night. There were two other dogs with free access to my space and my blanket. I had to stay alert to make sure they didn't take it. I didn't have much, but I had this and I was prepared to protect it and protect what it meant to me.

The following day the female came in again and fed the three of us. She simply put my food down near me, her soft words flowed over me as she did so. My ears pricked and twisted towards the sound and my nose twitched at the food, but I didn't move. She didn't show any signs of forcing me and she left. I came out and ate as I had done the night before. I licked the bowl clean and stood for a second watching the other two dogs play.

It had been a long time since I had seen two dogs playing. Most dog interactions I saw were fighting or breeding. Play was something that was almost alien to me. I watched the two dogs roll around the big cage room, all teeth and play bows. It reminded me of rolling around the shed floor with my litter mates. That was probably the last time I had played with another dog.

The floor of the big cage room was scattered with brightly coloured rubber things and rope. The other two dogs would grab the rope and tug, flinging each other round with glee. Sometimes the humans would come out and play too, throwing the brightly coloured things around. I usually stayed in my spot and they never tried to move me or force me to leave it

I would come out of my space to eat, and dart quickly back to it, but I was learning that nothing bad happened outside of that space. That the other dogs didn't always try to steal my blanket, or the humans wouldn't try and put a lead around my neck and drag me away or hurt me. So, I came out when there wasn't food, and when the humans were still in the room. I walked around the big cage room tentatively, twitching at every noise. I didn't get far before I went back into my safe space, but I had done it. I had gone out of the safe space, with the humans around, and I was OK. They hadn't tried to do or say anything bad to me.

I went back into the safe space, my confidence in the big cage room had grown a little but this had happened before, and I was careful not to trust too quickly. I knew things could change in the blink of an eye so most of the time I still stayed in my safe space.

One morning I was outside the safe space eating my food when the two dogs started to play. They were chasing each other at the other end of the big cage room. They were both sprinting backwards, forwards, left, right and every direction in between. I watched as I licked the remainder of food from my lips. It really did look like fun as they zoomed around each other, stopping occasionally and then charging off again.

One of them took a bigger circle and ran past me, I dropped to the floor as the second dog shot past too in pursuit. Something in me took over and suddenly I was charging after them. The three of us did laps of the big cage room and I had never felt so free in my life. I felt the air rush past my face and I felt it cool the saliva on my tongue as I panted. My fur flew in the breeze and my ears flapped as I charged around the kennel. I had never felt that feeling before. It was one of utter exhilaration.

We stopped, and I stood still. We all panted, and I suddenly realised my tail was wagging. It wasn't held low and underneath my abdomen like it usually was, it was up and swaying from side to side. My tongue lolled out of my mouth as I panted. That was amazing. I walked back to my safe spot and lay down, but this time the ball I curled myself into wasn't quite as tight.

And so, the days continued. I spent a lot of time in my safe spot, but I would come out and play as and when I felt like it. There was no force of any kind and the humans just let us get on with what we wanted to. I didn't bond with these dogs as I had with deformed leg dog, and I had no real interest in doing so. I was happy (as happy as I could be, in the circumstances) to interact as and when it suited me and that was the extent of my relationship with them. I was allowed to make my own choices about what interaction I took part in and sometimes I even played with the humans. I liked my own space, and I liked being left alone. I still didn't feel quite one hundred percent, but my confidence was beginning to grow, and I could feel that I was starting to think that may this life wasn't quite so bad after all.

The journey to...where?

There is a recurring theme during this part of my life. Just as things seem to settle into a routine, everything gets turned upside down and I find myself back at square one with no idea what was happening. That's what happened one cold day when a truck turned up outside the big cage room.

Trucks, vans and cars turned up outside the large cage room all the time, it just became background noise. Initially whenever I heard something approach I would immediately go back into my cage and try to hide, assuming it would be coming to take me somewhere new, or fear. Whilst living on the streets sit wasn't uncommon for cars to drive at us on purpose, and on more than one occasion I had been forced to eat canine roadkill where a dog hadn't been able to avoid the car. So, the noise of a car wasn't a positive thing for me at that point, however so many of them came and went with no negative outcome that I wasn't so bothered any more. So, when this truck turned up outside, I didn't think much of it.

The woman came in to the big cage room carrying leads. This was unusual, it wasn't often she would put leads on us and my stress levels automatically rose. This wasn't part of the normal routine, what was going on? I stayed in my cage, unsure about what was happening. One by one all three of us were led out of the large cage room, tails down and ears close to our heads. None of us knew what was going on. I had no idea what had happened to the other two dogs in the large cage room but from their responses it looked like they had had similar journeys to me. They both had tails down and tried to make themselves small, a stance that I, unfortunately, knew only too well.

The female human stopped me before I was put into the truck. She knelt in front of me and looked me over with a sad smile. She gently stroked my head. I had had very little positive human interaction up until this point, but this human was always gentle, she always gave me the choice to walk away or be left alone. I never felt like I was pressured to do anything or interact when I didn't want to, with her or with the other dogs. I always had the freedom to make a choice how to respond. The first few times it had happened I was terrified, but there was also an underlying curiosity and inquisitiveness.

As much as contact with humans mainly came with pain or distress, contact with this female was pleasurable and relaxing. Lying in the small cage room the contact with the deformed leg dog had given me a huge sense of comfort that helped me deal with the situation I was forced into. Here there was a human willing to give me that interaction and that contact, but all I could think of when she came close was that I was going to be hurt. Gradually, as my confidence began to grow a little, I allowed her hand to touch me. Just briefly. Very briefly. I would remove myself within seconds before the inevitable pain or fear came. That choice to leave gave me confidence, it reduced some of my fear, so I was able to accept the interactions more.

In that one moment next to that truck, as other dogs barked and whined, the human looked at me with a look that was filled with a melancholia mixed with a hopefulness and it was the strongest connection I had ever felt with a human. Unwittingly, she had given me confidence and an experience that had helped me learn and be at least a little more comfortable being myself rather than constantly being poised to fight or run. Those feelings were still there, they were ingrained in me, but they had been lessened through this human's kindness, and the kindness of the people she had around her.

I pushed my head into her hand as she stroked me, and she smiled. Then, she stood, and I was placed into the truck. It was happening too quickly. I didn't want this. I didn't want to move again. I liked it here, I was safe here and I was safe with her. It was the first time I had felt like that in months and I didn't want to be torn away from that. In a small cage in the back of the truck I could see the human looking at us through the open doors. I stared out at her, feeling a heaviness in my chest as our eyes met. Then the doors were shut, and I was plunged into darkness once more. She was gone, out of my life just like that. The human that had made me feel so safe was gone. Or rather, I was gone. Who knew where I was going to end up this time, and as the truck began to pull away all of the confidence and sense of calmness quickly faded away as the more recognisable and accustomed stress and fear came back to the forefront. It had never truly gone away, it was always lying underneath like a snake under a rock waiting to pounce.

That day it was absolutely freezing. I had never been that cold before, if I had been back on the streets chances are I wouldn't have made it through those nights. It sickens me to think how many street dogs became victims during those intensely cold nights. As I was placed onto the truck the snow was already thick on the ground and still falling. The truck bumped and swerved as I tried to lie down in my cage. The dogs around me whined and barked with each bump. It was pitch black in there which only made it worse. The noise indicated we weren't the only dogs in there, could see the other dogs and none of us knew what was going on.

The truck felt like it was moving slowly and there were lots of stops. It continued to be freezing in there and as I lay there shivering I thought back to the deformed leg dog in the large cage room. Had she made it? Was she in the white chest or had she been taken to a big cage room too? I hoped she was at least safe, if not happy. I hoped she realised how much she had helped me through those days in the dirty cage room, and I hoped I helped her too.

I was in that truck for the longest time, shivering and terrified of what was happening or might happen. Hunger had crept back in too. Why were we on this truck for so long? Where was it taking us? The longer we were on that journey, the more bumps we hit, the more times we stopped, the more intense my anxiety got. Any sense of calm I had achieved in my time at the large cage room was almost completely over shadowed by anxiety. It was almost comforting to feel something so familiar in such unfamiliar circumstances. I had almost forgotten what familiar circumstances were.

When I was a pup, we would often have to hide in the shed, be as quiet as we could underneath sheets or in the shadows where it was dark. It wasn't like darkness bothered me. On the streets darkness was usually your friend because it acted as a cover. It meant you couldn't be seen and could become invisible which reduced the chance of you being a target. The last thing you want to be on those streets is a target.

I couldn't have been more than six months old when I saw first-hand how brutal life on the streets can be if you become a victim of humans and their desire to inflict pain and misery. I was on my own at the time, it was before I had met Shimeka and I was in between groups. I was scavenging near some bins in an alleyway when I heard something moving. It sounded like someone dragging a bag across the floor. When I turned I saw a young dog, younger than I was at the time, dragging its hind quarters along the floor. The more time went on, especially once I went into the dirty cage room, seeing deformed and abused dogs was a common occurrence, but at this young age to see a dog younger than me in such a state was shocking.

The dog dragged itself across the alleyway towards the bins, it was obvious the dog, barely more than a pup, was aiming to get food. I couldn't help myself, I couldn't let this poor animal struggle. I made my way over to it and bizarrely he seemed cheerful. His ears were up, his eyes were bright, and his tongue hung happily out of his mouth. His facial expression completely went against how I thought this dog would be feeling.

He didn't flinch when I neared him as I assumed he would do. I pulled a bin bag across the alleyway, tearing it and letting the food remnants fall out. I nudged some towards the puppy who gratefully dug in to the food. I watched for a second before heading back to my own scavenging.

Suddenly I heard shouts and yells and I turned to see a group of people running at the dog, who immediately tried to desperately drag himself away. Before I could even register what was happening they were on the dog, beating and kicking and punching. They were beating a dog that had no way of escaping and no way of defending himself. I barked and howled from my hiding space in the shadows behind a bin, too scared myself to get too close. I tried to make as much noise as I could and eventually a man in a uniform ran into the alleyway. He shouted, and the people ran away as fast as they could leaving the small, lifeless body of the pup on the floor covered in its own blood. I watched as the man in uniform carefully picked up the pup and carried him away.

I have often wondered what happened to that puppy and if he made it. Could I have saved his life if I had done more and left my safe shadows? Now, here I was in another dark place with absolutely no control at all surrounded by distressed dogs. There was nothing I could do to change the outcome of this situation, because the outcome was a mystery to all of us. This wasn't a defenceless puppy that I had the potential to help. This was a group of dogs in a dark truck heading to somewhere we had no idea about and no control over.

Eventually, hours and hours after we were loaded on to the truck it stopped, and the doors were opened. My anxiety levels shot up as I saw humans enter with leads. Where were we? Why were we here? Was there a white chest? Two dogs were led off the truck, but the rest of us were left on. The door were closed again. I started whining. I had no idea what to do or why we were suddenly being split up. Why weren't the rest of us being taken off the truck? That fear that had been such a deep rooted aspect of my life right from the day I was born was back in full force.

The journey to...where?

It wasn't long before the truck started rumbling again and the bumps began once more. I was so hungry by this point and minute by minute the distress grew, especially as intermittently the truck would stop, and more dogs were taken off. As much as I didn't want to be on the truck, I was also apprehensive about what lay outside of it and where I would end up. I had been awake for a long time, and the majority of that time was spend on edge, so I was exhausted too. All those old street dog feelings were coming back with a vengeance.

Pretty soon I was the only dog left in the back of the truck. I didn't even have the comfort of knowing I wasn't the only dog on the truck. The loneliness was made worse by the sudden silence. The constant whining, crying and barking was stopped, and I was plunged into a blind silence. Trembling from the cold I curled up into a ball to try and stay warm. Although I had eaten whilst in the big cage room, I could still feel my bones digging into myself. I was pretty miserable.

The truck stopped again. My ears pricked as I heard footsteps outside then the doors opened and a sudden rush of cold wind made me flinch. A lead looped around my neck and I was suddenly outside the truck headed into a house. Everything was so different. It looked and felt nothing like the place I was used to. It was glaringly obvious even in my confused state that I was a long way from the streets I grew up in. I was led through a house and back outside by a lady. I was put into a big cage on my own, but there were other big cages around with dogs in. Some of them looked similar to the dogs I had grown up with. When you live on the streets you learn that street dogs have a particular 'look' and you can spot them when you see them. There were definitely a few in those cages.

Food was left in the cage for me. I sniffed at it, licked it but, despite the hunger that had got worse and worse during the journey, I was too nervous to eat. Then, the cage door opened and the human woman that put me in the kennel put the lead back on me and I was led out again. At this point I just wanted to sleep. The human brought me back into the house and suddenly I was met by two other humans. I had no idea who they were or why they, or I, were there. Everything was thrown at me at once in that room and I had no idea how to react. As had been the case before I was too tired to run or fight, so I just let it happen. I felt heavy and washed out, like all I wanted to do was lay down ad sleep for a week.

The floor felt strange under my feet, it was cold and hard compared to the soft ground and straw I was used to. Both of the new humans came down to the floor as I entered the room, which made them less threatening and I stood near them, waiting for whatever was about to happen to happen. After a day in a truck and everything else that had happened over the previous months I didn't have the energy to do anything more than let them do what they wanted. I braced myself for pain.

None came. My nails were clipped, but that was as intense as it got. The two new humans lay on the floor with me and they stroked me gently. It felt nice to have some interaction, but I had no strength to give anything back. I wanted to be left alone to rest. I don't know how long we were on that cold, hard floor. It all blurred into one after a while and I retreated into my own head. Then, once again the lead looped around my neck and I was taken back outside and put into yet another new car. I felt like a shell, like an empty shell being moved to and fro with real reaction to it. Inside I was terrified, I was apprehensive, and I felt sick and tired. The humans had being putting some paste stuff on my food, and I had started to feel better, but I still didn't feel right, and I didn't want to be going through all this right now. I just wanted a straw bed and my own cage, so I could lie down.

The car headed off into the dark night as snow fell hard. I couldn't settle in that car, I was too tense, and I felt unwell. I tried to second guess where I was going but there was no way I could. I sensed that I was a long way the streets I used to, and I sensed the people I was with weren't a threat, but that didn't go far to ease my feelings of distress. It was so black outside that I couldn't see anything I recognised even if I was somewhere familiar. I can't remember anything particular about that journey. It all went by in a hazy blur. All I could think about was how tired I was and what could possibly be waiting for me when the car stopped.

When the car did stop we were outside another new house. I fully expected to be put into another small cage, which was fine by me. It would mean I could sleep until I was moved on again. I never once imagined this would be my final stop, or what would happen in the coming months.

Chapter Seven

AT LAST – THE ARRIVAL!

~ • ~

WENDY AND ANDREW found their optimism growing. There was still the danger of a huge disappointment but they had to prepare as if everything was going to run smoothly from now on although they were very well aware that it might not, as Wendy explained.

Back in the UK we had begun to make preparations for Fleur's impending arrival. We erected a crate so that there was a safe space ready for Fleur, but also so that we could prepare Nero and Marti for any changes in their environment. In all honesty the crate had been ready to go since October 2014, but I had started to think it would never be put up. The doubts had started creeping in.

It was on October 25th that we were told Fleur was reserved to us, and we were expecting her the following month. Then came the distemper diagnosis so it was postponed to December, and then January. It wasn't until January 24th that we were told Fleur would be arriving with Val on Saturday 31st January and we would be able to collect her on Sunday 1st February. It was at this point we decided we were probably safe to erect the crate, covering it with blankets and placing a bed inside to turn it into her own little den. It looked cosy comfy but that didn't waylay some of the feelings of guilt I had when I thought about the fact Fleur had spent hours in a crate in veterinary clinics and then in the back of a van travelling for hours to then come to her new home and immediately be put into another crate while, in contrast, Nero and Marti had free run of the house. It just didn't seem fair.

Andrew pointed out that this was what Fleur had been used to. It would help her to feel safe and secure, and to ease her into life at the Morris household. Running that mantra through my head made me feel better and we introduced new bowls and other furniture as combat indicators to all residents that things were about to change.

Nero paid little attention to the cages, whereas Marti would go in and out of the cage, and on occasion she would sleep in there too. We wondered if it stirred up memories for her and maybe brought on some nostalgic comfort for her, like tasting a sweet from your childhood or smelling a departed loved one's scent. Either way, there was little to no negative response to the new stimuli.

It's not as if we could sit them down around the dinner table and explain that a new dog was coming into the household, like you would if you had to explain a pregnancy to existing children. That said, there were conversations between us and Nero and Marti explaining that Fleur was coming home, and all that entailed. Why we did this I have no idea. Not because they were dogs and didn't understand English, but more because Marti slept through the entire exchange and Nero simply cocked his head to one side as if asking for his ball. Even the ninja cat seemed non-plussed, pretty much displaying the attitude that she did about Marti and Nero. Come near and get a slap across the snout. But, despite the lack of resonance, we had done our due diligence. We showed them pictures of Fleur, as well as showing them to friends and family, as if they would remember and welcome her across the threshold like a long-lost cousin.

By now all of the children had left home. Grant, being the youngest, was the last to leave having joined the army. In a sense Fleur coming into the household when she did had filled the void that was left when Grant moved out. It was the classic fly-the-nest syndrome, and the house suddenly felt empty and sad. The rooms felt bigger and bare, like immediately after the Christmas decorations taken down, only this came with an added emotional emptiness. A quiet that wasn't as easy to fill as putting up a new picture or added some flowers to a vase. I felt compelled to care for something, I guess I needed to be needed which is probably why I found nursing to be my vocation.

We kept the kids up to date with what was going on and all of them told us how happy they were we were taking on another rescue dog, given how we had turned Marti's life around for the better and the care and love we had put into Nero once his condition came to light. It felt as if the house was finally going to be complete. Nero had always been the family dog, Marti was Andrew's project and now I had chosen Fleur. Soon we were going to be one big happy, furry family.

The day approached and even though I knew everything with Fleur was OK, I was also very aware that things could, and often had, turn on a sixpence. As the date kept getting put back Andrew had had to keep re-arranging his leave from work. I, however, hadn't been entitled to leave as I had just begun a new role. Whilst on the surface this wasn't ideal, I wanted to spend as much time with Fleur as I could when she arrived to help her settle in and make sure everything ran smoothly yet having a new job to focus on meant I had to switch off those emotions and thoughts.

It was all very conflicting. I would go to work and be able to focus on something else although with this slight nagging in the back of my mind. Then, when I would come home, it would be all I could think of. Several times I had put myself on the edge of hope only to be disappointed and that pestering doubt that she wouldn't make it to us never left me. Andrew, ever the realist, didn't hesitate to point this out to me. As depressing as this point of view may be, it turned out to be one of appropriate self-preservation.

As F-Day (Fleur Day) got closer I messaged Val to ask if we were still on for the weekend. Andrew had taken the week off work to help Fleur settle in to her new home. It was finally happening. Our new baby girl was coming home. It had felt like a long time coming, and now it was so close we could hardly believe it. With Nero and Marti, the transition from adoring outsider to overjoyed dog owner had been relatively quick and non-dramatic compared to Fleur, so this felt like the culmination of a lot of work and patience on everybody's part.

But, this was Fleur, so of course nothing was straight forward or easy. The winter of 2015 brought with it some dramatic inclement weather conditions in Romania and on the day Fleur was due to leave there came snow and the conditions were freezing. Part of me wondered if we should give up, if maybe this was all a sign from some higher power that it wasn't meant to be, or that actually they didn't want to us to have Fleur and were waiting for us to pull out, so they didn't have to turn us down.

My mind raced with thoughts and I couldn't help but wonder if maybe Fleur was so ill that they wanted us to give up, so they could change the plan of action. So, when we were given yet another revised date of 31st

January my thoughts were contrary. Was this it? Was this really it? Or as it simply another date in a long line of never-ending dates? I don't think I really believed we would collect her, not after all of the setbacks we had had so far.

On the Saturday I was expecting a call from Val with all of the relevant information for Fleur's collection. Val rang, but instead of giving us instructions she told us that because of the weather Fleur's travel had been put back to Sunday. I wasn't sure how much more I could take. It felt like disappointment after disappointment and with each one a little bit more of my resolve was being chipped away. It was only a delay of one day, but it still hacked away another little chip of confidence that Fleur would ever set paw in the UK.

That Sunday we were playing cricket as part of the indoor league. I was playing, and Andrew was umpire so there was no way we could back out, much as we may have wanted to. A message from Val came through at 11:10 that morning:

'Run for AAFA today estimated times due to weather...'

Oh my!. Fleur was due to arrive with her by 4pm. Andrew suggested maybe we should postpone collecting her until the following weekend, but I was so gutted at the thought of having to wait even longer to see my baby that I called Val and explained the situation. She was as set on us collecting Fleur that day as I was, she felt that after the turbulent journey, and what had happened prior to that, it was important to get Fleur straight home so that she could settle rather than spending more time in kennels and being shunted to and fro. That was justification enough for me and we agreed that we would collect her once the cricket game had concluded. I warned Val it would be late but that didn't seem to be an issue. As we got back into the game, it started to snow, much to Andrew's chagrin. I saw it as a good omen as we had collected Marti in February whilst it was snowing.

All I can really remember from that game was that we played, and not very well if memory serves me correctly. Maybe I was just too distracted as I'm sure was I caught out. As soon as the game finished I dashed to my phone. The last message had come through at 6:35pm.

'No transport arrived as yet'

At last – the arrival!

The delays were getting less and less, from weeks to days to hours. It was progress. Now, somewhere in the UK there was a van full of Romanian street dogs, and one of the was our Fleur. The cricket game may have been over but there was still the post-game de-brief and deconstruction to go through, something that Andrew took part in. Players would talk about the negatives and positives, what could have been done better and what needed to be improved upon and how. It wasn't unheard of for these to go on longer than the match itself. Please, Andrew, not on today of all days. My impatience was thinly veiled, and I egged him on to be done as soon as possible.

After what seemed like forever I was finally sat in the car and I could really let Val know we were on our way and should be at Valgrays at around 7:50pm. My excitement at every update Val sent was too much for Andrew whose annoyance grew at commensurate rate to my giddiness. In return, he insisted on stopping at home for a pee break for Marti and Nero, however this wasn't just a nip out to the grass outside. This was a walk around the block whilst I passively aggressively made him a coffee with milk and impatient irritation. After what felt like three years and telling a disinterested Marti and Nero we were going to collect their sister, we were finally back on the road.

With each update my smile got closer to my ears. Then, at around 7pm came a message from Val;

'She has arrived...'

I practically jumped out of my seat with excitement, smiling like the Cheshire Cat. After all the setbacks, the fighting (On Fleur's part, mainly) the ups and the downs, our girl was finally at Valgrays and in the space of less than an hour we would meet her. Andrew asked what the latest update was, and his response was immediate;

"Let's go get her, kid."

We were forty minutes away at this point. Far too far away for me. I kept Val up to date as we travelled, which acted as a sort of communication-based countdown. It didn't help waylay my feelings of excitement which were interspersed with very audible sighs at Andrews strict insistence on adhering to the speed limits.

We were now just one mile away

At this point my heart was racing with excitement. Our family was about to get bigger and all of the previous weeks were about to be worth it. Just to add to any feelings of trepidation or anxiety that we had, it was raining, and it was dark. It was like a clichéd scene from a movie. But we were here. Back at Valgrays.

The last time we had been here was to adopt Marti and it had been a much different affair. That Sunday we had arrived during daylight hours, composed, groomed and prepared as if we were turning up for an interview along with Nero. We had barely introduced ourselves before Val was into Nero, giving him a full once over. After all, what better way to scope out a person's ability to care for a dog than to see what state their current dog is in. Once she had acquainted herself with him she checked ears, tops of his front legs and his backside and tail. Poor Nero, groomed to within an inch of his life, barely knew what was going on it happened so quickly, but as Andrew pointed out, if the tables were turned and someone was collecting a dog from us he would be into their dog to ascertain any secrets of their 'dogmanship'. If you can't turn up to a rescue with a clean and well cared for dog, why should they let you take one of their baby's home? Quite right too.

The day we collected Marti we were able to walk her with Nero along the lane outside Valgrays. They got on well, or rather neither was bothered by the other, and much to our surprise Val let us take Marti home there and then. Marti was calm and walked nicely with Nero, so naturally we were thrilled to be able to take her home. A visit to the cash point and two hours later and we were driving home with Marti.

So here we were again but this time on a dark, snowy Sunday night ready to take on our next challenge. We turned up in sports kit, sweaty, frazzled and with absolutely no idea what to expect. We didn't have the option of bringing Nero and Marti with us, and the weather would have prevented introductions anyway. We really should have realised then that things weren't going to go as planned. Isn't hindsight wonderfully 20/20?

Valgrays sits at the end of a road in the small town of Warlingham. Val herself is well known within animal rescue and agility circles and you would be forgiven for assuming that Valgrays would be some large premises given the amount of work she does. Surprisingly it is a modest semi-detached property with double garage and long garden with the kennels located at the back.

At last – the arrival!

Val greeted us at the door with warm hugs and questions about our journey. Our relationship had changed since we picked up Marti, and specifically since our journey with Fleur had begun. Even though all of our interactions had been online there was a new closeness and a mutual cause that had brought us closer together. Without any knowledge of it, Fleur had facilitated a whole host of new relationships and friendships.

Val invited us in and we made our way into the large, tiled kitchen. A large wooden table stood under window with a door out to the back garden. The house and the garden is 'Valgrays'. There is one room set aside for Val and her partner Keith, such is their dedication to the cause. The remainder of the space is utilised in one way or another to accommodate a fair number of furry waifs and strays. The house is homely, and it would be an easy mistake to make to not realise that there is a dog rescue centre operating from it, if it wasn't for the large van stood outside with outstanding purple lettering reading 'Emergency Transport'.

Val put the kettle on, for what would a British greeting be without a hot drink? Andrew eagerly accepted her offer of coffee. My heart sank just a little, not that I have an issue with Andrew accepting sustenance, but Andrew likes his coffee cool, which meant waiting which in turn would give Andrew an opportunity to talk a lot which then meant a longer wait until I got Fleur home. I swore he was doing it on purpose to wind me up. As if there hadn't been enough delays already. I just wanted to get her home and get on with the loving, caring life she deserved. If only I knew what was to come.

Val seemed eager to get Fleur to us too. The trip had been particularly tricky due to the awful weather which had made it a traumatic experience for the dogs. The weather had been so bad the trip was actually aborted a couple of times whilst in transit, so the dogs had been on the van for a long time. That meant the sooner we could get Fleur settled the better, coffee or no coffee.

Val vanished out of the back door into the snow towards the kennels. It was really happening. We were really here. This was something I had fantasised about for months, and now it was actually happening it felt surreal. Like waiting and waiting for a well-deserved holiday and when you finally get to the airport it feels like a dream. Only this was a bigger dream.

We stood in silence, staring out of the window in the back door. Thoughts began to creep through cracks in the excitement. What if she didn't take to us? Would she fit in to our family and life? What if she bit us? Were we really doing the right thing? We had no way of knowing how this was going to go. We had heard stories and seen pictures, but we had no idea what the dog that walked through that door was going to be like, how she was going to react or what state she would be in. Then, there she was. Our tiny, fragile girl tip toeing into Val's kitchen.

Both Andrew and I responded together: "Oh, how small she is."

Looking at pictures is one thing, but when you see this small, almost ghost-like dog walk into the room it's heart-breaking. This innocent dog was carrying all of the pain, distress and abuse that our species had caused on her back. It was painful to witness.

The colour of her fur struck me as soon as I saw her. Fleur is a white dog, but the dog that walked into the kitchen was a yellow colour, a staining that is apparently normal when a dog has been sleeping in straw, as Fleur had. A tainting reminder of where she had come from, and what she had been through. As if the physical (and more than likely, mental and emotional) scars weren't enough. There was a strong odour and the poor thing looked like a rabbit caught in the headlights. She obviously had no idea what was going on, or what the previous twenty-four hours had been all about.

Her hair had been hacked at, presumably to remove faeces and/or dirt. More disturbingly it was apparent that the tip of Fleur's tail had been chopped off. Maybe she had been caught and had to pull it free, or something more sinister had occurred, that tail was to act as a constant reminder of Fleur's less than savoury past, like a childhood scar.

On top of all this, Fleur looked tired. Yes, she had just travelled from Romania which must have been tiring but this was more of an emotionally wrung out, exhausted type of tiredness as if she was almost at the end of what she was able to carry without collapsing under its weight.

Andrew mentioned he saw that same dullness to her eyes that he saw in the original photos when he quite rightly predicted she was harbouring an underlying illness but all I saw was my girl. Despite the smell and the state of her fur I was smitten from the second my eyes saw her and from then on she had my heart. Andrew also told me to remember that she had been on transport for hours upon hours, probably without toilet breaks

At last – the arrival!

so she had been laid in her own urine and faeces. There was nothing that couldn't be fixed by a warm bath, some food, a clean bed and lots of love. That was something I could do, in fact it was something I was desperate to do.

We lay on Val's floor (much to Andrews delight) as Fleur ignored us. We let her come to us and investigate when she was ready. Everything was calm and quiet, ensuring it was the least amount of stress on Fleur as possible. Seeing her build up the courage to approach us of her own accord was warming. We lay there on the floor and I stroked her gently, telling her gently that everything was OK. Andrew took pictures whilst Val clipped Fleur's nails.

The fact she was so accepting of human contact and inspection was astounding, given what she had suffered at the hands of humans up until this point. She accepted the attention, but there didn't seem to be any joy. She was almost empty; devoid of any remaining energy to respond. It was hardly surprising when you considered that in the last six months she had been violently ripped from her street home, incarcerated in a public shelter with little compassion and only a wooden pallet to sleep on, cruelly operated on and left in the most horrendous pain before being moved from one kennel to another at the hands of numerous different people and then loaded onto a van with more strangers and driven across Europe in hellish weather. It was impossible to imagine what could be going through her head, but judging from the outside, it wasn't good.

As we lay there cuddling our new fur baby it was pure, unadulterated joy. That whole day I had only had one thought on my mind, and that was cuddling my new dog. Even as we had played indoor cricket earlier that day all I could think about was how I wanted it to be over, so I could collect Fleur. Maybe that's why we lost. Now we were here, she was at last laying between us. I prayed hard that this wasn't a dream, that I wasn't just about to wake up.

Val gave us Fleur's passport and explained that Fleur had some sort of stomach bug. Details were sparse, or at least the details that I actually heard were sparse. Val's lips were moving and I'm sure there were more words than I heard but at that moment anything other than getting Fleur home was unimportant. I just smiled back at her like the penguins of Madagascar. All I knew was that she had tested positive for something, but for what I wasn't sure. A paste medication was given to us, with strict instructions. It was fitting that we should take Fleur home with an illness. As we had already found, speed bumps were par for the course.

Paperwork for microchip and adoption completed, and armed with some James Wellbeloved food, we headed out to the car. We were taking Fleur home. Finally, she was going to get the home she so desperately deserved, and the life she should have had years ago. At least, that was what we had planned.

Andrew lifted Fleur into the car and I climbed into the back seat with her. I wanted to make sure she felt safe and secure, this way I could reassure her the whole way home as I had done with Marti. As we journeyed home and I gently stroked the fur on Fleur's head, running it methodically through my fingers, I watched through the window as endless darkness passed by outside. I felt relief and I'm sure my shoulders had dropped an inch as the pressure and worry of the previous weeks floated away.

Even though there was relief, I was still worried about how Nero and Marti would react to Fleur. We had had no way to test them out, and it would be late by the time we got home. We wouldn't be able to take them for a walk together or spend time with them outside on neutral ground. It was all or nothing. We knew we were going to have to spend time with all three dogs, regardless of how late we got back. It was time for the hard work to start.

Chapter Eight

SETTLING IN THE NEW ARRIVAL

~ • ~

SETTLING IN THE new arrival was, of course, a shared experience. Fleur was the most involved but so were Nero and Marti and the ninja cat, not to mention Wendy and, naturally, Andrew who had tried to keep the lid on his emotional reaction and keep a more practical approach, as he explains.

Fleur wasn't the first dog I had rescued, and nor was Marti. As a kid I had a paper round which I would complete on my push bike. One day, after delivering a paper to a particular house, a large Bearded Collie type dog came out after me. Not knowing any better I tried to out pedal him, but of course I couldn't and soon I had a bleeding leg.

I'm not sure how, but somehow the attack got reported to the police (possibly because the policeman lived next door to the dog) and the local bobby was soon at my parents' door informing us that the poor dog was to be put to sleep. At that young age, I still made a huge fuss about the dog being put to sleep and the upshot was, the dog got spared. Even as a small child my empathy always leaned towards the dog, even if I was the victim.

Now, here we were driving through the falling snow in the pitch-black night having rescued another. Fleur sat on the back seat of the car staring out into the dark through the window. The journey took around an hour and for the entirety she stood, and she sat, but she never settled down. What was she thinking? I was probably anthropomorphising, but she seemed pensive, like so many film characters that stare longingly out of rain-streaked windows. Was she thinking about the horrors she had seen in her short life? Were there images flashing through her mind of all the hideous things she had seen and experienced? Did she wonder, or fear, what was to come next?

I knew Fleur would arrive at Valgrays in a state of severe stress. After the sea crossing and spending hours on end locked in a van with a number of strange dogs, not being let out at all, because that would run the risk of Romanian dogs on the hoof all over Europe, there was no chance on this earth that Fleur would arrive at Valgrays in any fit state at all. With this. combined with the photographs and videos we had seen in the days and weeks leading up to Fleur's arrival I expected her to arrive essentially broken. A mixed-up puzzle of a dog that we would have to then begin putting back together.

As I looked into her eyes for the first time outside of a photograph, they seemed sunken and immediately I saw Marti. They were the dark eyes of a dog that had given up, albeit to a lightly lesser extent. She seemed subservient as we went out to the car and I don't think she had it in her to jump into the car. When I picked her up to place her on the back seat she cowered, but she didn't tremble. This poor dog was so utterly exhausted that she didn't even have the strength to tremble in fear.

In the car was the first time she had sat up and her ears moved forward. She wasn't by any means a happy or content dog, but this was the first time her senses had really obviously kicked in and that gave me some confidence. It gave me belief that we had something to work off, that there was still a dog in there that wanted to come out, that needed to be brought out.

Aside from my and Wendy's subconscious wondering, the journey home was uneventful (which was an improvement for Fleur, given her recent luck). We spent the journey making sure we kept talking, both to her and to one another, but we just had conversations, nothing consequential and I honestly don't remember what they were about since they were so irrelevant. At no point did she scratch into the seats or try and bury herself into the them. She went from a distraught, almost given up husk of a dog to a dog that was sat up and relatively bright.

Once we arrived home we had planned to introduce Fleur to Nero and Marti on the grass verge beside our house, utilising the relatively neutral territory. Given how tired and emotionally wrought we were, and the darkness and snow, the meeting was much of a blur, but it must have gone well as nobody had wounds and there were no tears. Babe the ninja cat was well versed in new dogs coming into the home by now. She retreats to the sanctuary of upstairs where she can get her space, her food is put up there and the bathroom window is left open, so she can get in and out and she makes her own choices on how to deal with the situation. Cats are so aloof and independent, and she is no exception.

Nero has always been body confident and he felt no need to display anything towards Fleur whatsoever. There was a bit of a sniff and that was that. There was almost an air of 'she isn't part of my life, so I don't need to be interested'. Maybe he had spent too much time around Babe. Marti was content to be in Fleur's space, but there wasn't the confidence that Nero displayed. Fleur wasn't really giving off any signals or body interaction. These three dogs were the very embodiment of animals (including humans) being the sum of their experiences. Nero had grown up in a loving, caring home and held himself with a quiet confidence, Marti had a shaky confidence that appeared to be a mixture of terrible beginnings and the work we had put in to overcome that. Now here was Fleur who seemed to be letting everything wash over her with little to no real reaction at all. It was almost like seeing a living scale of how a dog can grow from anxious and scared to confident. From Fleur to Marti to Nero.

There is, of course, the distinct possibility that their lack of interaction with Fleur was simply because she absolutely stank to high heaven. A dog's nose is sensitive and if Fleur stunk to us, heaven only knows what Marti and Nero must have thought. She definitely didn't smell like any dog they had interacted with before, that's for sure. Marti also wears her heart on her sleeve when it comes to Nero and what Nero does Marti does, where Nero goes Marti goes, so her interaction with Fleur may have fed off what Nero was doing, which wasn't much. In fact, he soon took himself off into the other room to find something more interesting, like a sofa.

Once in the house Fleur had the freedom of the utility room and kitchen/coffee room. Her crate had been made homely with warm blankets, water and freshly cooked chicken. It had been a long day for everyone, not least of all Fleur, so we left her to settle and we went to bed. That night we fully expected her to be unsettled and stressed. We prepared ourselves for howling, barking and whatever else came, but nothing did. She remained silent for the entire night.

This continued into the next day. Babe remained upstairs only to be seen by us and Fleur found safety in the confinement and cover of the crate, only venturing out for food, water and walks. We both desperately wanted to hug her and give her that physical reassurance that she was OK, and things were going to be fine, but we knew she needed time and space to re-adjust and acclimatise herself to her new surroundings. Her new life was far from the turbulence and unease she had been experiencing recently but she needed to realise that for herself.

Interestingly, and pretty bizarrely from our perspective, Marti continued to go into the crate once Fleur had arrived. The door to the crate was open constantly so anybody had free access to it. Nero had no interest, I don't think he even knew what a crate was as he had never had any experience of one and it was far below ninja cat to go into a dog crate. Marti, however would often be found in there. She tended to get up and leave once Fleur went in but if Fleur came out for whatever reason, Marti would take her chance. It was bizarre because Marti detested crates. Absolutely hated them with the fire of a thousand Suns, to the point that when she first came to live with us we had to take hers down within a few days because it was causing her so much distress. Somewhere along the line something had happened to create such fear, and I dread to think what. Fleur, of course, had a terrible start but I often think Marti's was much worse in terms of abuse.

It became quickly apparent that Fleur was immensely observant. Living on the streets she had to be, she had to be acutely aware of her surroundings and any changes or threats. This bled into her life at the Morris house. She was incredibly sensitive to everything that was going on around her. If a door opened, a window closed, our movements, the other dogs' movements, anything in her immediate vicinity she would take in.

Whilst Fleur was inquisitive, her dark eyes taking in everything that went on around her, it was obvious she still had an underlying fear. Don't get me wrong, we both knew that taking on an unknown dog from rescue without even setting eyes on her outside of a photograph was a risk, but it was obvious that from that first photo Wendy felt something special about

Settling in the new arrival

Fleur. Something about that small, frail dog in the photo spoke to Wendy, and to me. When we saw her for the first time in Val's kitchen all those feelings flooded back. We knew we had done the right thing, despite the risks involved. It felt like kismet.

The first few days Fleur remained much the same as she had the night she arrived. They were non-eventful, and twenty-four hours of Fleur's day consisted of her being left to her own devices downstairs with open access to all of the rooms in addition to our usual routine of walks and feeding. She watched as we went about our business but she self-regulated her exposure.

We had set ourselves up for an almighty task and expected everything to change completely, and of course, to some certain extent things had, but Fleur slipped easily into our home without upsetting the apple cart. She wasn't a Kennel Club Gold Citizen, but she wasn't any trouble which was quite a surprise given her street dog roots. In the house she didn't really try to make any impact, as if she didn't see it as her home. This was just another place that she had been brought to that if I just lay here and do what they want me to do I'll end up somewhere else at some point, as if she was simply resigned to her fate. In all honesty, she just looked sad and dishevelled. Her coat had been hacked at to remove tangles or matted fur which gave her the look of a dog that had been dragged through a hedge backwards.

She lay in her metal fortress of solitude taking notice of what occurred around her but making little effort to move from that position. A lot of the time she lay at the rear of the crate. We kept a blanket draped over the crate to reduce her exposure but made sure she had a view of what lay outside her safe space. Again, maybe we are humanising. Who knows if she felt safe at this point. It's probably safe to say she didn't feel secure yet, not yet.

Above anything else in those first few days she was tired, and that was evident. She slept a lot, but it was never a full on, deep, snore out loud type of sleep. It was always a very shallow, low level type of sleep which is why I think she didn't have that security yet. Her body needed to rest but her mind kept on edge, it was ready to react if and when she needed to. She didn't seem to fully relax in terms of feeling secure and comfortable in her environment.

Fleur's activity was all sensory, all mental. There was very little physical activity other than going out for her walks. What she may have been doing, is noting every exit route to and from her sanctuary as well as taking in that each and every time a door carefully opened it was consistently and firmly closed again. Her harness was kept on at all times at this point. Given Nero's previous escapades, and our experience of rescuing Marti and the advice we were given then, we were vigilant not to allow Fleur any unfortunate opportunities. The long line remained attached for the first couple of days, as it was fairly evident that Fleur didn't want much to do with us so rather than stress her out trying to get her lead on three times a day we just left it attached, not that Fleur showed any indication that she would make a fuss. That was part of what gave her such a sad aura. I had expected some bucking bronco that I would need to lasso in order to tame like in a Western, not that I wanted her to flip out, but there was just nothing there and that's what made it so heart wrenching. She had no fight left whatsoever.

Neither of the other dogs seemed too bothered by Fleur in the days that followed. Neither Nero nor Marti paid much attention to the new little white dog in the crate, aside from Marti making use of it as and when she could. Much like we were doing, they let Fleur do her own thing in her own time whilst they went about their business. Each and any time she sensed any movement in the house Fleur would retreat into her crate, into her safe zone. As quiet as she tried to be the crate would make noise whenever she moved, and the flimsy plastic tray in the crate made noise whenever she repositioned herself, so at least we knew she was moving around. It was like a creaking comfort blanket.

Fleur showed little interest in adventure, but she was eating, drinking and sleeping so we had little concern. That was what was most important, and she needed to recharge her batteries. The poor dog must have been completely emotionally exhausted, as well as physically.

Anybody who has dealt with a deep emotional trauma, such as grief, will know how utterly exhausting it can be. Fleur had gone through some deplorable experiences in the past six to twelve months, and it was hardly surprising she needed to rest and deal with what we may describe as psychological burnout. She needed to rejuvenate and restore herself to factory settings.

We all slipped back into our normal routine, in fact we didn't really slip out of it. Having Nero and Marti around meant we had to keep that routine up, and Marti's routine was pretty simple. Do what Nero did. If she could do whatever Nero was doing, she was happy so that made things fairly simple. We would get up in the morning, walk and feed all three dogs then there would be napping. There would be another walk in the afternoon before lunch then more napping and pottering around the house. Nero's activity time would kick in around 4 or 5'o'clock in the evening. Nero was a bit of a night owl, much like myself, unless you introduced a ball to him. That was like an on switch any time of the day, his cue to go into over-drive.

So, a lot of the day was spent snoozing. Nero didn't actually have a bed, despite umpteen attempts to introduce one to him. He would find a spot in the house, be it one of the beds upstairs, next to the bed, the landing, and if he wore a hat that would be where he would lay it. Strangely, he never chose the utility room to lay down in despite the underfloor heating. The floor was tiled and if Nero lay on a hard surface it was usually a precursor to him not feeling well, something to do with body temperature regulation I assume.

Then there would be another walk in the evening before dinner which would be when his Nero wacky mode came to the surface. He wouldn't bother you during dinner but once dinner was over you were fair game, and he would bring you all manner of toys to play with him and he would nudge and bug you until you played. His favourite game was 'Border Collie in the middle' where me and Wendy would sit on opposite sofas and throw a ball to each other with Nero in the middle trying to catch it. If I threw it slightly short so Wendy couldn't quite catch it Nero would launch himself at it and suddenly Wendy would have 27 kilos of Collie on her lap. That would be him until the last toilet walk before bed time.

That routine stayed the same when both Marti and Fleur came into the house. Fleur slipped straight into the routine with no issues, although she was less playful than Nero, and she took to it like a duck to water.

As each day passed Fleur's boundaries would increase. She started only coming out of the crate at the offer of food, or in response to gentle tugging of the lead to indicate a walk, but otherwise remaining at the rear of crate. From this, she moved to laying her head alongside the open crate door, air scenting to gather more intelligence about her new environment. Nero continued to be aloof of, whilst every now and then Marti would stop at the entrance of the crate and gaze within.

In hindsight, this was probably quite intimidating for Fleur. By now Marti was older and slightly senile. She would often hold her gaze for an uncomfortably long period. Having an unknown dog glaring into your only escape route must have been akin to having someone you barely know staring at you through the only door to your bedroom.

When Marti was elsewhere in the house, staring at a myriad of other things, Fleur started to investigate the kitchen and the utility room. Both of these rooms are tiled and occasionally the light tip tapping of claws on the floor would ring out. The sound of impending independence.

In the evenings Wendy and I, along with Nero and Marti, would retire into the living room. We had our particular spots, like the characters in The Royle Family, and I would have my place on the floor, usually with Nero, whilst Wendy sat on the sofa and Marti curled up in a ball in her bed. All content in our respective spaces.

One evening, maybe three or four days after Fleur arrived, we were sat in our usual positions when we heard the unmistakable sound of the plastic move in the bottom of the crate. This wasn't unusual as Fleur repositioned herself in the crate. Then came a tip, tap, tip, tap. Dog claws on shiny flooring, it was a combat indicator in our household. Once you are attuned to the sounds in a particular area you notice what a change in sound can mean and in the Morris household a change in tip tapping means a progression from the tiles of the kitchen to the laminate of the hallway. As soon as we heard that change in sound we looked at each other. A quick surveillance scan of the room revealed Marti still in her bed and Nero happily snoring full stretch on the carpet. Wendy and I looked to each other, giggling like school kids who shared a naughty secret.

Her little head suddenly appeared just inside the doorway, her ears forward inquisitively. There was no real anxiety or trepidation, as if she had planned it and psyched herself up to venture further. Wendy and I were all smiles, stifling jubilant giggles so as not to send her scarpering backwards. Then her head would vanish and the familiar sound of the plastic tray in the crate could be heard. Then she would come back again and back to the crate again.

We softly tiptoed to the doorway, but not as softly as we thought and as we got to the hallway to peak at what our new little baby was doing, Fleur span on her paws, slipping and sliding like a deer on ice, and bolted back into her crate quicker than a vampire escaping the morning Sun.

We chastised ourselves for our impatience. Who knows how far we may have set Fleur back in her confidence because we couldn't sit on our excitement. We sat back down but kept our eyes and ears pinned on the door to the hallway for any sign that Fleur might find the courage to try again. Surprisingly, we didn't need to wait long. The tip, tap, tip, tap, then the change in tip tap and we knew she was in the hallway again. Fleur had obviously got a taste for the world outside her crate and suddenly BAM! She literally leaped into the living room as if officially announcing her presence in our family.

'Ta Da! Fleur is here'

It was a fantastic experience for us because it really cemented Fleur's progress. Marti, however, didn't even look up. As long as she could sleep, and Nero was close she didn't care. As for Nero, he was crashed out as well so neither of them really cared what Fleur was doing. They had no idea about the symbolic nature of what had happened, or they did, and they just couldn't care less.

Listening to Fleur tip tapping along the floor and being able to know instinctively where she was by the sound her feet made took me back to my time as a dog handler in Northern Ireland and Strong, the huge Rottweiler. He was a fantastic worker, however he we found he worked best with female handlers. He would always challenge a male handler, so Strong was placed with the female handler on the team. Unfortunately, she couldn't be there 24/7, none of us could, so the kennel duties were shared out between all of the handlers, male or female. Whilst Strong would tolerate this and tolerate male handlers coming to carry out the kennel duties, the male handlers couldn't let their guard down including myself. He enjoyed a good challenge.

One particular day Strong's handler had done a night shift with him. These dogs work hard during their shift and they get a final work, feed, kennel clean and then they get eight hours rest. On this day it was my turn to do the kennel routine and as Strong had been out working I prioritised him, so he could get his head down. He had a nervousness around water, including hosepipes so when I went into his kennel to clean he would stay inside whilst I cleaned the outside. To get to clean the inside, you had to get down on the floor and go through the dog door into the inside. At this point you're pretty vulnerable, especially when there is a walloping great Rottweiler waiting for you on the inside. I had the hose kinked in my hand so there is little to no water coming out, but it's still turned on. This was enough to keep Strong at bay.

I did what I needed to do, and I backed out to get back out of the kennel. Strong at this point is out in the run avoiding the hose, and as I exit he goes back into the kennel which was handy as it meant I could make good my escape. However, like a fool I turned around. My back was now facing the kennel, which meant it was also facing Strong. It was then that I heard the distinctive sound of claw clicking the steel that wrapped the step into the kennel. Instinctively I knew it was Strong who had evidently decided this was his chance to have a pop at me. I turned my head to catch him half way out of the kennel door like a rabbit in the headlights.

It was pretty obvious that his thought process was that he was going to have me. He was going to have that handler. But I had a thought process too. Don't worry, because I've got the hose. However, it is only now I notice that where I have been cleaning and crawling around and what not, the hose now has a double kink in it on the floor. Had Strong noticed that? I swear that he had. He knew something, I could see it in his eyes. He rushed me, and I let go of the hose, but because of the kinks the pressure had built so the hose starts spinning around like a snake whose tail has been trodden on. Water started spewing out of it and I can't control it because the pressure was too high. Strong suddenly charges back into his kennel, struggling to force his way through the small door. I'm in panic mode trying to escape the kennel run but the door opened inwards to stop dogs escaping so I pushed when I should've pulled, and water is spraying everywhere. I finally manage to get out as the hose dies down to s steady dribble on the floor.

This is when Strong thought right. I'm coming for you Morris and he sprinted back out of the kennel and began to slip and slide across the now ice rink floor as I manage to close the door behind me with a wry smile of 'Unlucky me old son' and he gives me a growl of 'No, you're the lucky one mate'. And that is why, or at least part of why, I'm pretty sensitive when it comes to picking up on noises and changes in noises when it comes to dogs. Especially when it's to do with claws tapping on floors.

From then on Fleur would flit between us and her safe bed in the crate. This was amazing. It was a huge bound in progress and now Fleur was confident to explore the house whilst we were in the room. On top of this, each and every time she entered a room her tail would be held up and her signature tail movement was present. That tail swish, held aloft with grace and flair, would announce her arrival. Soon she began using the bed we had set up outside of the crate rather than going into the crate, and then she progressed to using the fold down sofa-bed. This was really heart-warming to see, she looked so content and comfortable on the sofa-bed. In less than a week Fleur had come on leaps and bounds, literally, in terms of her contentment and confidence.

There were a number of things that surprised us in that first week. Fleur had no aversion to human contact and was always happy to receive some fuss. She didn't even flinch when a brush was introduced to her less than quaffed coat. What was most surprising, given her experiences and wounds, was that she was more than content to roll over for a belly rub. How can a dog whose trust had been so abused still show such love and acceptance of people she barely knew? It was astounding.

Fleur didn't mess in the house once, which is bizarre given her street dog past. We had already steeled ourselves for piles and puddles around the house, Marti had prepared us for that, but Fleur didn't leave us any presents. Not one. Training wise, she was a dream when we had expected a nightmare, or at least one of those bad dreams in which you walk into a busy room with no clothes on.

On the lead she walked beautifully, as if she had taken all of the training classes there were. She almost looked like she was tip-toeing as she walked which gave the impression of being tentative, yet she wasn't timid when she was out walking. She took things on board, she would react, but she wouldn't jump. As with toilet training, we had fully expected to have to put in hours upon hours of training to accustom her to walking on the lead. We envisioned spinning and bolting but none of that happened. We tended to walk her to the nearby recreation ground where she would bounce, hop and run with glee to her hearts content, whilst being attached to a long line clipped to her harness. We had begun her walks with double leads, as per Val's advice and our own paranoia following Marti and Nero's escapades. Within a week we were able to swap her to the long line because she walked so placidly and obediently on the lead.

She would walk perfectly fine with Marti and Nero and we coined ourselves the Oreo Pack because the all-white Fleur would walk between the black and white Nero and Marti. She met other dogs and humans with absolutely no issues. This wasn't the street dog behaviour we had expected, instead it felt like Fleur had almost been made for us.

That said, she did come with a few quirks. We quickly discovered Fleur did not like sticks, quick movements or loud noises, but most of all she despised drain covers or any metal work within the road or pavements. She would flip and manoeuver herself any which way she could to avoid walking over one. She was absolutely petrified of them and wouldn't go near them at all. We could only attempt to imagine the thought process which had led to that one.

One foible that was a definite throwback to her street dog origins was her confusion with the food bowl. For the first few days she simply wouldn't take to it and it took a fair few hand fed meals to get her to a point that she trusted the food bowl. It's a bizarre thing to think about, from our privileged pet owner's perspective but Fleur had most likely never even seen a food bowl before going into the vets a few months previously. There was no prior exposure for her to know what it was.

THEN CAME THE SECOND ARTICLE FROM DOGS TODAY

'We first met Romanian rescue Fleur last month. Brutally spayed and suffering terrible injuries because of it, she was fighting for her life as we went to press after diagnosed with distemper. Is there a brighter news this month.

After initially responding well to treatment things took a turn for the worse when the shy little girl developed a nasty infection probably due to the barbaric spaying she had endured.

It was a truly terrifying time remembers Val Philips, founder of Valgrays Border Collie and Animal Rescue, who are committed to helping Fleur find a better life. After her temperature was fluctuating constantly and she had no appetite at all. It really was touch and go as to whether she would make it.

But Fleur was in good hands under the care of Med Vet and slowly she started to improve. Then came the much-longed for news that she was finally free of distemper, and to everyone's relief she began eating again.

Against all the odds, Fleur had pulled through and at the beginning of December she was ready to leave veterinary care and start her rehabilitation with Ramona Apostal, one of Valgray's helpers in Romania. Over the past couple of weeks while her health has been closely monitored,

Fleur has been getting used to being handled and having fun, interacting with other dogs in a big enclosure, all in preparation for her new life in the UK. Val stated Fleur would be in rehab for about a month, so we are all hoping and praying that she keeps improving. She will have a Christmas with people who care. She is a gentle dog, responding to love and cuddles and she does not seem to be holding any grudges towards humans, which totally amazes me. In supporting Fleur each and every one of you are part of her and when she eventually comes to Valgray's UK, you can all pat yourselves on the back for helping her along this journey. The New Year for Fleur will be a new beginning.'

Unbeknown to the Dogs Today team, their words would ring true for both Fleur and us. The New Year brought us all a new beginning and a new dynamic in our lives. As Wendy had initially hoped for, Fleur brought Marti a new lease of life. It made walking more challenging, but we managed well. It was like having Mama Bear, Papa Bear and Baby Bear, with Fleur being the exuberant baby of the group.

As energetic as Fleur could be, she would also take herself for her own quiet time. Maybe she was reflecting on how her life had flip turned upside down over recent months. She would sit off to the side of us all and stare into the group. Watching her new family do whatever it was they were doing. I hope in these moments she felt safe and secure, but who knows?

Fleur's introduction to our lives was a stark contrast to Marti's introduction to the Morris household. Fleur seemed hungry for visual stimulation and would actively use her nose to seek out more information, whereas Marti would actively look to withdraw into her own soul. In those early days with Marti there were times we genuinely believed she wanted to curl up, close her eyes and never open them again. That was never a concern with Fleur, even in those first few days she displayed a quiet inquisitiveness that beheld an underlying zest for life that was wrapped up in a blanket of fear and anxiety.

At this point, of course, we knew little about what had happened to Fleur when she was in Romania, other than what we had heard from Val or found out on Facebook. We have since learned much more via a trip I took to Bucharest, but at the time we relied on second hand information to piece together what Fleur had experienced in those months leading up to her joining our clan. The third instalment of Fleur's story in Dogs Today helped with that.

'The last two issues we have been following the progress of Fleur; a Romanian stray whose survival has been on a knife edge...

After spending a very happy Christmas under the care of Ramona Apostol one of Valgray's helpers in Romania. Fleur has made a remarkable progress;
"The first day I took her from the Milhailesti public shelter, she was in so much pain that she bit me". Remembers Ramona. She was very shy and would crouch in the corner of the room cowering. Now she is such a sweet dog, full of love and affection for me and my team"
Ramona is currently looking after 45 dogs, all saved from public shelter, she says every one of them has a sad story and has suffered physical and psychological damage. You need to be very patient letting them learn to trust and feel comfortable with their new environment in their own time.
Depending on the case it can take up to 6 weeks for Ramona to see any real improvement in a dog's behaviour and interaction with people and other dogs. Fleur's rehabilitation has been even more problematic since she was under medical treatment at the time.
It was important that we took things slowly to build her confidence. By spending time talking to her in a calm tender voice and then progressing to being able to stroke her gently. She began to respond positively, initiating contact with us and feeling happy and healthy.
The presence of other dogs has also helped Fleur greatly and she has become firm friends with roommate Grivei, they have spent many fun hours playing in the snow together. Fleur loves to run and jump like a kangaroo laughs Ramona, but her favourite pastime is taking warm baths and snuggling up to the radiator. Valgray's and Ramona are now making the final preparations to bring Fleur to the UK, so she can begin her new life. Ramona says without the help and support of Valgray's both financially and morally none of this would have been possible. Our gratitude goes to all the wonderful people doing such amazing work to save these lovely dogs. Fleur will have her forever home soon, but she will always have a special place in my heart'

It was a strange sensation reading about a dog that was now living in our home and sharing our everyday life, in a national magazine. This article was more about what had happened to Fleur in Romania and less about Valgrays, as the previous article had been and reading about that was a bit of a wake-up call for me. Prior to Fleur coming into our home I had taken an interest in what was happening in Romania, of course, but it hadn't dominated my day or my thought processes. Now we had her in our home and I was reading about her plight, it hit me differently and being able to look at her, so small and fragile, I thought to myself 'this poor little dog'. It really hit home more being able to put it all together and the magazine was almost like waving smelling salts under my proverbial nose and it woke me up to the turmoil Fleur had been through. The issue then was how to stop thinking about because it really did affect me, and it was all a bit depressing.

It was apparent that in her short but traumatic life, Fleur had touched the heart of a number of people she came into contact with. These people had done everything in their power to ensure this dog had the very best chance of a fulfilling life and a home that cared for her.

It was because of these people that Fleur now lay her head in our home. Three weeks (one for each time she had had to fight for her life) into her time with us and Fleur was settling down well. She and the other two dogs found their places with Nero as King, Marti as Princess and Fleur was our Cinderella. She had found her happily ever after in Hampshire in England. Whilst we still checked social media every now and then, as far as we were concerned this was it. She was here. There was no need to post anything else other than the odd thank you or a picture here and there. She was home, no more updates needed. However, as you have already guessed, the story doesn't finish here.

Chapter Nine

THE HEARTBREAK OF ANOTHER SETBACK

~ • ~

NOBODY WAS MORE thrilled than Wendy as Fleur showed the very early signs of settling in but she was aware that the gentle approach would have to remain for some time yet, as she revealed.

It all seemed to be going so well but this is the story of Fleur, a little dog with a very chequered history. We knew it was still very early days and anything could yet happen.

Sundays in the Morris house tended to pass with little to raise an eyebrow. Sunday the 22nd February, 2015 was no exception. Except, of course, for the new four-legged addition to the family. Fleur had been settling in well, although we knew we had only seen glimmers of the dog she had the potential to be. Her stomach bug had cleared, and her bowel movements were back to something resembling normal. What is it about being either a parent or pet owner that makes you focus on what comes out of them?

Fleur's confidence in the house had grown, thanks to patience and cooked chicken. Gradually we would entice her out of the crate with the food and in time she would start coming out of her own accord when no one was in the room and laying on the sofa in the coffee room. If we appeared she would scamper back into the safe crate, but it was progress nonetheless. Occasionally she would creep into the living room, then scurry back to the kitchen, as if she believed we couldn't see her. Watching her transformation into a pet dog was as entertaining as it was intriguing and astonishing.

That Sunday had started as hundreds of others had, with coffee before saddling up the dogs and walking to the local recreation ground. Although Fleur was fantastic on the lead, she was still nervous when out and about and most definitely had no recall, unsurprisingly, so when we were out she was kept on her harness with a long line attached. This gave her some freedom but ensured her safety, and my nerves.

We had first used a long line when we brought Marti home and we discovered that she had a fear of men and sticks. This meant she would do anything to get away from Andrew, who had not long had hip replacement surgery so was walking on crutches. A man on two sticks was not a combination that Marti had any desire to be near.

So, while we were trying to gain Marti's trust we attached her to the long line, so she had the space the desired with the security we desired. We shortened the line gradually day by day until she learned that the man on sticks she found herself next to wasn't as scary as she had first though, plus, he kept chicken in his pockets.

Fleur had no such issues with Andrew, but what she did have was a change in gears; a desire to run and absolutely no concept of boundaries so Marti's long line offered her the freedom to run and charge around the recreation ground, thirty metres of freedom that she could use to her heart's content to gallop, leap, run and generally tear around the grass. However, we had the control to keep her out of trouble.

So that Sunday Fleur had happily charged around the field like a cat on catnip. She would run and jump like a kangaroo. It was fantastic to watch a dog that had had so much to overcome and so many restrictions finally be able to explore and enjoy her freedom. Every now and then she would attempt to understand why Nero was chasing a Frisbee, and why Marti was then chasing him (because she couldn't bear to be parted from him). The three would charge around the field after one another like a canine Benny Hill sketch on fast forward. Fleur, however, soon realised that that was pointless nonsense for domesticated dogs and held no interest for her at all.

Watching her in the field that day I couldn't help but laugh. She seemed to be full of pure joy and an exhilaration for life that completely overshadowed the illness and pain she had experienced. There were no signs of any illness as she ran through the dewy grass, happy as Larry. She looked more like a puppy than a street dog. It was then that I finally started to believe that everything was going to be OK, that all of the trials and tribulations of getting Fleur here were worth it and it had all paid off. It could have been so different, she could have been aggressive to the other dogs or towards us, but she wasn't. She was such a gentle little girl and had slipped into our life like a glove on a hand. She was happy, and that meant the absolute world to me.

That evening, after a day of cavorting, everyone had settled into their usual individual resting spots; Nero on the floor of the lounge with Andrew, Marti on her bed in the hallway and Fleur on the small fold down sofa-bed in the coffee room that she had now claimed as her own. To me, this in itself was a sign of Fleur's progress, of how far she had come in such a short space of time. She had gone from cowering under a chair in a veterinary clinic, screaming and snapping in pain any time anybody went near her painful stomach, trying to crawl into spaces that didn't exist, to laying peacefully on a cushion on her chosen sofa. She lay in her regal pose, ears cocked forward, eyes sparkling and nose twitching taking in all that went on around her. She was as far away from the life she had in Romania she could get as her tail offered a sweeping sway.

Although Fleur still looked for spaces to crawl into, they were available to her as she had free run of the house along with Nero, Marti and Babe the ninja cat. This suited Fleur. As much as she liked to be in our company, she sometimes preferred to take herself off into her own space, and this was one of those occasions.

We were relaxing watching TV when the most horrendous screaming noise came from the hallway. It was obvious either Marti or Fleur were in serious trouble. It was the most hideous, gut wrenching call for help; completely unrecognisable and it made both Andrew and I jump to our feet, but who was it? Had Marti and Fleur had a fight? I was the closest to the door and started to head to the hallway. I shouted out:

"Hey, hey girls!"

I assumed there had been an altercation and hoped my words would break it up or interrupt it, but then Fleur suddenly barged past me leaving a shocked looking Marti still cowering in the hallway not sure what to do. Fleur was panicked, darting backwards and forwards towards the kitchen then about turning to the living room as if she didn't know what to do to solve whatever it was that was causing the haunting, deafening screaming.

Something was obviously very wrong. She wasn't the nimble, agile

Fleur we saw earlier that day over the recreation ground. She was struggling to stay upright, up on her toes twisting her stomach and simultaneously arching her back. Her tail was pulled between her legs and the ear-piercing scream that got us to our feet emanated from her muzzle. Her eyes were out on stalks and filled with fear. It's an image that is burned into my memory. Her eyes looked through us, beyond us and were filled with utter fear as her head thrashed backwards and forwards.

Her screeching was interrupted by what appeared to be retching. When she wasn't retching, she was squatting. It was obvious to anyone that Fleur was in immense pain and distress. Any dog owner will tell you that seeing your furry baby in pain is abhorrent. It tears your heart out of your chest because not only are they in pain, but they have absolutely no idea what's going on and you can't explain to them. You can't comfort them or reason with them. All you can do is watch them and panic. Tears soon came, and my heart raced. After all Fleur had been through, to get this close to a safe life, was this it? Was it all over so soon?

In the centre of the living room was a wooden, glass topped coffee table my son had made. Fleur and all the other four legged household members of the Morris household have always successfully circumnavigated the table, it was usually the bi-peds that had an issue. Now Fleur was trying desperately trying to force herself into a space under the table that she simply couldn't fit into. She was reverting to that dog that tried to hide from everything, back to the dog that was terrified and suffering. It was as if I was watching her revert right back to the dog she was before all of the patience and work we, and everyone else, had put in. She was back to being that scared street dog.

She continued to try and vomit as she attempted to force herself under the table. Her back legs were giving way and her wide eyes displayed her absolute fear. She had no idea what was happening and neither did Andrew or me. When Nero had had his fit, we knew what was going on, the way he presented was terrifying, but it gave us a clear idea of what was happening to him, so we could respond to that. He was in a shaking heap on the floor, but we could make the area safe for him and do something to help, whereas Fleur was throwing herself around as if an alien was trying to escape from her stomach or possessed by Whirling Dervish on speed. There was no sign as to what was wrong and no logical way to ease it. That scream is still difficult to get out of my head sometimes.

The heartbreak of another setback

I was frozen to the spot with fear, but we obviously needed to do something. Andrew scooped her up from under the table, which was now being thrown around by Fleur's convulsions. She was burning out quickly and she slumped in Andrew's arms like a rag doll. She was losing ground quickly, we had to do something quick. Typically, it was Sunday and it was night, so not the most opportune time to get in touch with a vet.

I called our vets and as I predicted it rang through. It seemed to take forever to get to the automated message that provides the emergency vet number. We are well versed with this practise's emergency procedure thanks to Nero's prolonged fits. I dialled the emergency number, it answered immediately, and Martha introduced herself. Immediately my nurse training kicked in and I fell into medical mode. I gave a quick brief of Fleur's condition; suffering convulsions, retching and in serious distress. Martha responded instantly;

"Get her to the vets. Now!"

We needed to meet her at the Alresford branch of the vets, so she could assess Fleur as soon as possible. I hoped that it would be a quick in, assess, come home or that she could advise us over the phone, but I did stress to her that in my professional, medical opinion this was serious. Part of me thought it may be Bloat but I didn't mention that on the phone

Nero had growled when the commotion had begun but now he and Marti just sat silently. I'd like to think it was a testament to how well trained and adjusted they were, but I think they simply had no clue what was going on, and therefore didn't know how to react.

Whilst I was on the phone Andrew leapt into action and was trying to pick Fleur up, to try and protect her from injuring herself but the coffee table was making it difficult. Eventually he got her in his arms and tried to get her outside. By the time I got the front door open and they were headed outside, she was limp in his arms. It was hardly surprising. When I turned back into the house I saw that the contents of her stomach covered the living room carpet, along with loose stools. She must've been exhausted, much like a human after a seizure.

I desperately wanted to go with them and make sure my baby girl was OK, but I stayed behind to clear up the mess and reassure Nero and Marti that everything was fine. The smell was putrid, like something was rotten. It was at least some form of distraction from the terrifying thought that I may never see my special girl again. I opened all the doors and windows to let the smell out, but also to allow the dogs the freedom to come and go to escape the mess. They both stood at the garden gate looking out to where Andrew's car usually stood. Marti was quiet, but Nero barked, as if calling Andrew home. It was obvious they knew something was amiss.

The dogs being outside did make my life easier as Nero hates the carpet shampooer. Much like he did with the hoover he would chase it and try to bite it which in this situation would only have made matters much worse and acted like a furry muck spreader. I set to work with the carpet shampoo and Dettol and the time flew by. The dogs were pretty quiet, Nero had ceased his barking campaign when Andrew didn't reappear, and I walked them around the block to try and keep some semblance of routine and get them settled for bed. I gave Marti a lot of attention that evening, stroking her and kissing her. I apologised a lot as I still believed something had happened between her and Fleur to set off Fleur's episode and I blamed myself for any distress that had in turn been caused to Marti.

As I had done before, I was probably humanising it but to see Fleur go from OK to this level of distress was heart breaking. I cried a lot that night, mostly into Nero's fur as he gave me bear hugs. Isn't it astonishing how intuitive our pets can be when we are upset? And how much comfort we take from them in our times of need. That pure, unconditional and non-judgemental love and devotion is why we as people feel such a bond and closeness to our pets.

In that moment, sat in the quiet with Marti and Nero, I genuinely believed that the dog I had bonded so closely to over the previous three weeks was never coming home again, and my heart shattered.

Meanwhile Andrew was taking Fleur to get help.

As I picked Fleur up to carry her into the car I kicked into work mode. That's how I operate. I made the conscious decision that Wendy wasn't to come to the vets with me. Firstly, because the other dogs had just witnessed what had happened and for us to then just bomb burst out of the house and leave them alone wouldn't be fair on them. Secondly Wendy was an absolute mess and it would have been dangerous for her to drive to the vets in that state. I felt that if I was driving she would still be panicking and upset. I struggled with the decision because I knew that if I was driving and there was nobody else with me I couldn't do any medical interventions with Fleur should I need to. That said, I could pull over and do whatever needed to be done and that would have been more difficult if

The heartbreak of another setback

I also had to calm a distraught Wendy down.

I carried out a dynamic risk assessment and I worked out that if I placed Fleur on the passenger seat, I could rest a hand on her abdomen and feel her breathing. I could keep her mouth open and her tongue out for the short distance that I had to drive to the vets. It seems sterile, but this is what I am employed to do and it's almost a natural instinct to deal with situations in this manner, and thankfully it worked.

Don't misunderstand, I was distraught, but all of my training kicked in and I knew that there was a time and a place to be distraught, and this wasn't it. It wouldn't help Fleur in the here and now for me to break down. I had to do what was practical to get her the help she so obviously and desperately needed. I could be sad and distressed later but right then I needed to get on with the job in hand.

Wendy rang ahead to ensure the team were ready for my arrival so that when I got there it was clear Martha was ready to receive Fleur and I took her directly into the consulting room. She was tremendous and before I arrived she had already opened up the practice and prepared everything for our arrival.

I stood Fleur up on the examination table and she never moved. She just stood there. She was a little out of breath, but otherwise she just stood there. After all of the drama of the previous hour, from the screaming to the flinging herself around to the drive to the vets, there was a sudden huge anti-climax. Fleur didn't react at all. It was as if she was trying to make us both out to be lying hypochondriacs. She did, however, look like a sick dog. I could see that same look in her eye I had seen before as she stood there on the examination table. Martha looked at her.

"So, what seems to be the problem?" She asked.

It was a legitimate question. From Martha's perspective it must have looked like we were over protective, paranoid owners. I gave her a run-down of what had happened twenty minutes earlier, as well as a brief account of what had happened to Fleur in Romania.

Martha carried out an initial examination of Fleur. Her temperature was 101.4 and her heart rate was normal. She exhibited no pain or palpitation of the spine or any limb. However there were signs Fleur was in some discomfort and Martha watched as Fleur flank watched and licked her abdomen. She constantly stretched on the table into 'downward dog' pose and appeared uncomfortable, but in comparison to what had been explained to her on the phone, this was worlds away. If it hadn't been for my explanation of what had happened previously and Fleur's previous medical history there may well have been little reason to keep Fleur in, given how she presented herself.

Martha was concerned that the issue was internal, potentially a problem with the internal sutures given her experience in Romania. However, on examination there was no evidence that they had ruptured. Fleur was to be kept in over-night on pain medication and she would be reassessed the following morning. That was it. I could do no more. So, I gave her a cuddle and a kiss on the head and I headed home. Walking out of the vets without Fleur was no different to any high tempo style operation. You fight through and then you get the point of reflection, and that's what it felt like walking back to the car. It was time to look back on what had happened and almost debrief in my own head. That can sometimes be the most stressful part. During the incident itself adrenalin kicks in and there isn't time to feel stressed, just carry out the task in hand. It's only when you stop that the emotional side can kick in.

As I thought back on it walking back to the car Nero came into my head. We had had a wealth of experience of dogs in pain with Nero's epilepsy which had put us through the mill. Those fits were horrific to see but he got through them and got better with minimal intervention from us. With Fleur, she was getting worse and worse as we watched her and the screaming and the vomiting and diarrhoea and physical convulsions were all worse than anything I could ever have imagined.

Most of that drive home was focused on me trying to work out what I had missed that day. How could I not have seen a sign of what was to come? Surely there must have been something, some small indicator that Fleur wasn't right. When Fleur was throwing herself around and screaming it was obvious that on a pain scale of 0–10, 10 being the worst, she was experiencing multiples of 10. She was in absolute turmoil and I couldn't then. and I still can't now, fathom out how she couldn't have been in pain during that Sunday. Had she gone from a 1 or 2 to 10 in a split second or did we miss something during that day, or the previous days, that would indicate a higher level of pain? I kept going back and going over and over the events of that day and the previous day picking it apart piece by piece to try and find some sort of explanation, but there wasn't one. I couldn't think of a single thing.

The heartbreak of another setback

With all this running through my head I hadn't actually thought about what or how I was going to tell Wendy, which sounds bad in hindsight, but I knew after all of the work she had put into Fleur and Fleur's journey, and with her medical background she would be asking all the same questions of herself that I was. Wendy wears her heart on her sleeve and has no problem letting you know exactly how upset she is and I fully expected this to break her, no matter how I delivered the news. I expected her to feel like she had let Fleur down and that all of that work she had put in had been for nothing.

When I walked in through the door carrying Fleur's lead and collar, but not Fleur, Wendy's face dropped. It was obvious where her head immediately went, and probably where it had been all evening. There was an initial panic and almost instant tears. I think she had known for the whole evening that Fleur wasn't coming home, for whatever reason, but this was verification. She asked me a million questions about what the vet had said, if Fleur was OK?, what did the vet do?

Needless to say, we didn't sleep that night. We stayed up late just hugging and talking. Wendy felt like a failure as she pictured Fleur back in yet another crate in the vets all alone. She felt helpless and the not knowing what was happening stressed her out.

Fleur was back in a veterinary practice that she didn't know, back in a cage that she didn't know and there was no way of explaining to her that it was all going to be OK. She had gone from being one of three dogs in a relatively normal household to seemingly suddenly in catastrophic pain. We can assume that Fleur had actually been in pain for much longer than she had let on but had learned to cope with it (which is heart-breaking in itself) and now she had been transported somewhere new yet again. Maybe she had become accustomed to this simply being her life now, being taken from one place to another almost always in some degree of pain or discomfort. But we were the ones who were supposed to stop that cycle, we were supposed to be the light at the end of the tunnel and yet here she was back in the vets again.

We weren't expecting any call as we knew Fleur was being kept in overnight for Martha to observe her and do what she needed to do, but even so Wendy didn't sleep. We both stayed up late mulling over what we could have missed and what could be wrong with her. It was difficult to unpick medically what was wrong with her with so little to go on.

Needless to say, we didn't formulate any answers that night and whilst Wendy stayed awake and continued contemplating and deliberating I took the coward's way out and managed to fall asleep.

There had been an understanding with the vets that they wouldn't call us unless they needed to do something and need to talk to us beforehand, so we weren't on tenterhooks waiting for the phone to ring and the vets didn't open until 09:00 on the Monday morning. Calling before that time just gets you the automated message. Waiting for the practice to open so we could call gave us time to walk Nero and Marti. It gave us a distraction, a purpose. We couldn't suddenly change their routine, and I was adamant that we shouldn't. These two still needed us and Marti especially needed us in order to survive. Nero on the other hand was quite capable of walking himself, as he had done on more than one occasion in his younger years. He would also open his own tinned food given the thumbs up.

As we walked that morning both Wendy and I willed the time to pass quicker. Although we were doing our best to ensure as much normality as we could it was fairly obvious, to us at least, that we were a dog down on our walk. I don't think Fleur had been a part of the regular walks for long enough for it to impact on Nero and Marti. It was a sedate and subdued morning for all of us. We were both still numb with shock and we needed to know exactly what was going on with Fleur. It felt like we were in limbo until we knew what was happening. Yet again, we were left not knowing what Fleur was going through, what state she was in or whether or not she would pull through. It was like being transported right back to the beginning when we were waiting for Facebook updates or messages from Val.

After what felt like days, 09:00 came around and we were already at the practice eager to find out how our girl had been throughout the night. The response we got was prompt and straight to the point. Fleur was getting worse. She was panting; she was exhibiting pain in her abdomen, nausea and vomiting. We were advised that they needed to operate immediately. Of course, I gave them verbal consent. I headed to the vets and Wendy went to work. There was nothing she could do, and work would at least keep her mind off what was happening, as much as it could.

From the notes we were given, the operation opened Fleur up to reveal excessive turbid peritoneal fluid along with a large piece of black necrotic small intestine. She had adhesions throughout the abdomen and an intestinal full of strangulation at the distal small intestine adjacent to the caecum. There was also 60cm enterectomy and ileo-ileal anastomosis.

Of course, this meant little to us, more-so me, but in layman's terms it meant Fleur had to have 60cm's of intestine removed and then a repair to the stomach valve. When I entered the clinic shortly after the operation there was a disgusting smell, it was putrid. It hit me like a wall as I entered the building and my initial reaction was to throw up. Due to my work I have smelled death and dead bodies, I have smelled the burning bodies and the broken flesh with the smell of blood and innards but this was beyond the smell of death. In terms of something more civilian it was like walking in to some butchers or when you just start cooking mince-meat and it's just getting warm. If you multiply that by fifty you get something vaguely close to what hit me at the clinic. It was how I could imagine it would smell if you entered a room where a dead body had been festering for weeks in the heat. It was so bad it made my eyes water. It was then that someone told me that the smell was Fleur.

Fleur now lay in a crate on the floor at the back of the vets. She looked weak as she lay there lifeless with a distended stomach. I lay with her on the cold floor and as I watched her it was as if the life was literally draining out of her. When she had arrived at Valgrays she had looked weak and very much like the early pictures we had seen of her in Romania, but even that and the dull pigmentation in her eyes couldn't prepare us for how ill she was now.

We had written all of that off as effects of her travel and everything she had been through. We never saw it as an indication she would become ill again. All we had seen in the weeks she had spent at home was her going from strength to strength in terms of her health and personality, and now here I was trying my best to comfort a dog that could barely respond. Even with the medication Val had given us for Fleur's loose stools, there was no way we could have predicted the extent of Fleur's illness and the fact she had carried this for two weeks with absolutely no indication of the pain or discomfort she must have been in was complete madness. There was no way we could have put two and two together to make four, it just made no sense. All we could think was that it was a testament to Fleur's strength and her ability to hide her weakness and vulnerability.

I lay there with her for a long time on that Monday, being as much use to the veterinary staff as a chocolate fireguard. Not that they complained once. Maybe there were used to owners wanting to stay close to their pets, or maybe they were just too polite to tell me to move.

Either way, I was back on the floor where I was most comfortable plus the cage on the floor level that Fleur was in was big enough for me to crawl into in order to be close to her. I think I was appeasing myself more than Fleur or anybody else, I just needed to be close to Fleur.

We didn't really talk about what would happen if Fleur was to be PTS. I don't think we were really thinking that far ahead, nor had it entered our minds that it would need to be discussed. We knew Fleur was severely ill, but she was strong, we knew that too. We knew she could fight and, despite everything she had been through, we had faith that was just to be another wall she had to climb and climb it she would. She had to.

Oddly, considering my dislike of not being in control it actually made it easier in some way that she was in the vets because at least that way we knew that she was in the right place. She was much better off there at this point than she would've been at home and I knew that there was nothing I could do for her, other than try and comfort her when I was there with her so her being in the vets gave me piece of mind and put me in a much better mental place than I would've been had I been the one in control of making her better.

It helped that we knew we could get information as and when we needed it. We knew we could go and talk to people face to face or pick up a phone, whereas when Fleur was in Romania we were relying on third party information and misinformation. During the time that Fleur was in Romania there was a definite sense of detachment. Everything was happening hundreds of miles away under someone else's care, so the information that was coming through was a little more superfluous that the information coming from the vets.

t this point my relationship with Fleur was changing, it was beginning to evolve. There wasn't a strong bond there but there was a blossoming relationship. Fleur had only physically been in our lives for two weeks, so the word bond is probably a bit strong for what we had at that point, but the relationship was growing stronger every day which meant the dynamics were changing and the need for information was different than it had been when Fleur was in Romania.

Thanks to the updates from the vets, we had faith that although Fleur

The heartbreak of another setback

wasn't well by any stretch of the imagination she wasn't getting any worse. She was on IV pain relief and her stats weren't terrible, so although she wasn't improving she was holding steady. Then, on the Tuesday the update from the vets came in and we were told that Fleur was deteriorating. She was uncomfortable and vomiting again. The upshot was that Fleur wasn't recovering from her operation. One of the vets stated that the valve didn't look viable, and Fleur was becoming septic. Fluids were taken from her swollen abdomen which showed sepsis, so they suspected peritonitis.

Fleur's pain had increased over the abdominal area which was swelling. Wendy and I along with the vets discussed various tests and scans but the bottom line was Fleur was failing. The vets advised us to do what was kindest for Fleur, and that was to put her to sleep.

Chapter Ten

WHERE THERE'S LIFE, THERE'S HOPE

~ • ~

IT IS NEVER easy to translate exactly what is going on in the mind of an anmal, even a dog which is probably the closest four-leffed copanion known to man. However, the body language of Fleur seemed to indicate how she had felt about her new home and then her setback.

I knew being in a warm house with food and people who weren't hurting me was too good to be true. I knew I would eventually have to move again as that is what my life had been recently. I fully expected to be moved on again at some point, and that's what happened, I just wish it hadn't happened the way it had. As I lay barely conscious in another chemical smelling cage room I think I had given up. I had gone into a passive state many times before, extracted myself from a situation and just let it happen or wash over me because it was inevitable, and I didn't know how else to do deal with it, but this was different. This was now my choice to fight or not fight, and at this point I didn't think I had any fight left.

It had all started well, and from that first night I arrived at the house I felt comfortable. I felt like I wasn't in danger. I had a small cage, which gave me the safe space I needed and there was never any forced interaction, other than to go outside to the toilet. I spent a lot of time in the cage watching what was going on, watching the other two dogs wander around and watching what the two humans did. They just went about their own business and left me be, much as the human at the large cage room had done. It helped me feel safe and secure, knowing that my interactions with both the humans and the environment were on my terms. I was also able to spend most of my time recharging and resting, a wall of exhaustion had hit me when I arrived at the house and it took a while for me to shake off that constant tiredness.

As the days passed I started to trust that I wasn't in danger and trust that maybe I could venture outside my cage and into the wider world. So gradually I began exploring the immediate room, and there was nothing scary, nothing that presented any real danger. The other dogs had acknowledged me, but they hadn't displayed anything that worried me, so I didn't feel too scared about stepping outside of my cage outside of a toilet break. The floor was cold and hard, like the floor at the house I went to before this one. There were so many new smells and scents to explore including both of the other dogs and a cat that I had seen once or twice but who had completely disregarded me.

The further I managed to get outside of the cage, the more my confidence grew. It was different to exploring the large cage room. I could see everything in the large cage room, but this was a mixture of different rooms and areas I couldn't see, so my anxiety was increased, but the safety I felt within the house began to override that and eventually I started to feel comfortable coming out of the crate when the humans weren't there. One night I started to creep out of my cage to explore. I could hear noises from another room, so I knew I was safe, and suddenly something took over me, a confidence and a buoyancy that compelled me to go and find company, to seek out the humans and other dogs. So, I did. I followed the voices but then there were two face peering around the door and I assumed they were coming to grab me and take me somewhere else or hurt me or worse, so I spun round and charged back to my cage.

I looked back along the corridor and they had vanished. They had gone back to their safe space too. Maybe they weren't going to come after me at all. I took courage from this and leapt into the room they were in. It was a risk and it could go one way or another, but thankfully it was fine. I wasn't hit or hurt or dragged back to cage. In fact, they looked as surprised as I was that I had done it so dramatically. From here on any idea of threat was gone and I would happily go from my cage to where the humans were without too much worry. I always knew I had my safe space to go back to and it was always accessible. When outside of the house I could run

Where there's life, there's hope

and charge around as I had done in the large cage room. I could feel that exhilaration and that freedom that was glorious, but I always knew I had the safety of the humans near me and the comfort of having the other dogs around too. I was free to make my own decisions with the safety buffer of knowing the humans I shared a house with were trustworthy.

Those feelings of security and comfort that I had gained whilst staying in the large cage room all came back, and I had begun to feel like maybe this was going to be it. Maybe, despite my preconceptions, I was going to stay here and that nothing was going to change that. I wasn't going to be dragged out and taken somewhere else. But, of course, that night came and all that changed yet again.

I wasn't feeling myself that night, I knew something was wrong, as I had so many times before, so I took myself to my cage and lay down in peace until it passed. I was laying on the blanket, watching the cat eating biscuits from a bowl when I felt the most piercing, stomach burning pain I had ever felt. It was like a blanket of pain had been thrown over me and I had no idea what to do. I screamed out. I needed help. I knew that. What was happening? All I could think was that I needed help. Someone please help me! Make this horrendous pain go away. Why was it hurting?

I flew into the room where the humans were, still screaming and trying to find a position that eased the pain. It was like something inside me was dying and trying to escape to do so. All I could think of was how much it hurt and why wouldn't it stop. Why weren't the humans making it stop? Small spaces meant safety, so I found the nearest one and crawled under it trying my hardest to get away from the pain, to hide from it and escape it, anything to make it stop. But it didn't stop. It got worse and I only stopped screaming to be sick. I had experienced all kinds of pain in my life but nothing as utterly terrifying as this. I couldn't see any reason for the pain to be there, I had no clue or indication as to what was happening and that completely freaked me out.

I had no idea what the humans were doing, I just tried my hardest to get away, get into a safe space and stop the pain. I remember being in the car and thrashing around completely consumed by the pain and trying to get it to stop. Why was this happening? What was going to happen to me? Please, please make it stop.

The male human picked me up and carried me into another new building, it was another that smelled like chemicals. Suddenly the pain eased. I had no idea where I was going so I tried to hide as much of the pain as I could, I didn't want to appear vulnerable. He placed me on a cold metallic table where I just panted, utterly exhausted. Another female human looked me over and prodded and poked me. It didn't feel too bad, but there was a pain in my abdomen where the other people in the dirty cage room had hurt me. I licked at it to try and ease the pain and calm myself. It worked a little, so I repeated it.

I was put into a small cage and the male human left, after giving me some physical comfort. This was it, I was in my next place. I wouldn't see that home again, I wouldn't see the male or the female again. Instead I would be in this new chemical smelling room until I was taken to the next place. That night was hideous. I felt so bad physically as well as completely alone and in yet another new place. Where was I going to end up now? Was this pain going to stop? Why was it hurting so much? I was sick throughout the night and I couldn't stop panting; the pain was too much to bear without panting. It seemed to make it easier to cope with if I panted.

I barely slept, I was too uncomfortable to relax properly. I had the thing attached to my leg that had been attached the last time I was in a chemical smelling room. As the night passed it beeped regularly. As daylight broke into the room people started coming in and out and it wasn't long before a person came to my cage and I started to feel really sleepy. The next thing I know I'm waking up again back in my cage. My abdomen was painful, but now there was a new wound. I had absolutely no energy to get up or move. I felt completely and utterly drained.

I just lay there. There was nothing else I could do. It was as if I was looking at my life through a puddle, it was blurry and unclear. I had no idea how much time had passed but I remember hearing a familiar voice. My ears twitched towards it, but I couldn't move. The male human from the home had come back and was in the chemical-smelling cage room. He had come back! I wasn't alone any more as he lay with me on the cold floor. I felt his warm body next to mine as his hand rested gently only me and played with my fur. I couldn't really respond but just having that physical contact made the increasing pain more bearable. It was like having Shimeka or the deformed leg dog back next to me offering me some succour.

He left later, I had barely moved the entire time he was there. I wanted to, I just had nothing in me to physically be able to move. All I could

Where there's life, there's hope

do was lay there, motionless and terrified. It felt like everything was beginning to slip away, like the lights were slowly starting to go out. The pain got worse and my abdomen started to get bigger. I was so scared, what was happening to me? Why was I feeling like this and why was my stomach getting bigger? I didn't want to be here, like this. I wanted to be back in my safe cage. I wanted Shimeka next to me, her head over my neck letting me know everything was OK. Lying in yet another cage, hurting more than I think I ever had before and feeling sick with absolutely no understanding of why, I had had enough. I closed my eyes and a huge part of me hoped to meet Shimeka.

It was a nail-biting time for everyone, for Fleur of course, for Andrew who had been at the veterinary surgery, for their two dogs who knew that something was clearly wrong, for the ninja cat who grudgingly admitted that something was out of the norm and, of course, fpr Wendy who's work provided some distraction but little consolation as she recalled.

We had been told on the Monday that the next thirty six hours were critical for Fleur, and during that time I had been keeping Val updated via messages, telling her that Fleur had taken a turn for the worse and needed more x-rays and scans, and potentially opening up again. Every time I wrote her a message it was through tear-blurred vision. My girl had been through so much already, why was she being put through this now?

Val had then in turn posted updates to the Valgrays Border Collie and Animal Rescue page, as well as her own personal page. She posted that Fleur was responding well to treatment, and was pleased to see Andrew on his visits, but that she wasn't out of the woods yet and boy did we know it. We felt it.

I was, and still am, shocked at the rate at which Fleur's social media following grew. Her story seemed to resonate, and people were joining and following daily. With that came a feeling of obligation to keep the followers updated, so it was always in the back of my mind to that we needed to give everyone in internet land the facts as we got them, but at the same time to come across as positive as we could. We needed to give people hope, and in turn that helped keep our own fires of hope burning.

Although it sometimes felt like a duty to keep people updated, I did feel the love and support and knew I had made friends through Fleur's story. Ever the realist, Andrew was quick to remind me that I had never met these people, and wasn't likely too, so they weren't my friends.

He would always remind me to be careful about what I wrote, being completely security conscious. I think he was trying to protect me from any negativity, but at this point there wasn't any.

The house seemed quiet without Fleur there, not that she was a noisy dog, but there was something missing. Part of what made our house a home, what made our family complete, was gone. We both still had to work but we also wanted to make sure Nero and Marti were OK. Maybe what had happened had made us hypervigilant and more inclined to want to be at home with the dogs than before. Andrew was more flexible than me as I had clinics to run and patients to see when all I really wanted to do was be with my own furry patient. I struggled to concentrate, I missed meals and wasn't sleeping properly.

I found that I was walking the dogs for longer than usual and I would end up telling other dog walkers what had happened. As you know the Morris household is one of routine, and that goes for dog walks too, so we usually met the same people on the walks. They noticed the lack of Fleur and I was anxious that people would wrongly assume we had taken Fleur back to Valgrays, so I would end up talking a lot about what had happened, which helped.

Marti and Nero carried on as normal with their daily doggy tasks, but every now and then they would come up to me and rest a chin on my lap, cruising for a fuss. I am convinced they sensed something in me, or about the change in atmosphere of the home, and this was their way of comforting me. They would nudge my hand or arm to elicit a stroke and it kept me calm. It gave me a purpose to carry on for them; I felt wanted. Needed. I had to carry on as normal for them, even if on the inside I was tearing apart. Both of them seemed more excited when I was at home and they turned into my shadow, following me everywhere. They seemed more anxious when we would leave, and we made sure there was always someone at home for them. It was clear that Fleur's absence was not only felt by myself and Andrew.

Andrew wrote in a post following one of his Fleur visits that on the way to the clinic he came across a group of pheasants in the road. He managed to break in time, and in his post he stated that fortune favours the brave. To him it was like an omen for a good day. At the vets he was told that Fleur had had a good night and had taken on liquid food in the morning. This was progress.

She was passing urine and taking in water. She even rolled over for tummy tickles and allowed the veterinary nurse to brush her (Andrew had taken in the Dogs Today articles, so Fleur was getting the VIP treatment. Quite right too). Fleur was no pheasant, but she was brave, and Andrew wrote in his post that it seemed all of her followers' prayers and healing thoughts were working. The general feeling was positive.

However, Andrew was wrong. On Wednesday the 25th February I was on a half day, so in the morning it was my turn to visit Fleur. I sat with her inside the floor level cage and gently stroked her fur, but she didn't respond. My initial thought was that it was the drugs she was on following her surgery. I still believed she would be OK and I carried on stroking and brushing her, in my head she would be home by the weekend. That day they had already completed some tests prior to my visit, and I could sense the vet looking at me, as if waiting for the right moment to speak. In a vain attempt at self-preservation I tried to avoid eye contact, but of course that was impossible. When our eyes did meet he dealt a crushing blow.

Fleur was deteriorating, she wasn't responding. I was told that Fleur had become aggressive overnight due to the pain she was in, much like she had when she was in Romania. She had started vomiting and was now on the maximum pain relief. She had gone from wanting tummy tickles to resenting abdominal palpation and had heat all over her abdomen. Her temperature had risen to 102 and she was tachycardic. Tachynpnoeic fluid had increased in the abdomen and she was going septic. There was possible wound dehiscence and increased intestinal necrosis.

I took a photo of her and sent it to Andrew. This couldn't be happening, not again. I truly believed she was improving, and now they were talking about opening her up again. There was a whirlwind of information going around my head as I drove to work that afternoon. Four words stuck out. 'Do the right thing'. I kept seeing her, laying there in the cage lifeless and unhappy. I felt such a failure and most of that day at work was spent crying. That was probably the day that broke me. I was already run down and now I was unable to think rationally. I wasn't sure how much more I could take, and we now also had extended family and social media waiting on an update.

We, of course, kept Val up to date with Fleur's progress. Her prognosis was not good, and it was getting worse. Back at home we tried to keep everything normal for the dogs, but the stress and emotional upheaval kept taking their toll. I cried so many tears I'm surprised there was anything left to cry. I had the support from close friends, especially those that lived close to us and had met Fleur out and about and of course there was more support for Fleur, and us, on the Valgrays Facebook page. There were daily prayers and well wishes and despite it just being words on a screen it helped. It gave me something to look forward to and helped me focus on the positives.

I was interested in what people were saying about us and Fleur and it cemented my belief that we were doing the right thing by Fleur. There was now even more of a reason to will Fleur to fight and to make sure she survived not just for us but for her ever growing extended family and fan base. I have been accused on a number of occasions of focusing too much on another people's happiness rather than my own, and that's probably what I was doing here. Even with the expanding online community I still felt alone, so I willed Fleur's story to have a happy ending, so that everyone else would be happy and then in turn, I believed, I would be happy. Inside I was completely miserable and part of me just wanted to give up. I was exhausted, and my emotions were all over the place, but I felt I couldn't share this with anyone, not even Andrew. So, I remained focused on ensuring everyone else was OK and updated.

I posted on my Facebook page after one visit to see Fleur. I told people following Fleur's story that she had taken yet another turn for the worse and she was potentially going to have further emergency surgery that afternoon. How this little girl was going to cope with yet more surgery was beyond me. Fleur's illness and recovery was taking over our life, but for so many people our pets are just as important to us as human members of the family. There is often a stronger bond with pets, especially dogs, as they love us unconditionally. They respond to our affection and when we are happy, they are happy, when we are sad, they are sad. They appear intuitive and, whether rightly or wrongly, that increases that emotional link we feel with them. So, when one of them is suffering, we do everything within our power to ensure they are as comfortable and cared for as possible.

Andrew called in to the vets after work that night, as I had told him Fleur was deteriorating. I stayed at home, as I always did when Andrew visited the vets, and cuddled Nero and Marti whilst checking FaceBook, acknowledging comments and well wishes. I would often walk them too.

Images of Fleur

Smiles all around. (Photo copyright MojoElMundo.com)

Fleur – the dog that refused to die

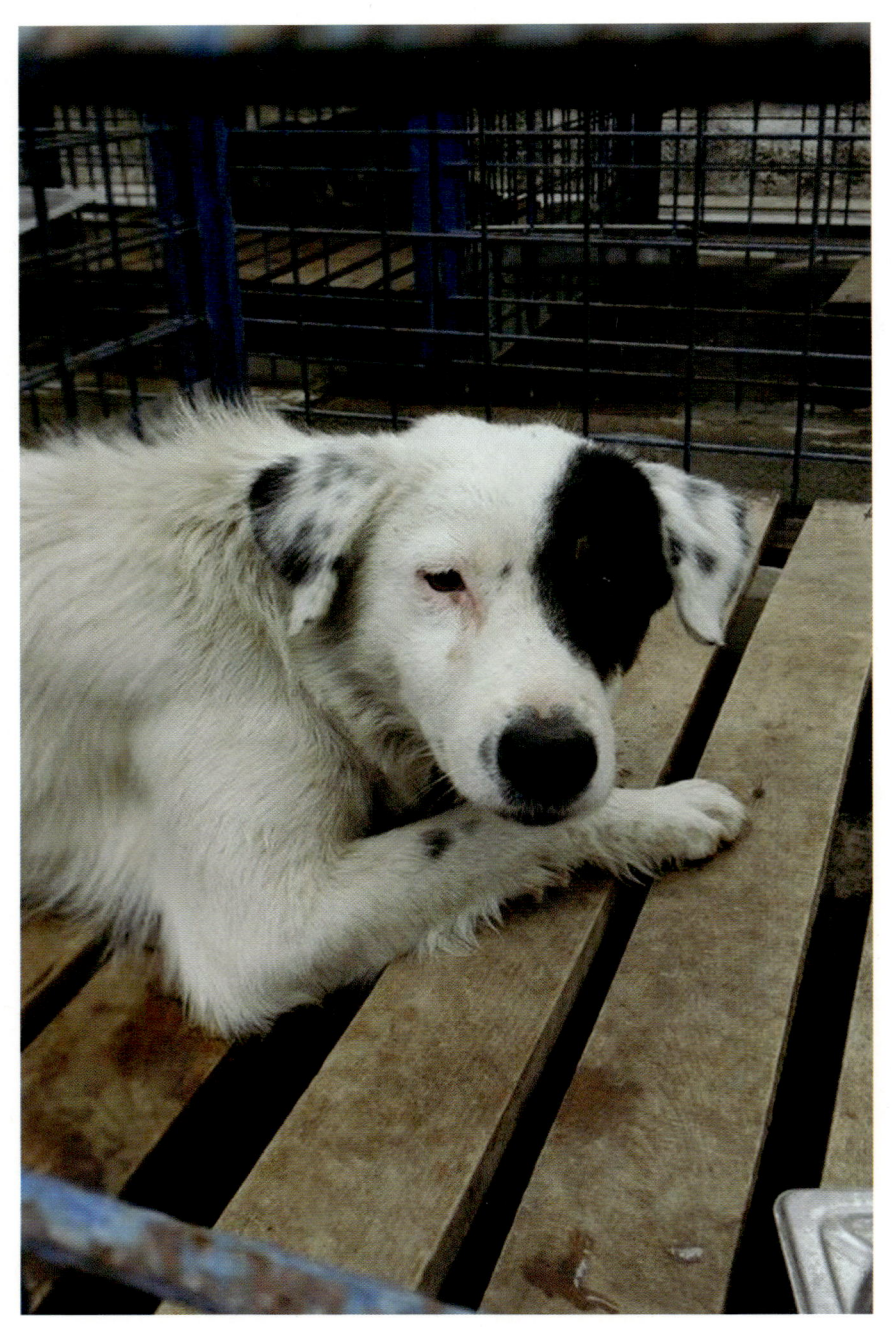

Fleur looks so depressed in the pound.

Images of Fleur

Will she survive? Andrew admits he wasn't sure when he saw these photos on social media.

Fleur – the dog that refused to die

Left: *The botched operation meant poor Fleur had her intestines falling out of the gaping hole that hadn't been properly closed when she was spayed.*

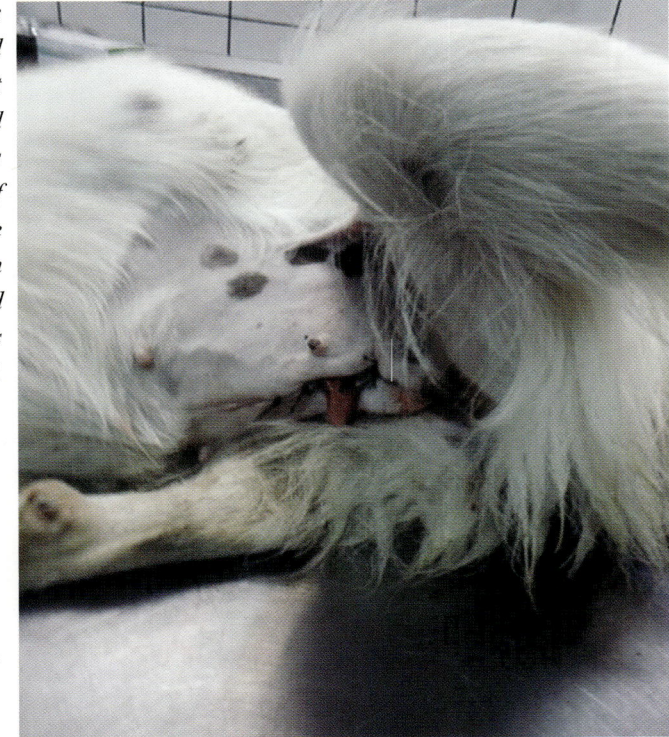

Below: *Poor Fleur wearing an identifying tag in her ear that shows she has been crudely neutered and vaccinated.*

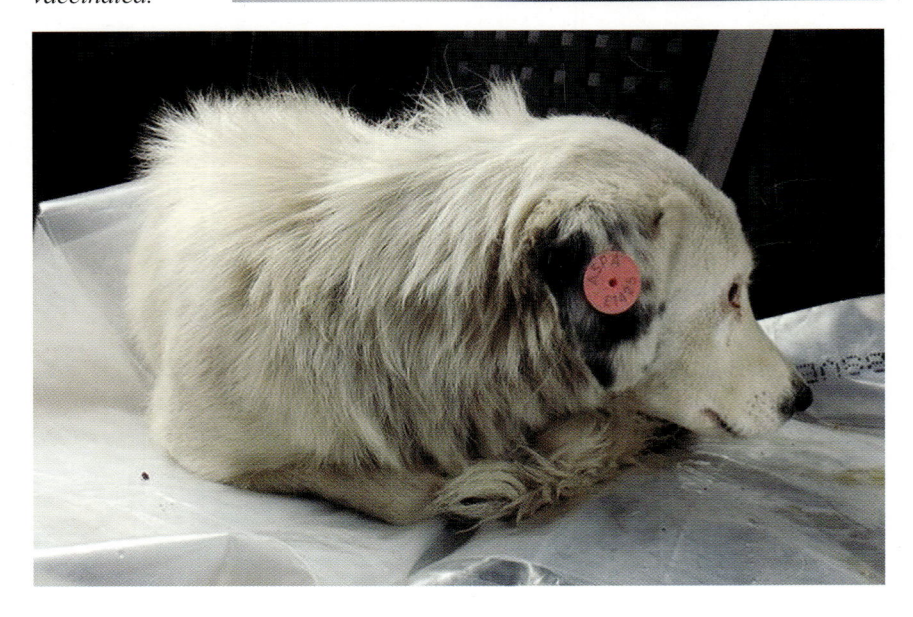

Images of Fleur

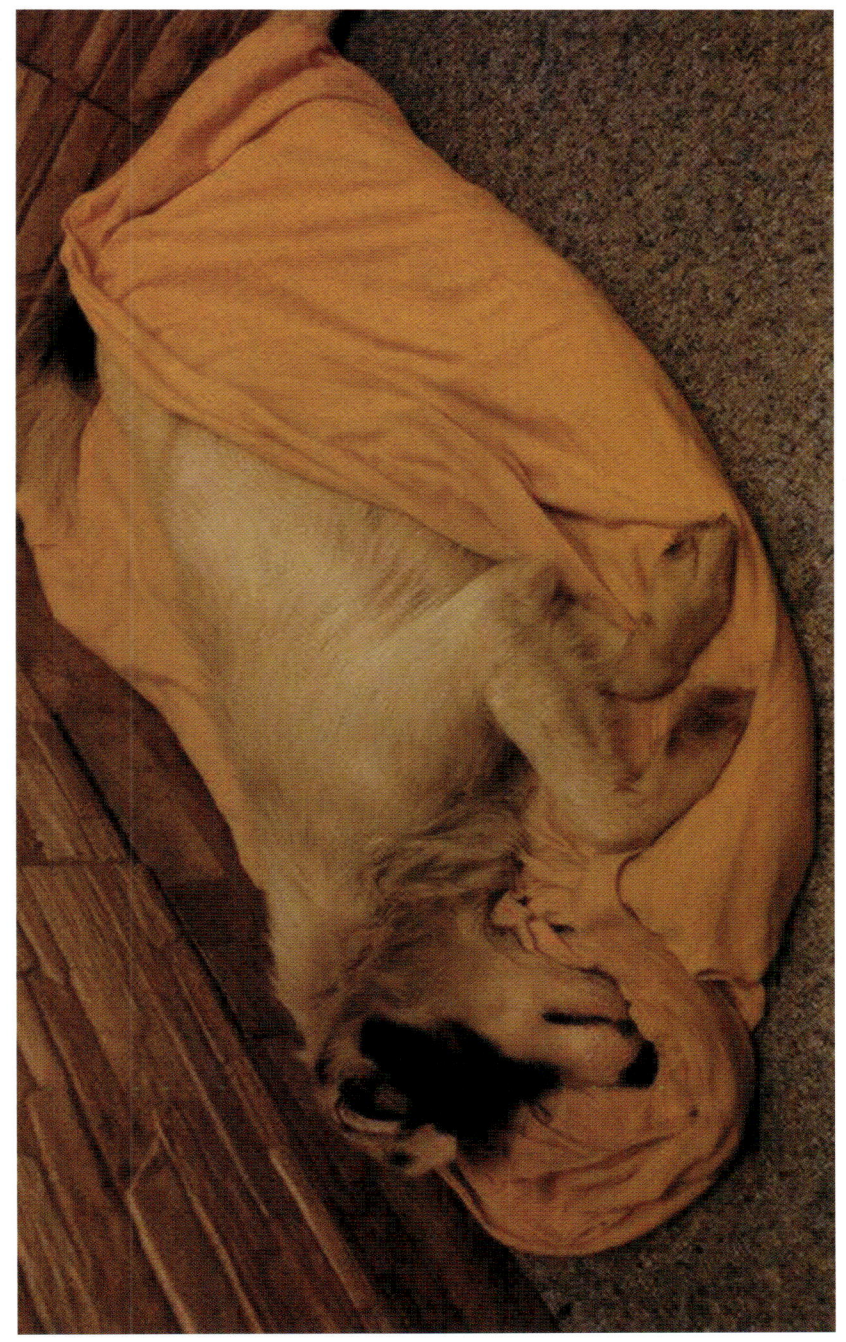

Very weak, Fleur fighting both distemper and infection.

Fleur – the dog that refused to die

Above: *Fleur survives and has Christmas in Romania, waiting to be allowed to come to England.* Below: *At Romana's place, looking much stronger.*

Images of Fleur

Left: *Wendy meets a very tired Fleur for the first time in Val Phillips' kitchen.*

Below: *It was Val of the Valgray's Border Collie rescue who had first spotted Fleur and offered help. Val already knew the Morris family, as they had coped so well with a previous rescue from the charity.*

Fleur – the dog that refused to die

Left: *Andrew and Fleur bond!*

Below: *Fleur really warms to being a pet.* (Photo copyright MojoElMundo.com).

Images of Fleur

Above: *Fleur fits right in with Marti (left) and Nero (right).* Below: *Fleur enjoys her walks, everything seems perfect. But no one knew that inside her intestines are dying. Fleur was soon to become dangerously ill.* (Photos copyright MojoElMundo.com).

Fleur – the dog that refused to die

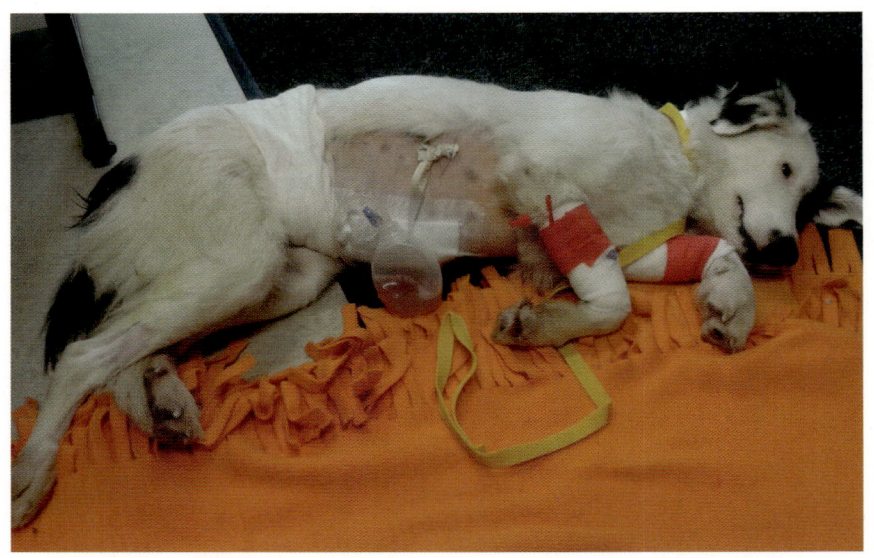

Above: *Fleur needs emergency surgery to save her life. A team of the best experts in the world operate on her all night. No dog had ever before survived this operation.* Below: *The Royal Veterinary College staff fall in love with brave Fleur. The dog lovers of Facebook raise the money for her life-saving surgery in record time.*

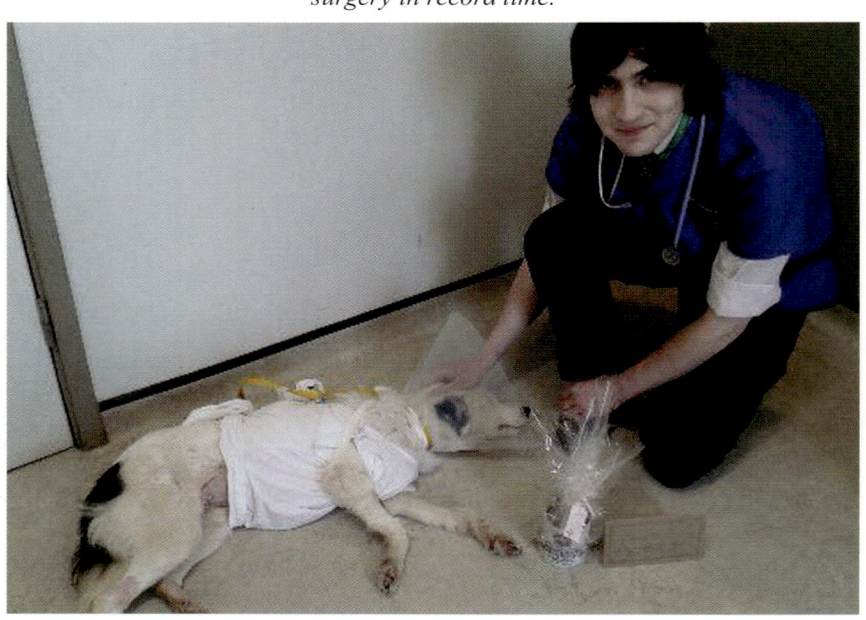

Images of Fleur

Fleur becomes a cover girl after a photo session with famous pet photographer Penelope Malby.

Fleur – the dog that refused to die

Left: *Noel Fitzpatrick, the Supervet, presented the award to Fleur. In the audience was another super vet, one of the team who had saved Fleur's life.*

Below: *Fleur met up with vet Vicky Lipscomb who had brought her kids to the London Pet show and was delighted to see her very brave and famous patient honoured. Vicky had been the lead vet that long night when they had all fought to save her life.* (Photos copyright MojoElMundo.com).

Images of Fleur

Above: *Of course, Fleur won!* Below: *Fleur met some of her fans at Crufts.*

Fleur – the dog that refused to die

Left: *Fleur enjoys being on TV.* (Photo by Val Phillips)

Above left: *Actress Rula Lenska was a little star struck meeting Fleur and Wendy at the launch of Wet Nose Day.* Above right: *Fleur and Andrew were slightly star struck when they met Matisse at Crufts, one of the winners of Britain's Got Talent.*

Images of Fleur

Fleur enjoying her new life with her dear friends Maggsie and Nero in 2017.

Fleur – the dog that refused to die

Fleur becomes a doggie Kate Moss, appearing on the cover of Dogs Monthly for the Crufts issue.

Where there's life, there's hope

They must have been exhausted with all the walking, but it helped to be doing things. Especially things that involved caring for the two dogs that were still at home.

At the vets Andrew found lying on the floor gives you a unique perspective of the veterinary clinic, and Andrew being Andrew he had spent a fair amount of time lately on the floor of the veterinary practice. The practice is very similar to a hospital, from the layout to the smell and the clinical sanitation. It's no wonder so many pets have an anxiety based reaction to going into them. At least if we go to hospital it is usually nominal. We have made a conscious decision that we understand the logic behind. Whilst we may explain to our pets why they are going into the vets; those explanations are lost in translation.

So, there was Andrew, laying on the floor of the back room of the veterinary practice which almost gave him a dogs-eye view and an understanding of why it elicits fear in patients. In the room along with Andrew and Fleur was a large male collie that had traits of Nero. He was eye level with Andrew and clocked him as a soft touch straight away and a full on charm offensive was unleashed. He barked. He whined. He pranced and there was some intense tail wagging. He couldn't have made his message clearer to Andrew.

'Spring me out of this joint'.

It was tempting, not in the least because above Andrew was an elderly tabby cat who had evidently been admitted for constipation. Unfortunately for all residents of the back room, this cat was no longer constipated, and no amount of Dettol was going to neutralise that odour. Andrew shared a look with the collie. They could both do with being elsewhere right now, for the sake of their suffering nostrils.

At the same time, there was nowhere Andrew would rather have been. He lay on the floor, half in and half out of Fleur's cage causing the busy vet nurse to step over him whilst juggling the soiled bedding of not-so-constipated-now kitty. Fleur was completely listless. Her fur was both the colour and texture of straw. Her skin had no elasticity and the only movement she made was caused by the fast and shallow rise and fall of her rib-cage as she breathed.

As Andrew lay his face close to hers he couldn't feel any breath on his cheek and the pigmentation of her jowls was white. Her normally glistening black nose was dry and dull. It was pretty obvious that she was spent. Andrew took no comfort from the fact she was hooked up to a drip and on medication. Our prayers, to whichever God would listen, weren't being responded to.

Andrew took a photo of Fleur on his phone as he lay with her. Looking at that photo when he showed me it was forgivable to think the dog being depicted had long since passed. It was haunting to see, as if Fleur had been laid to rest so owners could pay their respects. The picture of Fleur in Romania showed a dirty, scruffy, thin dog but there was hope and life in her eyes, and that's what had drawn me into her. This picture wasn't the same dog. She wasn't thin, she was emaciated. Her weight loss was dramatic, and she looked so weak. She had given in. It was a distinct slap in the face, a portent of what devastation may be to come.

We were taking every day as it came and trying to find positive aspects of hope wherever we could, it was a survival tactic and a way of moving from one hour to the next without completely giving in. We knew she was in the right place and we tried our hardest to remember that Fleur had been through so much she deserved us to fight for her as hard as she fought to make it to us. She needed us to ensure that we were prepared to do anything to help her and give her every chance of survival. It was the least she deserved. We trusted our vets, having had plenty to do with them with Nero and Marti, and it was a comfort to know they would do everything they could for her. Every day that she survived meant she was another day closer to coming home, at least that's what I told myself in my head. That's how I got from day to day and I expected her to be home by the weekend.

Whilst Fleur was still there hooked up to machines and receiving medication there was still hope, right? Surely?

Chapter Eleven

FLEUR AND HOPE FADE FAST

~ • ~

I USUALLY FIND strength when laying on the floor with the dogs. But on occasion, being both physically and mentally low means vulnerability can creep in. And as I lay there staring at what felt like an empty outline of a dog that had already pulled herself back from the brink more than once, the vet who had originally operated on Fleur came into the room.

He asked me to move so he could do some cursory checks on Fleur. I have no idea what checks they did because I was distracted. As he did his checks and adjustments he verbalised his medical opinion on Fleur's care and prognosis, and this was what I was focused on.

The vet made it very clear that Fleur was not making progress. He stated that it was his and his colleague's opinion that they needed to open Fleur up yet again and he expected to find that Fleur's problem would have deteriorated, and the tissues that had been joined together were probably infected and breaking down. He conceded that if this was the case there was nothing more that could be done, and Wendy and I needed to consider doing the right thing.

"What do you mean by the right thing?" I asked, already knowing what the vet was eluding to.

"Well, if we cannot do any more for Fleur, euthanasia is the only option," the vet replied, confirming my fears.

I just stared up at him trying my hardest not to hate the poor vet who had just basically told me I needed to make the decision to kill my dog.

I understood it was probably the right decision if the procedure had not been successful, which it was fairly obvious it hadn't, but that didn't make me hate him any less in that moment.

So, I continued my vigil over a dog that gave no output, but my presence was quickly becoming a hindrance to the staff. I was laying half in and half out of Fleur's cage which caused the staff to manoeuvre around me to give care to the other patients. I could feel myself becoming more and more of a physical obstruction, but I was on the verge of becoming an emotional one too. I could feel my mood slipping and I was in danger of becoming very verbally negative.

I needed to leave, but not before I made it clear that the practice had our agreement to conduct further exploratory surgery to find a way forward for Fleur. Furthermore, regardless of what those procedures discovered, Wendy and I were to be contacted before any further decisions were made. No decisions were to be made on my behalf

My fear was that I had absolutely no control over the situation or what was happening. I could not be there during the surgery which in my head meant those that were there could make decisions and take steps in which I had no say. The veterinary staff assured me they would keep us informed, but Fleur was my dog. She was my responsibility and without that control I felt helpless.

Now I had to relay the message to Wendy. Thankfully, although Wendy may be more emotional I am more pragmatic and methodical in my thinking than she may be, when it came to the medical and veterinary side of caring for our pets she had her head screwed on the right way. I didn't have to worry about trying to protect her from the truth of the situation because the fact of the matter was Wendy would probably have a much better understanding of what was happening than I did, and it would more than likely end up being me that had to ask the questions rather than the other way around.

When vets talk it just doesn't make sense to me, the words they use go in one ear and out of the other purely because I don't understand what they are telling me. If a vet calls us about one of the dogs now I always tell them to call Wendy, or I pass the phone to her. I didn't have to pre-plan how to tell her because I knew that when I did tell her, she would have questions and my immediate response would be to call the vet. Then she could explain it back to me in layman's terms, so I understood it too.

Still, it was never going to be a pleasant conversation to have and that night when I got home I sat Wendy down. I kept my tone soft and hushed, almost as if just saying the words was hard, like they didn't want to come out because it would make it more real.

"Fleur is dying, you do know this don't you?"

Of course, it was not something Wendy wanted to hear, neither did she really need telling that the news was as bad as it gets.

Thursday morning on February 26th was Day Four of Fleur's unwanted sojourn at the vets. Andrew had an important meeting in London that he had to attend, in essence he had to fight to keep his job, so this wasn't something he could pull a sickie from. Up until this point he had been fortunate enough to be working close to the vets, so he had visited Fleur every day.

I still wasn't feeling great, I wasn't really eating or sleeping much, and I think, looking back, I was definitely suffering from exhaustion. On top of this, I had started a new job and was in daily contact with people suffering from common colds, coughs and minor illnesses. Exhaustion lowers the immune system's effectiveness and I began to feel worse as I pushed forwards. I am certain I picked up a viral infection from work, my temperature rose, I was aching constantly and there were flu type symptoms. I had pushed through until the Wednesday evening shift, but early that Thursday morning I called in sick for my morning shift.

I only worked half days on a Thursday, but I couldn't shake the feeling of guilt. I hate calling in sick. As a nurse you are acutely aware of other's needs before your own, plus I hate letting people and patients down. I knew Andrew had to be in London that morning, so it offered me the opportunity to visit Fleur, however I was in no fit state to make clinical decisions or prescribing drugs without one hundred percent focus. My colleagues completely understood, and it probably helped that I sounded awful.

Andrews words were still running around and around in my head:

"Fleur is dying, you do know this, don't you?"

It was this comment that had hit me hard, I suddenly had an understanding of the 'wall' runners talk about hitting. I was done, I'd taken all I could take and hearing those words from Andrew were the straw that broke the camel's back. I just sat and cried my eyes out that night, Whilst I knew Fleur wasn't looking good when I visited her that Wednesday morning, the vet had said 'We need to do the right thing'. This was ambiguous, the meaning and outcome was left open to interpretation which afforded me the opportunity to believe Fleur was still getting better. Andrews words were blunt and left no room for misunderstanding.

All I could do was sob. I desperately didn't want to be the one to make the decision, to make THAT decision and I knew Andrew didn't either. For all intents and purposes Fleur was my dog, and so the decision should lie with me. Sharing your life with a dog comes with a multitude of benefits and perks, but the responsibility of ensuring that when the time comes you have the strength to make that decision is one hell of a kick in the teeth.

Andrew held me as I cried, he didn't like to see me cry and his words weren't coming from a place of malice, more a place of brutal honesty. Nero and Marti could sense I was upset and that evening there were a lot of cuddles and kisses as I cried into their soft fur. The kids were kept informed but by now they had their own lives away from home, and whilst they sent their virtual love and hugs, reminding me that Fleur had had a great three weeks with us (is that really all it had been?), it was still Nero and Marti who took the brunt of my tears without flinching or wavering.

Back to that Thursday morning and Andrew was ready to set off into London. The meeting was for him to fight for his job, so he couldn't rearrange and as I was home I was able to go in to see her. Andrew made me promise to spend as much time with her as possible and send him pictures and updates. I wasn't feeling great, but I had promised Andrew I would go to see her and I knew this might be the last time I had the opportunity to see Fleur. Andrew had taken the lead role in terms of visiting Fleur prior to that so this was my time, and I was going to make the most of it no matter what my health circumstances were.

Having not seen much of Fleur since she was admitted to the vets (Andrew's work was more flexible than mine and had a greater ability to keep his emotions in check and deal with the situation objectively, whereas I just cried a lot), I was anxious about what was waiting for me inside. Although I had seen her the day before and seen the picture Andrew had taken the previous evening, seeing her deterioration in person filled me with trepidation. I hoped she would be happy to see me, and I prayed for a wagging tail.

I went in to the practice and what greeted me was nothing like what

I had hoped for. There was no wagging tail, in fact there was no real response at all. She was laid on the floor, lifeless. She didn't even raise her head to look at me. It was gutting to see her like that, I remember thinking it looked as if she had already started to slip away and it terrified me.

I spoke to Chris, the vet on duty who was open and honest with me. He told me that Fleur had what was called a 'poor-grave prognosis'. Val had also put in a call to her vet for the second opinion and he stated that, in his opinion and following his duty of care, given his professional accountability and integrity and keeping to their area of competence Fleur's needs had to come first. She was dying, and the best course of action would be to put her to sleep.

The bottom fell out of my world with those words. It was the last thing I wanted to hear. Everything became blurry. The vet may have kept talking, but I wasn't listening. The tears came quickly, and I struggled to breathe. I couldn't believe this was actually happening. We had known this was a possibility, but there was always an underlying hope that Fleur would tap into that strength that had got her this far and pull through, but everybody has their limits. Fleur seemed to have reached hers and I was utterly devastated.

I tried to phone Andrew, but to no avail. He must have been preparing for his work meeting, or 'Fight Club', as he described it. I needed to speak to him, to hear his voice. I needed something to ground me, bring me back to the moment and help me focus on what I needed to do but it was looking like I had to face this alone. I couldn't call Val. I felt completely numb and as if my whole world was being turned upside down. I was already feeling run down and weak. I was emotionally vulnerable and now I had to take in and consider all these new opinions and options and process all the consequences without my partner to bounce them off. Not only that, but now I had to consider the financial aspect as well. I had no idea where to go or what to do. Everything was running around my head and I couldn't focus on what I needed to. How could I make this decision on my own? Why should I have to make it on my own?

I couldn't give up on my baby, and that's how it felt; like I was sentencing her to death and giving up on her. How could I do that? In that moment I felt completely alone. The vet told me I could go away for a couple of hours and think about it. I ended up at a friend, Trish's house. I have no idea why I ended up there, I just drove and that's where I got to. If anyone was going to understand it was Trish.

We both knew Trish well, and we have similar opinions and interests, plus she knew Andrew to a tee which means she understands the dynamic of our home and relationship. I could talk to her frankly and she wouldn't judge. Our friendship was one of those where long periods of time can pass, but when we meet it's as if we have been talking every day. Trish is one of those rare finds, a friend where everything just seems to click, and you fit together like two jigsaw pieces and not matter how long you go without being next to each other, you still slot into place perfectly. She even hosted family at her house when we got married and helped organise the event itself. She is a wonderfully creative person and made all one hundred of our wedding favour herself.

Right then, with so much flying around my head, I just needed to talk to someone and she had listened and given great advice on so many occasions, so she was the perfect choice in this instance. She had been in a similar situation when her dog Jake, Nero's best mate, was suffering from cancer and she had to make the heart-breaking decision to send him to Rainbow Bridge. We had looked after Jake a number of times when she had been travelling, and in turn she had helped us look after Nero and Marti.

Jake was a black Setter/Collie cross, but with a distinct Setter look. People often say dogs mirror their owners in terms of looks, but in this instance Jake mirrored Trish's personality. He was so kind and calm, yet so full of vigour. Despite having had two major cruciate ligament surgeries to his hind legs he still loved to chase a ball. He and Nero adored each other, they would play together and whenever Jake slept over at ours he and Nero would sleep together. As Jake began to fall ill, Nero seemed to respect his space as an older dog. Once Jake had passed we took Nero to Trish's house so that he could smell that Jake had gone. He seemed sad, and he never got that close to another dog. Their bond was special, unique.

I sat in Trish's house, a trembling cup of sweet tea in my hand, as any good English person in shock would have, with tears streaming down my face and a tissue in my other hand. Trish just listened as I rambled. My head was spinning from all the information I had received, and I talked myself in circles. Everything just spilled out in a fit of emotionally charged verbal diarrhoea. I think the vortex of thoughts had been swirling around my head for so long it just had to find an exit, and when it did there was no way of closing it. Trish just sat patiently.

She suggested contacting Val, who had then advised a second opinion. I was so tired and unfocused that I didn't really take in the message. Was she saying that our vets had got it wrong? I wasn't sure if she was telling me what we should be doing or asking me. I didn't want to move Fleur to another vet, the poor little thing had had enough upheaval as it was. Thankfully Trish came to the rescue. I was confused and not really thinking straight. She read the message for me and simplified what Val was saying. She confirmed it wasn't Val dissing our vets, but more like if we, as humans, don't like what we are being told by a Healthcare Professional we go straight to another doctor for a second opinion. I, of course, knew this happened all the time and it helped to think about it from a perspective of which I had personal experience. It brought some clarity.

I was brought out of it by a second message, which was surprising given the distinct lack of signal at Trish's house. A one line message from Val;

'Message from an Amanda Slade. A possibility for Fleur'.

What? Who? How? I had no idea what this meant. Who was Amanda Slade? How could she help Fleur? How did she even know Fleur needed help?

As it turned out, Val had rung Beverley, who had been collecting her son from school at the time. It's weird how, in the middle of one of the biggest crises of your adult life, life still goes on. People still have lives to go about and not everyone stops to react to what is happening to you. What happens to you is all encompassing and it's so easy to forget that it doesn't encompass everyone else. However, as we had already realised, Fleur's story had the ability to latch on to people and not let go.

So, after the call from Val, Beverley had in turn written a piece for Dogs Today as it went to press as well as including and sharing links to FaceBook pages. This was starting to get big, but it was all completely unbeknownst to me. I had been so caught up in the immediate that I hadn't realised that both Val and Beverley Cuddy had been sharing Fleur's current situation in order to try and find a solution. And a solution had been found in the form of this Amanda Slade.

Thankfully a second message came through to give the first text some context. She forwarded the original message from Amanda;

'Hi Val, I hope you don't mind, but I spoke to Potters Bar about Fleur and they have a 24 hour emergency care team all specialists and very experienced. They have soft tissue specialists on the team and they think there is a possibility they may be able to help her'

At first, my brain couldn't compute the message. Once again, Trish had to simplify it for me and she offered to come back to the vets with me. I just couldn't get my head around what was being said. I wasn't sure how to feel or react, but I knew I was angry that people were interfering and putting in their thoughts, opinions or acting on our behalf. It clouded my judgement as I started to consider what other people were thinking rather than my own thoughts and what was best for Fleur.

Everything I was now hearing conflicted with what my vet had told me and to be honest just caused even more confusion. I didn't want to upset anybody or give the impression I thought that they weren't doing the best by Fleur. My instinctive feeling was to take Fleur to the specialist vets as Amanda had suggested, but there was this nagging doubt somewhere in the recesses of my brain about the cost and on top of that there was no guarantee she would survive. Did I really want to put her through even more, including a fairly long journey, for nothing?

'They said to get the vet to call them as soon as possible and ask for the emergency care team and give a full history. Dan Burden is on as head of the emergency care team and he is an amazing vet/surgeon. Very well respected and well liked too. He saves animals where others can't. I hope you don't think I'm interfering, just can't bear the thought that Fleur will die, and they may be able to help her.'

How was I supposed to make this decision? I spoke to Trish, but I felt completely alone. Andrew was out of communication in London, so I couldn't lean on him. I tried and tried to call him to no avail.

People were trying their hardest to help, even people I had never met or spoken to, but I still felt utterly isolated. I didn't want to give up on Fleur.

Fleur and hope fade fast

I trusted our vets and believed that they had done everything they could. What I had never been aware of, however, was that there were specialist vets out there in all manner of disciplines and one of those may be able to help Fleur.

How had I not heard of these vets? Why did my vets not refer Fleur to them in the first place? Was she an unsuitable candidate? Did our vets not trust the specialists, and if they didn't, should I? I had so many questions flying around my head, but Trish managed to bring me back down to earth.

"As a nurse, what is your gut reaction? What are you thinking, feeling?"

I considered for a minute before I answered.

"If she has just one percent chance, that was still a chance."

I knew if I didn't give Fleur that chance, no matter how small it was, I would never forgive myself. It was better to try than not to try, after all. I knew in my heart I would regret not giving Fleur that one percent chance and I didn't want to give up on Fleur just because someone said I had to.

I had no desire to be the one who put Fleur to sleep without trying all the options available to us. With that in mind I knew that as long as there was a chance with this new lifeline, then I wanted to do it. Fleur needed me to be strong and make a decision for her. I would much rather look back knowing I at least tried than look back kicking myself for not trying. Fleur deserved much more than that, she deserved someone to be as strong as she was.

At this point I didn't really have time to consider other people's thoughts and opinions but looking back its astonishing to think how many people who had never met us, or Fleur were throwing themselves into the story and offering help. Once again, Fleur had angels out there looking out for her, and Amanda Slade is one of those angels. As it turns out, Amanda had been following Fleur's journey via Val's FaceBook page. She had seen Val post on her page the day Fleur collapsed and read that Fleur may well be PTS, and she wondered, much as I did following the event, why our vets hadn't put a call in to Potters Bar.

She had hoped our vets would make the call before they made the inevitable decision, but it quickly became apparent this wasn't going to happen and Amanda, through her purely selfless concern for our dog, contacted them herself. She related Fleur's entire story to the Potters Bar team and asked them if they would see her, if our vets contacted them. They informed they would have a team standing by waiting to get the information from our vet and if Fleur was well enough to make the journey. Blanche Dubios was right about relying on the kindness of strangers, especially given what was to happen over the following days.

I knew I had to head back to the clinic, I had told them I just needed some time to think and they were expecting me back. Trish drove as I was in no fit state. In the veterinary clinic I wasn't really sure what was happening, or what the next step was. The vet was surprised about my decision to refer Fleur, and he confirmed my underlying fear about the cost. I knew that to get Fleur to the RVC took a referral from the vet, and he seemed reluctant to give one considering Fleur's state of health. I had already resigned myself to the fact that if they didn't give us the referral I would walk out with fleur then and there and go to the RVC myself. If that was the only hope for my little girl, then that's where she was going by hook or by crook.

Thankfully, despite his reservations, the went to make the call to the RVC and left us in the waiting room, wringing our hands and nervously jiggling our legs. He returned and dropped yet another bomb. They would see Fleur, but it would cost £4000–£8000 and we would need to pay half of the bottom end of the quote upfront – £2000. I had to make the decision, it was now or never, so I agreed.

Did we have to wait for an ambulance? Did they provide us with transportation from the practice to Potters Barr? The vet informed me that that wasn't the case and we could go now and take her myself, but not before he warned me yet again how bad an idea it was and that he didn't believe Fleur would make the journey.

"You'll be lucky if she makes the car journey," were his exact words.

His bedside manner left something to be desired, and if my anxiety and upset wasn't already piqued, it certainly was after that.

So, we loaded Fleur into the car with one proviso from Trish – she had to get petrol. That was one fence I wasn't bothered about jumping. Fleur was barely conscious at this point and she lay on the back seat with me. She looked so small, so weak and frail. This was turning into a race against the clock to get her to the RVC. Her eyes were dark and eyelids white. Her bones dug into me as we sped along the motorway and she didn't move at all. I could easily have been holding a dead dog, and that thought made my blood run cold.

Fleur and hope fade fast

She didn't really respond until we stopped at a service station, where she sat up to look out of the window. I took the opportunity to take a photo so that I could post it to Val later and Fleur's growing fan base could get an update. Fleur already had people that followed her story online, but little did we know how much this would grow over the coming weeks and months and the path it would lead our lives to. People we didn't know would share the pictures and updates of Fleur's journey. I changed my FaceBook profile picture and prompted others to do the same to show support and belief in Fleur. The response was phenomenal, and we received messages from all over the world including America, Australia, New Zealand and all over Europe and Asia. The photo of Fleur in the back of the car whilst Trish filled the car with petrol was all over FaceBook. Just as it had with us, something about Fleur and her unyielding desire to survive had touched people far and wide.

During that drive I finally managed to get hold of Andrew and explained what had happened and that we were on our way to Potters Bar. Andrew had abandoned his meeting and was on the train from London headed home. He seemed as confused about the messages from Amanda Slade as I was, but he has a very practical brain and he urged me to calm down and explain everything to him. I told him about the cost and, thankfully, he just said do what you have to do, and we will worry about paying later. He even said we can re-mortgage the house if we have to. I think he was mostly disappointed that it wasn't him driving Fleur to Potters Bar, that he couldn't be here when both Fleur and I needed him most, so he was doing the next best thing and heading home to care for Nero and Marti.

Sat in the back of that car, it was obvious to me that her desire to survive may not be winning. I held her in my arms and the frailty of her body was deeply upsetting. All of the progress she had made in her first weeks with us, all that hope we had gained by watching her flourish, had gone and it looked like soon Fleur may be gone too.

Chapter Twelve

THE LAST CHANCE FOR A BRAVE LITTLE DOG

~ • ~

ONLY FLEUR REALLY knew what was going on in her mind while she was fighting for her life but probably it was something like this.

Everything is a blur about those days. I remember the male human being with me for a lot of it, but I was constantly teetering between conscious and unconscious. It felt odd, like I was dreaming but I was aware I was dreaming. People came and went, I was prodded, poked and stabbed but it all passed in a fog of semi-reality. I would never become fully conscious long enough for anything to gain any traction or make an impact on my memory. The only thing that I do remember, the only thing that was a constant was the male humans voice. It was that that tethered me to life, that that made me continue to come back to consciousness rather than slip into a permanent unconscious.

A little part of me remembers times when I felt so bad, so unutterably destitute, so completely bereft that I had no desire to come back to consciousness. I could almost feel Shimeka calling me to her and I wanted to go. I wanted to feel her warmth and her soft fur next to mine. I wanted to feel it tickling at my nose as she lay over my neck, and more than anything else I wanted the pain and the fear to stop. I wanted to know it was over and I was free. But then I would hear that voice and it would pull me away from Shimeka and for the time the male human would talk, the fear eased, and I felt better.

I remember hearing the female human's voice. It was faint, like it was a long way away or the other side of a door. Then it was gone. I wondered if I had imagined it, maybe it was wishful thinking that she had come to take me home. Home. Was that place home? It was the warmest, safest place I had ever been, but now I was here and once again I had no idea where I would end up. They kept coming back to see me though, so maybe I was going back to the house. Maybe it was home.

Later her voice returned, but I assumed it was just in my head. It would be gone again as quickly as it came. But it didn't go away. She didn't go away. The voice got louder and suddenly I was being picked up and carried away from the cage I had been laying in for days. I could still hear her voice, it helped me feel safe. I could be going anywhere but hearing her voice there with me helped me know that I was safe. It was like an anchor keeping the ship safe. Her voice was my anchor at a time that I had no idea what was happening.

I was placed on a more comfortable seat. I opened my eyes as much as I could and realised I was in the back of a car…again. There was no telling where this journey would end, but I desperately hoped I was going home. If this was my time to go, I wanted to go at home with the humans and the other dogs I had grown to consider family. I had never really thought much about how I would die. I knew I would, and probably sooner rather than later given my beginnings, but I had put so much effort into not dying that I had never thought about how it might happen.

Soft hands lifted my head and I felt my head rest on a warm lap. That was nice, it was similar to Shimeka's warm neck covering me against the cold nights. The warmth seeped into me like eating warm food. One of the soft hands rested on my bony rib cage and despite the fear, despite the pain and despite the sickness I felt secure. I drifted between consciousness and unconsciousness to the rhythm of the car engine as we rode along. It didn't take me long to realise we weren't heading home, the journey was too long. If we were headed home we would be there by now. I had done this journey before and I knew how long it took, and what turns were where. This felt different. That didn't help my stress levels, because it was out of my window of experience, but having the female human there gently stroking my head somehow made me think things were going to be OK. She wasn't going to take me anywhere like the dirty cage room, right?

The car stopped and the change in rhythm brought me to consciousness. I needed to have some idea of where we were and what was happened,

The last chance for a brave little dog

so I struggled up into a seated position and looked out of the window. It was bright, the sun's glare made me squint, having been under artificial light for so long. I watched as someone walked their dog along the grass verge. That was where I wanted to be, I wanted to be out with the other two dogs running around the field, charging through the damp morning grass without a care in the world, free and unrestrained. Or laying in my warm cage at the house as the humans made dinner, watching my new family doing whatever it was they were doing.

I heard a click as the female human pointed something at me, but I was too tired, too lost to care what she was doing. I lay back down and soon the engine started to hum again and I was quickly back in that place between conscious and unconscious. Part of it was intentional, if I gave in to the semi-conscious state I didn't hurt as much, and I didn't have to feel the fear and stress that had been there ever since that night the pain started. As much as the humans helped ease the fear by being close to me, it didn't make it go away completely. That only came with the blackness brought on by unconsciousness.

Once again I was brought out of the blackness by the car's rumbling stopping. Quickly I was lifted out of the car and I felt myself being passed to someone else. Was I going into a new cage room? What was this one going to be like? I wish I could understand more of their words, so I could have at least some idea of what was going on. It was the unknown and the lack of being able to predict what was going to happen next that caused the most stress.

Everything happening felt panicked. I was quickly passed between people and rushed into a building (I assumed it was by the change in temperature and the by now all too familiar smell of chemicals). I felt my body being placed on a table and yet again I was poked and prodded by people I couldn't see. I didn't have any sort of energy to be able to respond. I could barely register what was going on, let alone react to it. I did notice that the female human's voice had stopped. Had she gone? Had I been left here? Was she coming back? I hoped she wasn't too far away.

Wendy, of course was not going to abandon Fleur.

I wasn't too far away at all, I was just the other side of the doors, but I couldn't tell Fleur that. When we arrived at the RVC the security guard was expecting us. I had no idea what to expect. I had never heard of the place, nor had I any idea where it was or what it looked like, so I had no way of knowing what to expect. I had assumed we would get there, park up and take Fleur in as we had done with our other many visits to the vets. What we didn't expect was a sudden rush of uniformed staff surrounding the car as soon as we pulled up. Before I could even get out of the car Fleur had been taken from my arms and rushed into the building. It all became very real, and very urgent at that moment and the severity hit me. This was life or death, and Fleur had just been taken into the animal equivalent of A and E.

Once Fleur had been taken there was a huge breath of relief. She had been taken into safe hands and now the experts could do their thing and we could hear their second opinion. It was only then that the thought of actually paying hit me. I obviously knew we would have to cough up the £2000 but everything had happened so quickly I hadn't even picked up my purse before heading to the vets. I had nothing with me, how was I going to cover the costs? This was quickly becoming my worst nightmare. All I wanted to do was get Fleur the help and care she so desperately needed, not keep hurdling over fences that stood in my way. Once again, Trish stepped in and without question she paid the bill. I don't know what I did in a previous life to deserve a friend like Trish, but I cannot express how grateful I am for her support. She was a steady rock I could cling on to as hard as I needed in a stormy ocean of confusion and emotion.

They had taken Fleur off into the examination room and I was left with student vet Simon Cook who took me to one side and tried his best to get a full history from me. I struggled to focus, Fleur was gone. Just like that, she was gone, and I hadn't said goodbye. I hadn't told her I loved her. What if she never came back? What if I never saw her again and I never got to say goodbye or tell her she was loved? Tell her she had a family that adored her? She had already been through so much I couldn't bear the thought of her dying in there, all alone with no one there that loved her, not knowing how much we cared for her, how big a part of our life she had become. I had counted every single mile on our journey to the practice, all 76.6 of them and every single minute. Ninety-two to be exact. All that time I had kept in physical contact with Fleur and now she was suddenly gone, and I hadn't had chance to tell her everything was going to be OK.

Simon asked me another question and brought me out of my own anxiety-ridden thought process. He was calm and understanding, as were all of the staff. The atmosphere there was completely different to that of our own vets. It felt more tranquil, more professional and it was clear they were used to handling hysterical and emotionally charged owners. Their empathy shone through and I felt confident I had made the right decision.

I gave Simon as many details as I could, but I found focusing very difficult. So much had happened in the past few hours I wasn't really sure where I was. I had never experienced anything like this, either with dogs, family or myself. I had never had to talk to health professionals about a sick relative or had any medical issues myself to this extent. The room was very clean, there was a desk and chairs and two double doors. It's often bizarre the details the mind records in these situations, seemingly pointless details yet they stick in the memory.

Then Simon hit me with it. They were assessing Fleur as we spoke, behind those double doors, as it turned out, to see if she was strong enough to undergo further exploratory surgery and initial tests. If Fleur did need the operation, the risks were huge. He said words like 'deterioration', 'untreatable disease', 'anaesthesia risks', 'blood transfusions' and then the one that was like a slap in the face – death. Of course, I knew this was a very real possibility but to have this vet, in this hospital that was supposed to hold her miracle, say it made it very real. This was where we had brought Fleur to save her, to hear that death was still such a high possibility filled me with a coldness.

Being a nurse, everything he said made sense. My training helped me recognise that Fleur's situation was serious, but it also meant I understood words such as 'sepsis', 'blood count' and 'observations'. I knew what these meant in a medical context, and that meant I was always preparing myself for the worst news, rather than focusing on positives. Not that there were any positives at this stage.

I understood the terminology and what it all meant, but this was the first time I had seen it all down in writing and had had to sign that I understood the risks and potential outcomes. I couldn't sign it, I just couldn't. I needed to think, to take my time. It was as if signing it made it a done deal and I was signing Fleur's life away. We were ushered back into the waiting room where we sat for what felt like hours. All the time I sat there I tried to imagine what Fleur was going through, what they were doing to her and how scared and alone she must be feeling. I hoped she knew I was there waiting for her, and that maybe that might help her pull through. To know she had a loving home waiting for her would hopefully give her some strength and a reason to keep fighting for just a little longer.

Intermittently my head would deviate from Fleur and focus on the cost. Where were we going to find this money from? As much as Andrew reassured me we would find a way and that making sure Fleur got what she needed was paramount, I couldn't help but question where we were going to find such a large sum of money from. Unbeknown to me at the time as I sat silently in the waiting room with Trish, back at Valgrays people were having similar thoughts, and they were taking action.

Nickie, a staff member at Valgrays, had heard of Fleur's current plight and had set up a specific FaceBook page to keep people up to date with Fleur's progress; 'Help for Fleur' and it spread like wild fire. The numbers soon shot up, the membership grew and grew and within hours came messages of support and offers of help and goodwill from the world over. The Fleur worldwide whirlwind had begun. 'Help for Fleur' started with a description written by Nickie;

'This brave and loving dog was cruelly mutilated in Romania – where state-sponsored barbarism has been encouraged to clear the streets of stray dogs. People are mutilating dogs and killing them in unimaginably cruel ways. Fleur survived the cruellest treatment against all the odds once before, she had been so crudely spayed that her intestines were left hanging out.

She has found a loving home in the UK, but she needs our help one more time. The repair to her damaged intestines has failed and now only the best vets in the world at Potters Bar can give her any chance of survival. We can all probably think of lots of reasons why we shouldn't help this one dog, but it would be a cruel world where we did all just all look the other way.

It's true, we can't save them all, but is that any reason to let Fleur die?

We might not succeed, she might still lose her battle – but we think she deserves the best possible chance. Even if she does lose the fight she will be remembered, and new people will have heard of the atrocities that are happening every day in Romania. Seeing her trusting face will give people a vivid connection to the suffering of so many others. This is the grim reality for many strays in Romania. It should be stopped, of course.

No dog should be left with her intestines hanging out. No dog should have her crude wounds sewn up with string. No dog should be injected with paint because it's a cheaper way to kill them than using proper veterinary drugs. Compassion fatigue?

It's entirely the individual's choice whether to help Fleur or not. Despite all the cruelty she has lived through, she's survived mutilation and then even distemper, but she has never given up loving humans and hoping to live for another day.

Please tell your friends about what is happening in Romania. And let Fleur's hope spread and make everyone believe that tomorrow will be a less cruel day on this earth. Let's all try to save her. Just give something, anything, even if it's just sharing this link and wishing her well if you can't spare any money.

If she loses the battle or we raise more than is needed to put her back together this money will be used by Valgrays to save other dogs like brave Fleur. Here is the link, please if we all just give a pound we'll get there – share this message and show the world it matters what happens to these dogs, every life is precious'

So now everyone knew our story and the position we had found ourselves in, but Nickie then took further steps in rallying support for Fleur and for us. She set up a BT 'My Donate' page and pinned it to the 'Help for Fleur' Facebook page with the following brief;

'Fleur was mutilated in Romania, where state sponsored barbarism has been clearing the streets of strays. She was so crudely spayed her intestines were hanging out, and that 3 weeks into her new life tragedy had struck. It's through Fleur's name people will hear of the atrocities in Romania. Fleur's lovely face will make the suffering of so many others personal. No dog should be mutilated, none should have crude wounds sewn up with string. No dog should be killed with paint because it's cheaper than injecting proper veterinary drugs. Despite all the cruelty, Fleur has never given up loving humans and hoping to live for another day. Let Fleur's hope spread and make everyone believe that tomorrow will be a less cruel day on earth. If more money is raised, the money will be used by Valgrays to save others like Fleur'

Sat in the waiting room at the RVC, counting the seconds as they passed, I had no idea what was going on, on the internet. I wasn't really thinking about checking social media, I'm not one hundred percent sure what I was doing, other than sitting and waiting. Waiting and sitting. I didn't have the energy for checking messages and responding to people. It's not that I didn't want to, as such, I just couldn't face it. I was too drained to do anything other than sit. And wait.

I was brought out of my thoughts by Senior Clinical Vet Andrew Phillips calling me and Trish into a consultation room. My heart started racing, but I took a little hope from his name. Andrew, my husband's name, and Phillips, Val's surname. Maybe it was a sign. Maybe I was grasping at straws, but it helped a little. It didn't help me focus, and the vet's words were background noise to my busy head. I managed to pick out particular bits. They were going to operate on Fleur. She was holding her own but if Fleur deteriorated during the operation then they wouldn't wake her up. That was like walking into a glass door. Suddenly I was very much in the room. I could feel my eyes get hot as I was asked to sign a consent to give them permission to operate. My hand was shaking as I handed the pen back to the vet.

This time I took the opportunity to ask if I could say goodbye to Fleur, knowing it was entirely possible this could be the last time I would ever see my miracle girl. It was the most heart-wrenching, emotionally wrought and surreal moment of my life up until that point. Fleur was brought out to me and Trish. My cheeks were damp before she even appeared, but when she did it hit hard that I may never see this girl again. After going through so much just to get her in to our home and seeing her begin to settle into a new, secure and comfortable life to then see that being so brutally and undeservedly ripped away from her, and her from us, was devastating.

One of the first things I noticed was that she wasn't wearing her usual collar and lead, instead she was sporting a yellow slip lead. I was handed her lead and collar and it felt symbolic, like they were handing me part of her to take home and remember her by. A memento. Everything came out at that point and Trish started to cry too. It was awful, truly and completely awful.

Poor Fleur didn't have a clue what was happening. She wasn't really with it when she came out but nevertheless I buried my head into her soft fur and breathed her in. Much like people, dogs seem to have a specific smell, something that's familiar and individual. I didn't want to forget it, so I kept my face buried into her, my tears dampening her fur, as I repeatedly told her how much I loved her, everything would be OK. I didn't want to let her go, if I let her go that was it; it was happening. I clung on to her collar and lead for dear life. Eventually I pulled my face away and looked her in the eye. They were so pale, so lifeless but there was a hint of a glint there. Somewhere in there my girl was listening to me, I just knew it. I told her once more that I loved her before I stood back up and she was taken away. It felt like a dream, or rather, a nightmare, that I was looking in on from outside with no control over the outcome.

Right then I honestly believed that would be the last time I saw her. Maybe it was selfish, but all I could think of was Fleur and myself and how I didn't want to let her go. It felt like I was leaving her behind and what if she forgot me? There were none of her blankets, nothing with our or my smells on it. We had only had her for three weeks, so I really had no way of knowing how she would cope. It made it heart-wrenchingly tough to leave her there, so far away from home.

Then I was in limbo, stood in the reception area with no idea what to do, still in tears. It was like I was in some sort of emotional vortex and I couldn't think or see straight. I didn't know if I was supposed to wait here or go home or what. Did I really want to go home and leave her here? At least if I stayed here I was closer to her if something should happen, and maybe she would be able to sense I was still close. The reception staff told us we should head home, and that someone would call us as soon as there was any news. But home was so far away, what if we needed to get her quickly? What if something happened? The women behind reception were incredibly kind and understanding, I doubt I was the first emotionally hysterical owner they had dealt with, and they told me there was nothing I could do. Go home, rest and they would contact me as soon as they had any news on Fleur.

The drive home was a silent, sombre one. It was dark outside by now and that matched the mood entirely. I questioned everything, constantly asking myself if I had done the right thing or if I was letting Fleur down. Was I putting her through too much? Was I being selfish, should I just let her go and stop her suffering after she had been through so much? Did Andrew have enough money to reimburse Trish? All this was running through my head and I was completely exhausted, as was Trish. Despite that, and my emotional state, Trish never stopped trying to ease my feelings of guilt and reassuring me things were going to be OK.

We stopped off for food on the way home but all I could manage was a coffee. As I sat there hugging the steaming cup I yearned to be at home, hugging Nero and Marti instead. I had a strong urge to hold them and tell them I loved them. Plus, I knew Andrew was at home now, and I could do with his reassurance too.

To try and distract myself I checked my phone and was over whelmed by the messages of support and well wishes that had come in, especially through the Fleur FaceBook Group and page. They were only words on a screen, but it was comforting to know so many people believed in Fleur and believed in what we were doing. I took warmth from what I read, from all the prayers and virtual hugs, and I felt less alone. I wasn't go through this on my own but for all the comfort those messages gave, I just wanted to get home to Andrew and the dogs.

For the rest of the drive home I prayed that Fleur would make it through the surgery and wake up the following morning. I prayed that they wouldn't put her to sleep and I willed her not to give up. She had come so far she couldn't give up on herself now, and neither could we. Not only were we waiting for Fleur to wake up the following morning, but so were hundreds of dedicated and devoted fans.

Chapter Thirteen

NEWS OF FLEUR'S 'DEATH'

~ • ~

WHILE ALL OF this was going on, Andrew was in London trying to save his job while in his head the fight for survival of a little dog was dominating his thoughts.

I had been in London that day to fight for my job. The company I was working for was doling out redundancies and each staff member had to go in and basically convince those above them that they were worth keeping. So, I was pretty tense that day from the start, but it was before I had gone in to my meeting that I got the news about Fleur literally as I was about to head through the door. I had barely heard anything from Wendy that morning. Information came in dribs and drabs as we either kept missing each other or I was otherwise engaged with work things. When I did hear from her, it was to tell me Fleur had been dropped off at the RVC and they were headed home.

Wendy seemed a lot better during that call. Maybe upbeat isn't the right term, but she sounded much more confident about the situation. She told me that we had brought Fleur to the place where, if there was something wrong, the right people were there to deal with it. What she neglected to tell me, be it on purpose or not, was that if this didn't work this was the end. There was no other option for Fleur. There was nobody else that could do anything for Fleur. Wendy left this piece of devastating until we were face to face at home. I took from Wendy's tone that she was happier with the situation, she wasn't doing cartwheels around the car park of course, but she didn't sound as down as she had that morning. We still didn't know what was wrong with Fleur at this point, or what they were going to do.

Thankfully, I managed to catch my boss as everybody was going in and told him what had happened, who completely understood my adoration of dogs and my bond with the dogs I shared my home with. I had to get home to Hampshire. I didn't actually wait for a response before I turned on my heels. He seemed nonplussed and more focused on the job in hand than my sudden departure, but I kept my job, so something must have worked in my favour.

At home I made sure Nero and Marti were OK. It was easy to forget that they had gone through a lot of changes over recent weeks too. Our house was one of routine and it was a routine that the dogs thrived on, especially Nero. They were walked at a certain time, they were fed at a certain time. We came and went at certain times which generally stayed similar. In the space of a few weeks we had brought in a new dog which had changed the house dynamics, and then they had witnessed her horrendous outburst of pain and then she had vanished for days. Now they were left alone, and Wendy probably was going to come back without Fleur, so they needed one of us there to provide them with some stability, some form of normality. As owners we had a responsibility to ensure that our dogs felt secure and that any anomalies were buffered by our care.

At home I tried to ensure things were calm and I went about things as I would do normally. I knew Wendy was on her way home and I knew what had happened but when she walked through the door without Fleur it stung. Seeing the lead and collar in her hand and not attached to Fleur made it seem suddenly a reality. I had always been pretty pragmatic when it came to Fleur getting to the UK, but now she was here it was hard to bring that pragmatism to my response. I had forged a bond with her in the time she had spent with us.

In hindsight, mine and Fleur's relationship had probably come from a familiarity she provided. Taking her out to the field for a run, her behaviours and mannerisms reminded me of the street dogs I saw in Kabul. It immediately transported me back to those streets and our bond grew quickly. By being able to relate her behaviours and movements to the dogs I had seen during my work meant I could get some sort of idea of what she had gone through, which in turn meant I could almost put a story to her which gave me something tangible to attach to. As far as we were concerned, Fleur's history pre-shelter was unknown, but this meant I could conceive some of what she may have gone through. I had felt an empathy for those street dogs and now I could channel that empathy into Fleur, and know I was helping.

Seeing that empty collar when Wendy arrived home was a stark reality check and made me realise how Wendy must have felt when I had left Fleur at the vets originally and arrived home with a dog-less collar and lead. She got back quite late that night, and a lot of coffee was consumed as she talked me through everything that had happened that day and what had actually led to Fleur ending up in Potters Bar. The coffee helped, as she had to explain it to me more than once because I just couldn't get my thick-as-mince head around it.

Wendy spent a lot of time with Marti and Nero that evening, as we both did. It was a surreal atmosphere and it was as if there was a grey cloud hanging over the house casting a shadow over us that we couldn't shake. We were just waiting for the sun to shine through, or the storm to erupt. That wasn't the only thing that was erupting. I had no idea about the Facebook page that had been set up, but I was absolutely blown away by the sheer volume of messages and the level of support that was being offered. In such a short space of time. It was unbelievable that this many people were so attached to Fleur's story.

Going to bed that night was more of a routine gesture than a necessity. Neither of us were likely to sleep, but it offered normality for Nero and Marti and it at least diminished some of the odd atmosphere that the day had ended with. Wendy had put Fleur's collar around her wrist and wore it to bed that night. It was her way of keeping Fleur close by, a physical manifestation of Wendy's emotional closeness to Fleur, and her desire to be with her.

I tried to sleep but I could feel Wendy checking her phone every few minutes. It was by doing this she realised she wasn't the only one having a restless night, the Help For Fleur FaceBook page continued to be updated with messages of support and prayers. I appreciated them, but they really meant a lot to Wendy. It touched her heart to see that Fleur's story had resonated with so many people, and that so many of them had seen in her baby what she had seen. What we hadn't realised that it wasn't just well wishes that people were sending.

At around one thirty in the morning the phone rang. Now, we had been told that they would not hear from the vets until the morning unless it was bad news and they had to discuss options. So, when that phone rang in the early hours Wendy was really nervous. This must be it, no one else would ring at that time of the morning. Were they ringing so late (or early, depending on your view point) because it was really bad news?

What we were given was a bittersweet explanation that Fleur had made it through surgery, but it was touch and go. She was better than when she had gone in to the RVC, but the percentages were still massively stacked against her and she was by no means out of the woods yet. The following twenty-four hours would be critical. The point was, she had survived thus far. She was still there, she was still with us. We both breathed a huge sigh of relief, and then prepared ourselves mentally for the next twenty-four hours, and of course Wendy, having done her best to try and explain it to me in words I could understand, was straight onto FaceBook to give everyone the update they had been waiting for.

The operation had consisted of cutting out more rotten intestines, as had been done the first time round and joined healthy gut to healthy gut. They discovered that she had had faeces leaking into the abdomen as well as the presences of abscesses. The surgery had been more complicated than it should have been due to Fleur's complicated medical history.

In the UK we have little knowledge of distemper, because we never see it. In the vet's words, Fleur was an exceptional case. With that, we could not argue. She needed intensive nursing and had been catheterised and her abdomen washed out with antibiotics. The vet finished by telling us she was in a bad way but presented well. She was remarkable. Again, we couldn't argue.

That period during Fleur's recovery at the RVC was difficult. Potters Bar wasn't just down the road and of course we felt that someone should be with Fleur as much as possible. Wendy was an emotional wreck at the uncertainty of her her baby's life and she was still physically ill. She was strong in that she could understand the medical side and what needed to be done but she was struggling to eat, and she wasn't taking on fluids. Ironically giving her profession she wasn't caring for herself properly, she was putting Fleur and others before herself and that was taking its toll both physically and mentally.

I was concerned for her health, so I took on the task of travelling back and forth. One trip I had to call into our vets in Alresford to pick up a parcel that a well-wisher had sent to Fleur, it contained a purple teddy bear that Val stated was their good luck bear, a symbol of all of the hope that people across the country, across the world, were putting into Fleur's survival.

It was on one of this sojourns to Potters Bar that the joy of social media caused another hiccup in the story of Fleur. As I have spoken about before, misunderstandings and confusion on social media posts is rife and easy to fall victim for. On this particular day I had gone to visit Fleur whilst Wendy stayed home with Nero and Marti. We were still trying to keep some form of routine for them, so it made sense for one of us to stay at home with them. Wendy would post the updates to the Help for Fleur page based on my feedback. On this particular occasion, when Wendy logged in to check the page she read a post that made her heart hit the floor.

'Has she passed away? It looks like she has, so terribly sorry to see this. Poor girl. Xx'

Wait! What? Below this post were two posts, one from Trish;

'What? Where did you read this?'

One from Val:

'????'

Wendy immediately started to panic. What was she talking about? Her girl couldn't be gone, and She couldn't be reading about it on a FaceBook page for the first time. She tried to get hold of me but because I was with Fleur I didn't have my phone with me. Wendy couldn't get hold of anybody. Whilst I was enjoying some Fleur cuddles Wendy was beside herself with fear that she had lost her precious baby girl without getting the chance to see her, and as far as she was concerned nobody had told her. Thankfully it didn't take long for Val to come to the rescue, as she had a habit of doing.

'Denise sincerely apologises. She read it wrong when someone said they were going to miss her. Xxx. Phew'

Phew indeed. There had only been around ten minutes between the first post and the rectification, but it felt much longer to Wendy. It was ten minutes of panic, of complete heartbreak and for that brief period Wendy knew what it would be like to lose Fleur. She needed a cup of tea.

When I would visit Fleur, the vets would tell me about her progression. On that first visit they told me that she was looking good considering what she had been through. Her parameters were OK, but she wasn't eating. She had a gastric tube fitted but due to regurgitation they couldn't use it. She was being closely monitored and the drains were draining well. Her progress was slow, but it was progress. They assured us if there were any significant changes they would let us know, but the lack of control was maddening. I wasn't there, I couldn't have any effect at all on the outcome. Not that I could if I was there either, but at least if I was in the room I would have some pseudo control and I could at least control the support and love Fleur was receiving, as it would be me giving it. At home, I could do nothing. She was without the people that loved her, and that was a hard pill to swallow.

Don't talk to Fleur about swallowing pills – she had had enough of medical treatment and was resigned to whatever was going to be the conclusion.

Despite being left in this chemical smelling room, I had an underlying confidence that the humans from the home had not left me forever. I had an instinct that they would be coming back, and that helped me stay calm when I was placed into a new cage in yet another chemical smelling room. It was warm and comfortable, a far cry from the first cages I had experienced.

My instinct was right and the male from the house came to visit me as he had in the previous chemical smelling room. It reduced the fear and whilst he was there the pain seemed less. Just him being there made things seem less stressful and less painful. It gave me a little surge of energy, which was severely lacking after I woke up with a new wound. It freaked me out seeing all the drains and tubes coming from me, but there was no energy at all to react to it. I just couldn't bring myself to do anything, and I still felt sick.

I lay there looking at the male as he gently stroked my head. I wished we were out in the field, me running hard with the wind running through my fur rather than stuck in this cage. I felt trapped, both in the cage and within my own body. Everything in me wanted to get up but my body wouldn't let me. It felt familiar. I had felt this lack of control, this feeling of not being able to escape, before.

I couldn't have been more than six months old and scavenging behind some bins. I caught a smell. It was fresh, warm and meaty. It drew me in, right in to a cage. This was my first exposure to cages, I had no idea what it was or what was about to happen. What I did know, is that I wanted what was inside that cage. The smell was enticing, I could almost taste it as the drool dripped from my mouth. There it was, staring back at me, calling me too it. In that moment I had never seen anything so delicious, so beautiful. I was so close to it. BAM! A cage door slammed closed behind me, catching my tail as it locked shut.

The pain was intense and flew up my tail into my spine. I span and flipped and went completely mad, screaming and yelping trying to free myself. I pulled and threw myself around, the pain got worse, then I felt a coldness. My absolute terror eclipsed the pain and I refused to stop until I knew I was free. I must have been making the most horrendous noise, I was piercing my own ears let alone anyone else's. And then there was a POP and I was free. It was then, in the relief of freeing my tail, that the sharp pain hit again. I looked to my tail, or what was left of it. The white fur was now a deep red and I realised I had torn the end of my tail off in order to free myself. There, still stuck between the door and the cage was the furry tip of my tail.

I immediately pulled my tail into me and curled up against the back of the crate. The smaller I made myself, the safer I was. I started to lick around the tip of my tail as it continued to seep blood. It did help, and it was a coping mechanism I would employ throughout my life when things got tough or painful. My breathing calmed down and I began to recovery myself. But I was still trapped, and I had no idea how to get out of the cage, or what would come of staying in it.

I didn't have to wait too long to find out. A man in a uniform appeared at the front of the cage. He grabbed the handle and dragged the cage along the pavement to a van. The scraping noise of the metal on concrete will stay with me forever. At the back of the van he grabbed something I recognised, even at the age of six months. A catching pole. I was already whining and barking but the sight of the pole sent me into a frenzy. As he opened the cage door to place the pole around my neck I took my chance and I charged. I pushed passed the man before the pole could loop my neck and ran as fast and hard as I could. I didn't look back, I just ran and ran. I charged around a corner and stopped in my tracks as three dogs faces shot to me. One of them growled. I cowered, kept myself low and told them I wasn't a threat. One of the dogs stepped forward and lowered her head, looking away from me. She wasn't a threat to me, either. We greeted each other, and that was how I met Shimeka.

Back in my cage in the chemical smelling room I was trapped again, but at least this time it was warm, and I felt safer. Although I wanted to get out, it wasn't because I felt terrified, like I had in the cage in the street. I was anxious, I was scared but it wasn't as intense. I had no idea what was to happen, but at least there was the constant of the male and female from the house coming back regularly.

There had been times where I had been seriously ill and felt overwhelmingly exhausted and ready to give up, ready to just let it take over me and slip into the waiting darkness, but now, although I felt terrible and had no energy at all, I wanted to stay awake. I didn't want to slip away. I wanted to go home, I wanted to go back with the male and go out into the field and run. I wanted to fall asleep in my nice warm cage or wander around my home taking in all the smells and having the cat completely refuse to accept that I even exist. I wanted tummy tickles from the humans and I wanted my security back. For the first time in my life I really felt like I had something to fight for. A reason to keep a bite on the light and to not slip into the darkness.

Also, for the first time, I really didn't want to eat. Part of it was pure exhaustion, I was too tired and too overcome with full body fatigue to be able to eat, plus I felt like I was going to be sick which wiped my appetite. People in the same clothes kept trying to offer me fresh chicken but initially I just couldn't face it. What I did enjoy, however, was the never ending tummy tickles and physical contact. As a street dog physical contact came rarely, especially with humans, and yet it was something we as dogs were drawn to naturally. Usually any human contact came with pain or fear, so we began to avoid it rather than seek it out. If you touch a hot flame, you don't touch it again.

However, since leaving the streets there had been kind people, there had been gentle people and the flame began to cool down. The human contact was pleasurable and comforting and it became enjoyable. There was always a compulsion to gain physical contact, you just learned to fight it. It was much easier to allow that compulsion to carry itself out and it didn't take long for the trust we are born with to come flooding back. Although there was still some anxiety, once I knew I was safe there was nothing better than a tummy rub. Thankfully, the people in the same clothes seemed to feel the same.

    I didn't have to stay in the cage the whole time. The uniform people did take me out to go to the toilet but that was it. It was gentle and to be honest took a lot of effort. As much as I wanted to go tearing around the field on the inside, there was no way my body would allow it and it was always nice to get back to my cage and lay down. I was fighting, I knew I was fighting and I felt like I was fighting. That took energy and those toilet trips were all I really had the energy for. This chemical smelling room was the easiest to be in out of the ones I had previously stayed in, that made it easier to rest rather than panic, and to actually sleep rather than teeter on the edge of sleep but always keeping a foot in awareness, just in case. There was no longer a just in case.

    The time passed in a bit of a haze with little relation to how long I had been there as most of it was spent asleep. Every time the man from the house came in I hoped to see my usual collar and lead in his hand. That collar and lead always led to a walk and that meant I was going home, but that didn't happen. What did happen, was that he kept coming back.

Chapter Fourteen

GOOD NEWS AT LAST

~ • ~

WHILE ALL THIS was going on at Potters Bar there was an attempt to keep things as normal as possible back home, as Wendy picked up the story.

In the Morris home we tried to make sure everything stayed as normal as possible for Marti, Fleur and the Ninja Cat but our minds were never far from Potters Bar and our fourth baby who was there in the hands of people we didn't know. The staff were fantastic, and they provided regular contact with us and they would always let us know when we should expect to hear from them, which was usually around four pm. It meant that we weren't pre-occupied with waiting for a call all day and we could focus on our other daily responsibilities and chores. That said, it did not stop us panicking every time one of our phones rang until we could identify it wasn't the RVC. If anything out of the ordinary happened they would call us immediately. These daily updates would then be reiterated into text and shared on the 'Help for Fleur' FaceBook page.

We owed a huge debt of gratitude to that page. We had always posted regular updates on Fleur and we knew she had a strong social media following. Wendy specifically had always felt that we had a responsibility to keep these followers updated as often as possible as a recognition of all of their prayers, well wishes and messages of support. During her stay at the RVC each update averaged 350 likes and 130+ comments. Occasionally someone would mention about telling Fleur's story on a show such as This Morning or Paul'O Grady to highlight the atrocities that happen to dogs in Romania, but at that point all we wanted to do was make sure Fleur lived and we were focused on her recovery and making sure Nero, Marti and Ninja cat were cared for. It simply wasn't in a consideration at that point.

It was a little surreal to think how many people were involved in supporting our dog. Little did we know how that support would manifest itself when we really did need it. Whilst Fleur was at the RVC, the latest issue of Dogs Today was released with the following press release.

'Other breaking news as went to press Fleur the beautiful Romanian collie that we have been following every month had a relapse. She had been mutilated in Romania, allegedly by a vet who had spayed her badly that her intestines were left poking out. The fantastic Valgrays charity had saved Fleur, who had gone on to contract distemper, sadly just 3 weeks into her new, happy life in the UK, she suffered a terrible relapse and was fighting for her life again. All hope was close to fading, but Fleur's spirit was still strong. Her only hope was at the hands of Dan Brockman, one of the best surgeons in the world.

A mercy dash to the Potters Bar veterinary hospital had three surgeon's operating on Fleur overnight, and, as we go to press, she had come through the operation but was still critical. Miracles don't come cheap and an appeal to raise the funds to pay for her surgery and nursing care was launched, raising more than £4,000 in less than 24 hours. But more will be needed, as she will need intensive care round the clock nursing for some time if she pulls through – it was a big operation'.

Four thousand pounds in less than twenty-four hours. It was insane. Absolutely insane, but the insanity wasn't over yet. Four thousand pounds was an incredible amount, but by the end of that twenty four hour period Help for Fleur had raised almost ten thousand pounds. In less than a day ten thousand pounds had been raised for Fleur. It was overwhelming, not only that that much could be raised but more so that it was raised by people we had never met. These people were donating their precious money, money that they had earned and was there to feed their own pets, to look after their families to make sure our girl survived. The kindness of the people that had invested both personally and financially was incredible. It took our breath away to think about the amount of support we, and of course Fleur, had. This amount didn't include the auctions that were being held on the Valgrays FaceBook auction page.

It was very humbling to consider the amount of work that had gone on behind the scenes, or rather behind the keyboards, to ensure Fleur made it. Val and Nickie and countless others had promoted, and shared Fleur's story and it had touched people the world over. Whilst we had tried to live in some vague attempt at normality for the benefit of our other pets, little did we know they had worked tirelessly to ensure we had what we needed to help Fleur. And that doesn't mean money, it includes the support buffer that we knew we had via the messages and posts from people. Since the pages conception there had been forty four pages of messages and donations varying from pennies to hundreds of pounds. Every donation meant the same and went towards lifesaving treatment, all four hundred and fifteen of them.

All of the good luck messages meant something to us, but two messages in particular struck both Andrew and myself.

'My sincere apologies, but I am unemployed and have three doggies of my own to feed. I know my donation is a very small amount, but it is still a contribution. Thank you for helping this special girl'

It was indeed a contribution, and it carried meaning because this person had their own problems, their own struggles and yet they could spare some of their limited means to help Fleur. Every donation was relative to the circumstances it came from, and in that context this donation was huge. It's always those with the least in the cupboard that will give you the last slice of bread.

'The strongest oak tree of the forest is not the one that is protected from the storm and hidden from the sun. It's the one that stands in the open where it is compelled to struggle for its existence against the winds and rains and the scorching sun'

If ever there was an epitome of this sentiment, it's Fleur. She had spent the entirety of her short life weathering a storm in order to survive. All of her experience and given her the strength she now needed to tap into in order to get through this latest storm, the difference being she now had people to lean on, and the safety of a warm caring home to act as a storm barrier.

The days that Fleur spent at RVC were critical in her recovery and in regard to the tissues joining up, but the daily messages we got from the RVC and the chats I had with Andy the vet were generally positive. Fleur was popular at the hospital, and Andy admitted to having a nap with Fleur on the floor during the twenty eight thousand hours a day Fleur slept. Another final year veterinary student, Phil, had developed a bond with Fleur and he spoke of the care and love she got whilst there. It was a relief and a comfort for us to know that not only was she getting medical care, but she was getting interaction and love to help her come to terms with where she was and what was happening. Then came the update we had been waiting for. Fleur was eating well, and as that was used as barometer for her progress, she was to be discharged from the RVC. Fleur was coming home.

That night the update on Val updated Fleur's FaceBook page that Fleur was coming home. Amongst the myriad of comments was the following poem by Andrea Rooqui Russ;

Fleur

Out from the darkness and into the light,
Came a little dog, so full of fright,
She battled and fought and tried to get well,
So, she could travel to England away from that hell.
To Valgray's she came, where she was showered with love
With Val's magic touch and some help from above.
She blossomed and grew into a beautiful hound,
It wasn't too long before the perfect home was found,
Off she went with a spring in her step,
She now knew what it was like to be a loved pet,

But now she has fallen again so unwell,
Because of those vets in the place of hell,
So please help Fleur to win her battle,
Buy in the auction, the sale or raffle.
Every single penny that you can give
Will help this precious girl to live.

The donations came in, from far and near,
Then came the update we wanted to hear,
Fleur, was fighting in her own unique way,
And improving with every passing day,
It's thanks to all that bought and gave,
This precious life was one to save,
The skill of the vets, and nursing staff,
Absolute masters of their craft,
And today, amidst cheers and songs,
Fleur is home where she belongs.

Both Wendy and Andrew were totally overwhelmed by the support and interest and were almost lost for words in describing their gratitude to all concerned. Andrew explained some of how they felt.

The exact date Fleur was due was Friday 6th March 2015. Of course, this couldn't just be a straight forward 'Fantastic, let's go and get our dog'. No, no. This was Crufts day and we were due to be there. We had attended Crufts for a few years at this point with our friends Pete and Pauline, and we had always attended on the day that the working and pastoral breeds were showing. Back in 1989 Pete had won the prestigious award of Best in Show with a Bearded Collie he owned at the time. It's the equivalent to winning Best Film at the Oscars, or Album of the Year at the Grammy's. It's a big deal, so they had a vested interest in the show.

We were torn. Both Wendy and myself wanted to travel to Potters Bar to collect Fleur, but I felt that one of us needed to go to Crufts and speak to Fleur's followers and fans. We were fast turning into her PR team, but we felt it was important to be able to thank Fleur's friends and those that had helped her in person.

I was more than happy for Wendy to go to Crufts without me, encouraging, in fact. For me it was just a chance to go and lie on the floor with a bunch of dogs and avoid as many people as possible, whereas Wendy would actually interact with other people there and engage with Fleur's followers. So, the decision was made that I would go and collect Fleur, and Wendy would go to Crufts as Fleur's official representative. Plus, the silver lining was Wendy could offer my ticket to Trish as a thank you for everything she had done for us since Fleur's arrival, not that it came close to what it would take to recompense her unfaltering kindness and generosity.

Wendy packed some Fleur T-shirts and keyrings to sell on the Valgrays stand and help raise some money for the charity, and both she and Trish donned Valgray's purple polo shirts with pictures of Fleur on the front. They were walking billboards promoting Valgrays and Fleur, and quite right too. Since Wendy had got a partner in crime to attend Crufts with, I roped in another friend, Jackie, to come along to Potters Bar with me. Much like Trish, and a plethora of other people before and after, Jackie jumped at the chance. This meant I could sit in the back with Fleur and comfort her on the way home and Wendy didn't need to feel like she had to rush and leave Crufts early.

Before Wendy set off she posted a video to the Fleur FaceBook group with Trish, saying yet another thank you to everyone on the group (there aren't enough 'thank you's' in the world to counterbalance the immense amount of kindness shown) and then off they went. We were due to arrive at Potters Bar before two pm, so I had some time to sort Marti and Nero out and make sure they were OK and settled before we headed to the M25. My military training has made me allergic to being late, so we left early, which of course meant we arrived early. The added extra for Jackie was that this meant I put my hand in my pocket and stretched to an eye wateringly expensive sandwich and coffee at the expansive South Mimms Services. Ironically this service is often used as a hand over point for dogs being transported from Europe to the UK.

My military precision came in to play and we arrived at the RVC bang on two pm. As soon as we mentioned 'Fleur' to the receptionist there was recognition and a confirmation that they were expecting us, which was reassuring. We were placed in the waiting area, but we didn't have to wait long before Vicki Lipscombe made her way over to us. She was dressed in a blue clinical over-shirt and introduced herself as the tissue viability surgeon that operated on Fleur. She, alongside a team of surgeons, nurses and carers had made sure Fleur had stayed with us. It was because of these amazingly talented and selflessly caring professionals that we were here to take Fleur home.

Vicky was very matter of fact, which was refreshing. She explained that Fleur had undergone an exceptional procedure that came with a world of its own complications as it hadn't really been done before. Fleur had undergone a re-sectioning of the non-viable tissue and that close to the defect where the junction between small and large intestine (ileocaecocolic junction) was removed as the tissue here was not viable. The upshot of this surgery meant that, because of the removal of the section of the intestinal tract, lifelong diarrhoea was a distinct possibility. At the time, Fleur was suffering with diarrhoea and Vicky told us this may never resolve itself, but she would reassess it once Fleur had been at home for a week and settled a little more in her home environment and her usual diet.

It was important that we followed strict instructions following the major abdominal surgery. She needed to be rested in a small room or crate when unsupervised (hardly out of the ordinary for Fleur) She could only go outside on the lead solely for toilet breaks for the following two weeks. This could then be increased to three to four five minute walks on a short lead for the next six weeks. For the whole six weeks there was to be no uncontrolled exercise such as running, climbing or jumping. So, there would be no tearing around the field for the next few weeks for Fleur.

The wound needed close monitoring. We needed to be conscious of any signs of heat, discharge, swelling or redness. If these signs did become evident then we needed to inform the RVC straight away. Fleur wore a t-shirt that held her feeding tube in place which needed to be flushed twice daily. I was suddenly wishing Wendy was with me, taking this all in. Her nurse's brain had its benefits.

It became quickly and brutally apparent that Fleur was far from being out of the woods yet. Sometimes there is an automatic assumption that because the dog is allowed home then they are out of danger and everything is suddenly going to be fine, but with invasive surgery in particular, there is still a long way to go in terms of recovery. The next ten days were going to be crucial and if Fleur became in any way unwell, lethargic or starting to vomit then we would be back on the road to the RVC.

As Vicky finished her very professional and acute explanation my first words back to her were;

"That's all written down, right?"

Thankfully it was all incorporated into the discharge report that Vicky had already prepared. I had already mentally earmarked it for Wendy and her medical thought process. I had started to glaze over during Vicky's explanation, not because I wasn't interested, or bored, just because I am a practical person. Listing a ton of medical terminology to me isn't going to mean a great deal. As I took the report from Vicky, as if they had been listening behind the door ready for their cue, X-Factor style, appeared a vet nurse and next to her; Fleur.

I had seen her in the cage a few times but to see her saunter along the corridor with that characteristic swish of her tail made it all fade into history. Here she was, up and about and seemingly herself holding her head high. Graceful as ever. How on earth did this dog do it?

As she came towards me I couldn't help but marvel at this dog's absolute tenacity and resolute desire to survive no matter what curve balls were thrown her way. There was a regal flair to her presentation that was only spoiled by the fact she was sporting a cone of shame, half her midriff was shaved along with both her forelegs, which now both sported yellow bandages, and she had what looked like a colostomy bag attached to her side. It didn't seem to effect Fleur as she trotted towards me.

I didn't really expect any recognition from her. She had only been in our lives for 3 weeks before she was admitted to the RVC, and the times I had visited her here she had been asleep or barely with us. On top of that, the previous six months she had been in various locations with multiple people coming in and out of her life all the time, so I was a little taken aback when she made a beeline for me, tail wagging away as she did so. She was our girl, she was part of the family it and seemed like she knew that. I, of course, filmed the whole thing ready to update her loyal followers later that evening.

I was loaded up with medication and a tray of prescription tinned dog food like a Buckaroo donkey, and then came the painful part. I think I may have physically winced as the receptionist informed me of how much needed to be paid. We had fronted up to the accountant about the lack of funds, but also that there were charity collections via Valgrays and there had been a stay of execution as the invoice still needed to be finalised. Then came the amount. £25. Wait, what? That was it? As it turned out, the RVC was happy for us to pay the administration fee and then take payment for the rest direct from Valgrays. Thankfully the house didn't need to be re-mortgaged after all, and more importantly Fleur was coming home. Again. Hopefully for the final time. Maybe.

Chapter Fifteen

HOME, SWEET HOME

~ • ~

THE VETS SEEMED happy, Wendy and Andrew were cautiously happy and Fleur's many friends were cheering her on. But how did Fleur herself see things?

The female uniform wearer came to my cage with the familiar lead. It wasn't my home lead, but it was a lead I recognised that meant I was going out for a toilet break, which meant some fresh air and getting out of the crate. It also probably meant a tummy tickle. We left the room, but we didn't go the usual route, we headed in the opposite direction. Six months ago, this would have terrified me, and thoughts of where I was going to end up and what was waiting for me would have flooded in. Now, they didn't. Although I wasn't home I still felt fairly safe and secure.

We waited as two sliding doors opened and there he was. The male from the house was sat waiting for me, and he had my lead and collar! I was going home! He was here! I could feel my tail swishing in glee as I made my way to him. It was a weird feeling, walking with a big plastic thing around my head but I didn't care. I just wanted to get to the man and go home. There was another female human with him and we went outside.

It felt nice to be outside again, not just out for a quick toilet break but outside for a walk, albeit fairly brief. Despite everything that was attached to me, and the wind on the bare skin that had been shaved, it felt as if a bit of the normality from the home was coming back. The female gave me some belly tickles and head rubs, and then we got into the car We were actually leaving. I was definitely going home.

This journey was completely different to my last journey. I remembered nothing from that journey, other than sitting up and looking out of the window. Everything else was a complete blur. I didn't lie down once on this journey. I wanted to take it in, I was excited and wanted to make sure I remembered it. The male from home sat with me and together we watched the world pass outside.

We stopped at a place with a lot of other cars. The man took me to an area with grass and I relieved myself. Suddenly the area was full of other dogs of every shape and size you could imagine. Had they all come to see me? That's what it felt like. I lapped it up as various dogs approached me to say 'hello'. It was a stark difference to how dog interactions happen in cage rooms and on the streets. So different that I wasn't scared or nervous at all. I loved it. The man, however, seemed nervous every time a new dog approached. He seemed eager to get back to the car, so I reluctantly left my adoring public and headed back across the tarmac. Then it was full steam ahead to home.

The world outside flew past quickly. It was so green. On the streets the main colour we saw was brown or grey, or sometimes red on a bad day. I watched as it passed by and soon we were back at the home. This was the first time I had ever been relieved to return somewhere. It felt familiar, warm and welcoming. I'd never had that before. As we went inside the other two dogs came up and sniffed a hello, and that was that. Given the response the other dogs on the grass had given me I had hoped for more, but nevertheless it was good to be back. First thing was first. I needed sleep, so I found the comfy blanket and that was it for me. I had slept at the vets but sleeping somewhere you feel fully secure and relaxed is the only real way to sleep. I had never known real sleep until I came into this home. Plus, the man slept with me and I could feel his hand resting on my neck. That night I dreamt of Shimeka and her head on my neck.

It was a deep sleep that night. Being back at home meant my appetite came back with a vengeance, but unfortunately it wasn't the only thing that came back with a vengeance. I had had stomach problems at the chemical smelling room and they hadn't eased with coming to home. It wasn't the most comfortable of times, but I was getting a lot of attention from both the male and female human which helped ease a lot of the discomfort.

Stomach problems didn't really phase me anymore, at least not on their own. Living on the streets as I had, food was so hard to come by that I

Home, sweet home

would eat whatever I could get hold of, this meant that often what we ate was old or not the best thing for my stomach, but it was eaten out of necessity and survival. That outweighed any painful or uncomfortable consequences. This was the first time I could remember eating for pleasure rather than to make hunger pain subside; eating because I wanted to rather than because I had to. Eating when you weren't forced to by crippling hunger was a whole other experience.

There were times over the next couple of days, laying on my blanket whilst the male human and one of the other dogs slept next to me, when thoughts of street life kept me awake. Things that had happened ran through my head in that time between being awake and falling asleep. It was a show reel of how much my life had changed in the past six months.

Before going into the big cage room, the streets were my comfort blanket. I knew them inside out, I knew how to survive and how to traverse the city to make the most of it. They were all I knew. The thought of living in a home didn't even cross my mind, it wasn't something that happened to us. As far as we knew dogs that were taken by the dog catcher, or anyone else, just never came back. It never even crossed our mind that any of them would end up in a home.

I wondered if the deformed leg dog was laying on a warm blanket in a loving home somewhere. If she was I hoped it had been more straight forward a journey than mine had been, but however traumatic it had been it had led me to something that was better than anything I could ever have dreamed of whilst sleeping under cars or behind bins. Whilst I felt a type of security on the streets, this was different. This was a comfortable security. A more relaxed security that came from knowing I didn't have to be afraid, or anxious, or on the verge of fighting for my life. I was home.

If Fleur was happy to be back at her new home, Wendy was delirious, as she recalled.

Having Fleur home was fantastic. Finally, we could settle into life with our new baby girl. Not that there was much settling between the drain flushing, toilet walks and diarrhoea cleaning. And, my goodness, was there was some diarrhoea. Aside from taking care of our miracle girl, a fair amount of time was taken up updating the Fleur Facebook page. Since Nickie had set up the 'Help for Fleur' page it had grown to over one thousand members. The page started as an open page where anyone could join and post, which aided the quick growth of its members. Sadly, amongst every bunch of grapes there are bound to be a few sour ones.

Trolls don't just live under bridges and they would pop up in the group every now and then, posting pointless adverts and approaching members directly but what was worse was the negative posts and comments we would get, especially when people found out how much had been raised for Fleur. Everyone is welcome to an opinion, and of course everybody has their own viewpoint and that is fine. However when these opinions cause hurt and offence, and are purposefully posted to do so, it crosses a line.

There were a number of people, those that had seen the FaceBook shares or read the Dogs Today articles, who felt that the amount raised would have been better spent helping a number of dogs rather than one dog. One Fleur. Their viewpoint, which they are perfectly entitled to, was that that amount of money could be used to help dogs still in Romania, those that were still suffering in the shelters or on the streets. Whilst we did understand that perspective, from our point of view helping one of them was better than none and after everything Fleur had suffered at the hands of man, surely, she was entitled and deserving of a new, loving home, no matter what that took. On top of that, the stir that her case was causing was drawing more attention to the plight of the dogs that were still in Romania. Wasn't that justification enough? If Fleur's story could then inspire people to help more dogs in need then we felt that justified our actions.

It put me in mind of a parable I had heard years earlier., the starfish parable.

One day, an old man was walking along a beach that was littered with thousands of starfish that had been washed ashore by the high tide. As he walked he came upon a young boy who was eagerly throwing the starfish back into the ocean, one by one.

Puzzled, the man looked at the boy and asked what he was doing. Without looking up from his task the boy simply replied, "I'm saving these starfish, sir"

The old man chuckled aloud, "Son, there are thousands of starfish and only one of you. What difference can you make?"

The boy picked up a starfish, gently tossed it into the water and turning to the man said, "I made a difference to that one!"

That summed up how we felt. There were thousands of dogs throughout Romania that were suffering in shelters or on the streets. Thousands that we had absolutely no hope of helping, however we were helping this one. We were helping Fleur and we were giving her the life that they all deserved. There was no guarantee that if we had taken on another dog that the cost would be any different, and although we would have loved to help more dogs it simply wasn't feasible. Of course, we were pained that we couldn't help more dogs in need, but we knew we were doing the right thing by Fleur.

It was because of these trolls that the decision was made to change the settings of the FaceBook group from public to closed. The trolling was changing the atmosphere in the group and causing upset and tension, which was the opposite of what the group's ethos was. People had become passionate about Fleur and were seeking daily updates on her progress and her toing's and froing's. The group was the perfect platform to provide them with just that, and so began the daily ritual of writing and posting about Fleur's roaming's and activities.

This task usually fell to Andrew who would scribe the day's events and post them on the page. I always surprised how interested people were in the goings on of our girl, but then we were also acutely aware of how Fleur and her story could take a hold of your heart and never let it go. Despite this, it soon became apparent that daily updates were not only physically unfeasible with other commitments, but most of the time Fleur did typically dog things, nothing that would necessitate a group entry. It wasn't Bridget Jones' Diary or Sex and the City (or maybe that should be Bridget Bones' Diary and Rex and the City) so we began to only write an update when something significant had happened.

The Chronicles of Fleur would focus on Fleur's health, as that was what people were most interested in, plus any events that she attended such as dogs shows etc. and any funny or unusual stories that occurred as Fleur settled into life with us. Of course, it wasn't exactly that smooth or fluid. And smooth fluid was the appropriate phrasing, giving what fleur would produce during her convalescence at home.

Andrew's Chronicles of Fleur would often include an update on the consistency of Fleur's doings, or lack of it. A competition had begun in the Morris household as to who would witness the first solid poo. Isn't it weird how changes in conversations occur when you have pets and kids?

Suddenly instead of sending flirty text messages, you send faecal updates including consistencies and colour variations.

And so, whomever would have the pleasure of taking Fleur on her morning walk would also keep their fingers crossed that that walk would be the one. That would be the walk that would result in that ever elusive and coveted solid poo. Needless to say, this took time. I would return home from taking Fleur out and Andrew would ask me;

"Was it solid?"

My reply would be something along the lines of, "It would have passed through the eye of a needle". I'm not on for beating around the bush, which is exactly what Fleur would do when trying to find the exact right spot to do her ablutions, whilst one of us waited on crossed-finger tenterhooks trying to get a glimpse of what that day's poo looked like.

Fleur had spent a huge portion of her life in a crate in one way shape or form, and so, since returning from the vets, we had decided to banish it from Fleur's world. Although initially she had used the crate to find her place of safety, to hide away and to regain her confidence but now she was safe. She was safe in our home and she no longer needed the crate to provide security. There is a line in Agatha Christie's 'Death on the Nile':

'Dogs are wise. They crawl away into a quiet corner and lick their wounds and do not re-join the world until they are whole once more'

This is how it felt with Fleur. She had spent time in her quiet corner and her (significant) wounds had been licked. Although she may not have been completely whole at that point, she seemed a lot closer to whole than she had when she arrived with us. Our house was now her crate and she felt safe enough to see it as such. It felt like quite the milestone, a physical acknowledgement that Fleur had now accepted that this was where she belonged, and this was the family she was part of, and we had accepted that to. There were no more hurdles to jump or mountains to overcome.

Things did seem to be moving forwards well. Now home, Fleur's wound management was down to me and everything appeared to be progressing nicely. I continued to flush the wound twice a day and the staples that were used to hold the wound together were doing their job and it seemed to be messing together well. Fleur had been attired in an elegant and incredibly fetching cone of shame, which she seemed to take to surprisingly well. It was probably a little superfluous considering she never bothered with her wounds at all. Maybe she felt safe in the knowledge that we were taking good care of her, so she trusted us enough not to try and clean the wound herself. Maybe she was just used to having stomach wounds, or maybe she realised the buster collar meant it wasn't worth even trying. Whatever her reasoning was, Fleur left her wound alone.

That doesn't mean she was a model patient, however. When Fleur first went to the vets in Romania the issue was fear and biting, now, the issue was completely the opposite. It was a warm March Tuesday in 2015 and the sun shone down on the Morris household. We went about our daily routine as normal. At least, most of us did. The sun seemed to have gone to Fleur's head as she did her best to convince us that her six-week recovery period had passed, and it was definitely time to play. Whilst she slept well, her waking hours were spent trying to illicit play in any way she could. We had to put all the dogs' toys away in a box to stop her unleashing her 'Arctic Fox Mode' and launching herself, dive bomb style, onto any and every toy she could find.

Andrew called a pack meeting and, as he lay on the floor with them, explained to everyone that the jubilations and gleeful partying need to come down a few notches. He talked them through Fleur's recovery plan, again, explaining that it took weeks, not days. They seemed to take it in, heads tilted in that way dogs do to show you they are listening. Of course, they could just have been intent on getting access to the biscuit Andrew held in his hand. Marti had already given Andrew's head a lick in an attempt to soften him up. If non-animal-owning people could be a fly on the wall in our homes sometimes, I'm sure they would have us committed when they see the conversations and interactions we have with our furry family.

We were convinced that Nero and Fleur were trying to hatch some sort of plan. Considering Fleur was supposed to be on bed rest with restricted exercise, imagine our surprise when we found Nero stood at the gate with Fleur's purple ted (that had so kindly been donated when Fleur was at the vets, and Andrew had delivered) with Fleur and Marti stood either side of him as if plotting some sort of escape plan. All three looked shifty, with a 'We weren't doing anything' look on their faces. Andrew took a photo and shared it onto Fleur's FaceBook page for her followers to try and deduce what was happening.

On that same day, just to throw a juxtaposing reality check into the equation, we were given a short sharp reminder that Fleur was still unwell, and definitely not recovered. It was evening and as usual we were all in the living room relaxing. Suddenly Fleur leapt up with a yelp of pain and quickly took herself under the coffee table. Instantly my head went to that horrendous night not that long ago and my heart started to race. No. Please God no, don't let this be happening again. Panic rose quickly, feeding off the trigger stacking I was witnessing. The yelp, the table, it was all far too familiar.

Thankfully Fleur quickly recovered herself without any real intervention, and the status quo was resumed. It was a stark slap in the face to remind is that Fleur was by no means out of the woods yet, despite how she may be presenting herself. She still had a lot of internal stitches and staples and she was still in recovery. Sometimes it was all too easy to assume she was fine, given how she ran around and went about her daily life as if nothing was wrong. This made us realise what was on the outside didn't necessarily mirror what was happening on the inside. Maybe we should've been more aware of that given how well she had hidden her illness the first time round. I think at that point Fleur's illness was more likely to be the death of me than her.

Thankfully Fleur had an appointment for a progress report at the RVC the following morning, so I hoped any fears that the incident may have provoked were unfounded.

Chapter Sixteen

MORE TEARS IN THE MORRIS HOME

~ • ~

GOING BACK TO Potters Bar brought back to life the recent memories of anguish along with the worry that things were not progressing as well as they should but the hope that Fleur was progressing even better than expected. So, with mixed feelings Andrew explains what happened.

The following morning, March 12th 2015, we made the now very familiar journey to Potters Bar for Fleur's check-up and, of course, we both prayed for good news. That morning there had been a sudden intake of breath from both of us as Fleur brought up some white, frothy bile. This wasn't something we needed to experience but at least she was off to the RVC. My other concern was that Fleur hadn't offered us a Bristol Stool Chart sample. Was there going to be an in-car explosion? I prayed we wouldn't see a back-end blow that would need internal windscreen wipers. Thankfully, Fleur was good as gold during the car journey.

We were met by Lindsey, a final year veterinary student and a Fleur fan. She even joined the Help for Fleur FB group, so she was very aware of Fleur's celebrity status. We had met Lindsey before, and she formed part of the team that had saved Fleur's life. The staff at the RVC were the reason Fleur was walking into their clinic that day, they were the reason she was here to wretch up bile on to our floor, which we dutifully handed to Lindsey. The entire staff were professional throughout, but more importantly they were empathetic, caring and compassionate. Every member of staff I had the honour to meet had been fantastic and it made the entire experience much more bearable.

Once again we watched as Fleur was taken into a back room. The difference this time was that Fleur was walking of her own accord into the room, she wasn't being rushed in folded in the arms of veterinary staff. All four paws tapped away on the floor as she trotted amicably through the door. Aside from her medical attachments she was the mirror image of the dog Wendy had brought here weeks earlier. In the back room the veterinary staff removed the clips from her abdomen and discarded the gastronomy feeding tube and finally the cone of shame was removed.

Then the consultant vet, Andrew Phillips, listened as we updated him on Fleur's progress. At home she was bright, and we had no real concerns. She was beginning to eat well which was promising, but she still had hosepipe diarrhoea. This had been an ongoing issue with Fleur and meant finding a food that wouldn't result in Exorcist style ablutions. That was a task in itself.

As we walked out into the reception with Fleur, it was almost like a Stars in Their Eye's make over. She went into the room a sick patient and she emerged Fleur, finally ready to take on her life in the Morris household. All that was missing was a smoke machine and Matthew Kelly (or Davina McCall, depending on your age). She definitely had a swagger to her trot now that she was free of accoutrements, and I could literally see her grow in stature as she walked out of the door. It was as if the real Fleur was emerging.

If you think that that was it and all was hunky dory, you obviously haven't taken in all of her previous story. Nothing was ever that straight forward where Fleur was concerned. This was really just another step in her recovery, albeit a big one. The vet gave us instructions to ensure Fleur was able to recover properly. Restricted exercise was a stipulation we had assumed, and one we were already implementing. We were told Fleur could have life-long diarrhoea which in turn could bring with it nutritional issues. There may have to be alternative diets and/or added medications to modify the gastrointestinal environment. It was a small price to pay considering what the outcome could have been, and even with these issues Fleur's quality of life was leaps and bounds ahead of what it had been in the rescue centre in Romania before she was taken by Ramona.

We left the vets with another reminder of just how lucky and loved Fleur was. The veterinary bill breakdown put some figures to just how much Fleur was loved. The RVC account stood at £4981.23 and our local veterinary bill with Cedar Veterinary Group stood at £941.78. Without the support of people, the world over, without their selfless devotion to Fleur's recovery and her journey it would have been infinitely more difficult to get her the care she needed. Her story had ignited some spark in so many people, who had then passed it on to others and it had grown like wildfire throughout the dog world and outside of it.

Incidentally, that evening I was chatting to one of our neighbours who had been in West Sussex that day. He had been in a shop and overheard a customer and a retailer discussing Fleur. He had immediately butted in to tell them that he was Fleur's neighbour. That's what Fleur's story seemed to do, it brought people together and it gave people a tangible way to help and get the word out about other dogs in Romania and what they go through.

Fleur had fans the world over, but there was one particular fan close to home who needed to know about the outcome of Fleur's visit to the vets, and that was Great Grandma Joan Morris. We took the detour to my birthplace to visit the matriarch of the family who was also a huge Fleur fan. However, given her ninety years, she wasn't one for social media so a face to face visit was due, knowing full well she would be more interested in Fleur's face than either of ours.

True to form Fleur didn't disappoint and headed straight to the cat's food bowl and wolfed down leftovers. Her strict dietary restrictions were off to a cracking start. Once she was finished she headed straight to Great Grandma Morris for some fuss and cuddles, it was difficult to tell who was enjoying the attention and affection more.

We left and headed back to the M25, but as we figured this was our last visit to Potters Bar (at least, we hoped) we headed anti-clockwise instead of clockwise towards Warlingham, Surrey. As we drove up to Valgrays HQ there was a distinctly different atmosphere. There was no snow, for starters, and the bright Sun shone down. If ever I believed in signs, then this really was one to take on board. The Sun truly had shone down on Fleur and this was her time. This was her time to come out of the shadows of her illness and into the light. Not that I believe in all that universe type stuff, but if I did…

Back where it had all begun, in terms of Fleur's physical entry into our lives, and with the person that had introduced Fleur to us there was a sense of coming full circle. There was still a sense of that quiet dog that we met and forced ourselves on that first night, but now there was a confidence and an inquisitiveness. She had put on some weight and her coat had grown out. She looked healthier and there was an all-round brightness that hadn't been there when we picked her up. That tired, dull-eyed dog was a thing of the past. There were tears in Val's eyes when she saw Fleur. There had been updates online but they often don't do the reality justice, and as Val hadn't seen Fleur in person (or in dog?) the difference was much more evident to her than it was us.

Val had been absolutely instrumental in Fleur's journey right from the very beginning when she posted that picture on the Valgrays FaceBook. That had inspired something within Wendy, something about Fleur had drawn her in and from then on it had been a domino effect. But without Val, none of those dominoes would have fallen and when one of them threatened to stay standing, she knocked it down. She had ultimate faith in Fleur and ultimate faith in us and it's because of her and those she inspired that Fleur is still with us, so for her to see Fleur on that day was an emotional experience.

We knew there was still a way to go in terms of Fleur's recovery, and there would probably be ongoing issues with regards to her health but that day it really felt like we had turned a corner.

For Fleur this was also a very special day of course

I was still there. I was still in the home with the same man and woman. I had had to go back to the small cage room, but they were with me and they had brought me back here, back home. I wasn't moved on to a new cage room or dragged into a car and driven somewhere new. I knew that when we left the home, we would come back to it. I knew that now.

Although I had spent more time on the street than anywhere else, I felt a calmness in this home that I never felt in my street life. I didn't have to hide or suppress hunger pains. I didn't need to keep moving to stay safe. The only moving I had to do now was to find which bed was most comfortable. That was my main goal the day after we went back to the chemical smelling place. The weird thing around my neck that stopped me from seeing had been taken off. That was a relief because it kept hitting things, especially walking through doors.

The tube thing was gone too, but where it had been taken out was really itchy. I tried to scratch at it but then the lady put some soft thing around it which meant I couldn't get at it and it drove me mad. Even with the itching, all I wanted to do that day was sleep. The day before at the chemical smelling place had been a long day. We had stopped off at a couple of places on the way back too, and there was something familiar about the second place we went. There were some familiar smells, I could smell a lot of other dogs. I had been there before. A woman came out to greet us and I immediately recognised her scent.

When we went inside the building I recognised where I was. This was the place I had come to after the long journey with all the other dogs. I was positive it was. I wasn't really sure what was happening. Was I going to be left here again? No, something about it didn't feel like that was what was going to happen. I knew the man and woman wouldn't leave me here and this time I wasn't scared or apprehensive. I knew I was still going to end up at home.

And I did. Later that evening we were back at the home with the other two dogs and the elusive cat. My new outfit was put on me and I was off to bed, it had been a long day. So, the next day the aim was to snooze as much as possible. The great thing about the home was the grat choice of sleeping places. Not only were there beds down on the floor, but there were bigger beds in almost all the rooms. There was one in the same room as my cage, but it was more comfortable. In the room where everyone seemed to sit there were all kinds of beds and then up the stairs there were even more beds on the floor and extra big beds. It was the exact opposite of trying to find somewhere to sleep on the streets. On the streets you could be searching for hours to find a safe space to lay, now the problem was having too many to pick from.

I had always been cautious about things that smelled like the other dogs. I knew from experience that going near things that other dogs had laid claim to was dangerous, but something was different here. The rules here seemed to be much different than those I had experienced on the streets. Things felt more interchangeable and free flowing, so I took advantage of this and lay on a bed in one of the rooms upstairs. It smelled like the female dog, but it was so comfortable that when she came into the room I let out a low throaty grumble. She turned and left, so as far as I was concerned the bed was mine and I fell fast asleep.

The rest of that day was spent in much the same state. A whole day slipping in and out of sleep is something that would be impossible on the streets. Days were spent hunting for food and generally trying to stay free and alive. That worry was non-existent at the home, and for the first time in as long as I could remember I could sleep without being on edge.

It felt like a different lifetime that I first arrived at the home. Back then I thought that I had finally found a place that I could truly relax, but actually I was just so dog tired that I just collapsed. I didn't have any energy in me to do much else but sleep. Yes, I didn't have to worry about what was going on around me as much as I had had to back on the streets, but I don't think I was still truly relaxed. The banging of a door or the sound of metal hitting the floor would always bring me back to life in an instant.

But after coming back from the chemical smelling room something changed. The man and woman never left me, they never took me anywhere in the car and left me. No stones were thrown at me and I never had to hide under a car. I never had to keep one eye open or look over my shoulder in case another dog was going steal my food or shelter, or the man with the pole was coming to catch me. As time passed I began to feel calmer and I stopped second-guessing everything with fear. I learned that not every interaction would result in pain or misery, and that I no longer had to feel hungry or cold.

There were still leftovers from the streets, still memories from which I couldn't escape and every now and then something would trigger them, bringing them crashing into my head and suddenly I relived that fear from being on the streets. Loud noises had always been something that made me scared, loud noises were usually followed by something scary or painful but that had grown better the more I heard loud noises and nothing bad happened, but one thing that really did bring back horrendous, painful memories was metal on the floor.

On the streets there were no people to teach you what was safe and what was not, and as a puppy without an adult dog to guide me I had no way of learning what was safe and what wasn't other than to learn what hurt and avoid it in the future. One day, at around three months old, I was walking along a quiet street. Coming towards me was a group of people. I already knew that people tended to cause pain, so my immediate reaction was to avoid them. To do that I needed to try and be as invisible as possible, so I crawled down into the road, keeping my body as low as possible. The people came close and I prayed that they wouldn't notice me, or if they did that they would ignore me.

They came level with me, everything inside me expected there to be pain or something scary. They kept walking. They had passed without anything bad happening.

Then there was suddenly an intense, sharp burning in my paws. I yelped and sprang backwards, whimpering and confused about what had happened, what had caused the sudden pain. On the floor was a metal grate. I hobbled away into an alleyway to lick at my burnt paws until they didn't hurt anymore. I sat in that alleyway for what felt like hours licking at the pads on paws, waiting until I could walk again without any pain. From then on; I avoided metal in the floor.

The first time the man and woman took me out of the home I was terrified when I saw metal in the floor. I didn't want to feel that pain again, I was desperate to try and avoid that metal, but I was attached to a lead. I couldn't just avoid or run away which was my first choice, so I flipped and made as much of a fuss as possible to try and tell the man and woman that this was dangerous and terrifying, and I didn't want to go near it.

It worked, but that fear never went away. I always had a rise in anxiety whenever I saw metal in the road. I was taken back to being that scared puppy licking her paws in the alleyway and I did whatever I could to avoid it. But something unusual happened. The man and woman listened to me. They understood, and they responded by helping me avoid it. They talked to me and reassured me and, although it was scary, I got past it and calmed down.

Although that fear response remained with me and every time I saw metal in the road my stress levels immediately rose, the man and woman would help me avoid it. Together we managed it. I knew now that I had people to help me learn what was safe and what wasn't, and to help me feel safe. As time passed I began to trust them and when I was around them I was calm.

I had started to enjoy going home, I liked being in the home. It helped that the food was so much better than the food I found on the streets. For starters, I didn't have to hunt for it, plus, it didn't have mould or bugs on it. On top of the food that was abundant within the house, the outside also often provided a buffet.

The big grassy area where we would walk was always a heaven of scents, but one morning in particular I hit the jackpot. The man and woman had stopped walking me on the short and long lead. The freedom felt amazing. I ran through the streets all the time but that wasn't freedom, that was that was panic. Running through the grass was a completely different feeling, and on this particular morning it came with a mouth-watering added extra. As I ran my nose twitched. Food. Fresh food.

My nose led the way as I flew across the field. There was a small building across the grass, and my nose was telling me that was where the smell was coming from. I heard a shout from behind me and I saw the man running after me. He must've smelled it too, but he wasn't getting it before me. Just to be sure, I sped up. His shouts got louder, he really wanted that food.

I got through the fence and into where the smell was strongest and there it was. Fresh bread. It smelled delicious, I could almost taste it. I heard another shout behind me and that made me launch myself forward and grab the bread in my mouth. At that point the male came into the garden, but he was too late. I won, and it was mine. He tried to get it off me, but he was too slow. That walk was so much fun, breakfast and a game. What more could I ask for?

It was in these moments that I really felt that I had found my home, and my family. Back home we would all lay in our spaces and we would all converge for walks or in the downstairs comfy room in the evenings. I was never forced into doing anything, I always had the space I needed but there was also the security of knowing that I could usually predict any outcome from most situations, and there were usually all positive. That was the complete opposite of my life before coming to the home. I had peace of mind in my environment and those I shared it with. Everything stayed the same and I could trust that it would stay that way.

Wendy, of course, was also much more relaxed, delighted in fact.

By the November of 2015 we had reached a pleasant, steady status quo in the Morris household. Fleur's health had settled down, aside from the ongoing diet/stool chart issues and the usual doggy stuff and life was what we had always hoped it would be with Fleur in the house.

In fact, it was better because Fleur came with opportunities that we probably wouldn't have had without her. We got to go to shows and agility and we had photo shoots and magazine interviews about her story. Fleur's impact on our lives was so big, so dramatic that it was sometimes easy to forget why we were looking to get another dog in the first place.

Almost a year earlier this tsunami had crashed into our lives but instead of being destructive it had brought with it a whole new branch of our tree to explore.

But Fleur's original story, in terms of coming to our house, began with Marti. It was because of the first signs of her decline in health that we began to look for another dog. Initially that had worked but as time passed and Fleur had grown stronger, Marti had begun to slow down. Maybe this was the explanation for the rift between the two, Marti feeling more vulnerable as her health dipped.

On November 1st I was sat on the couch at home. Andrew was working away so it was just me, the dogs and the cat. As Marti had begun to get older, she needed assistance to get up on the furniture, so with my help she managed to climb on the sofa with me and I gave her a cuddle.

As my hands worked through her fur I noticed how fragile she had got. Physically, she had almost started going back to the dog we collected from Valgrays all those years before. As I snuggled with her that day I noticed there was a smell too, but I just put that down to her age. I had done the same with the fact she had started to urinate more, especially inside the house. I just thought it was her age and her mental decline would of course mean her training would suffer, and that's where I pinned her new lack of house training.

Marti had always been energetic and so full of life. She didn't play as Nero did, she wouldn't chase a ball or a Frisbee, but she would happily roll back the years and bring out her herding skills, something Andrew would proudly, and regularly, show off to anyone that would watch. She always loved a cuddle and was very affectionate, so that day on the sofa I told her everything would be OK.

"Don't worry, Mummy will look after you."

Not only was I on my own, I couldn't even pick up the phone and call Andrew because he was away at work and communications were extremely sparse. I think Andrew preferred it that way, it was his way of dealing with being so far away from home and his family. His communications would be limited to checking his computer once in the morning after the gym, and then again in the evening after his working day. There could often be anything up to a twenty-four-hour delay in responses because of the time difference.

On the morning of November 2nd he turned on his computer and phone as usual, just like I had got out of bed and made coffee, as usual. These weren't the latest MacBook and iPhone, so whilst they booted themselves up Andrew did his usual routine of going to the gym and kidding himself he was still 22. Forty-five minutes later he opened his WhatsApp and read my message from the previous day.

'Marti is not good. I am really worried about her, will take her to the vets tomorrow'.

I took her to the vets for a check-up, and whilst I was worried I fully expected to be told she had a urine infection, given her new weeing habits. Andrew was as relaxed about it as I was and when his reply eventually came through it read;

'Hi Wendy, I'm sure Marti will be fine, let me know how she gets on'.

We had taken the dogs to the vets so many times during our life with them it was fairly run of the mill by now, and we expected run of the mill news. What I got was something much darker, and much more significant. The urine sample I had taken with me showed that Marti had a severe infection, but on top of that the vet found a large tumour and a swollen spleen.

I was knocked off my feet. But, surely she just had a urine problem. Yes, her back legs weren't great anymore, but she was old. Surely there had been a mistake. This couldn't be what I thought it was. This couldn't be it. Not like this, not this quickly without us getting to cherish those final moments, to make sure she was spoiled before she went.

Not twelve hours before I had told her I would look after her and that everything would be OK, and now I was being told that Marti was going toxic and septic suggesting there was cancer in the spleen. She had a couple of days left at most. I couldn't grasp what was happening. I hadn't prepared myself for it at all and it hit me hard. I felt like I was in a tunnel struggling to find my way out as the information swirled around me.

I knew what the ultimate decision needed to be, I had to do what was best for Marti. In my heart, if I stripped away all the layers of selfish self-preservation, I knew letting her go was the kindest thing to do. Of course, I chose to stay with her for the process, and the vet left to get the nurse and the necessary drugs. I leant my head into hers. I could feel the intense, tight pain in my chest.

'My Princess, you will always be in my heart'.

The vet came back, and the process was done. I held on to her tightly as her breathing got slower. I sobbed uncontrollably as her chest stopped rising and falling, then she was gone. The vet and the nurse left the room, telling me I had as much time as I needed. I was left in the room with Marti's body, alone and distraught. I felt bereft and confused and heartbroken all in the same sob.

That was it. She was gone. I felt cheated. I never got the chance to show her how special she was, how much she was loved. I never got to take her on her final walk or give her, that favourite meal. That evening I left the vets through the back door, clutching Marti's collar tightly in my hand.

If ever I needed to be able to grab a phone and call Andrew, it was then, but of course I couldn't. I sent him a message though I was torn. I knew he needed to know, it wasn't fair not to and to spring it on him when he got home but at the same time I didn't want him to be angry I made the decision without him, or to have to deal with it on his own.

'Andrew, I'm really sorry to tell you that Marti really wasn't well at all. There is nothing they can do for her. I've had to let her go. Please don't be angry. I'm so sorry'.

And I was. I was so sorry.

It was not our only sorrow, there was also another loss – Marian Shepherd.

Let me please explain. Val has run the Valgrays charity since the 70s and has saved countless dogs. To do this Val has had the support and friendship of many people. One such lady, Marian Shepard, had been a great friend and fellow dog rescuer with Val for many many years. Marian was the epitome of how far some will go in their pursuance of rescuing dogs from pain and cruelty. Marian summed up her own passion in the following message:

"As most of you are now aware I am at the Rowans hospice, Purbrook under palliative (end of life) care. For more years than I care to recall I have been involved in dog rescue & I fully intend to go out still doing all I can for the dogs!

I have always said I don't want flowers at my funeral but instead donations to a good cause, so whilst I am still here I would love it if you could help me. I want to try to raise money for the following 3 dog rescue charities:

1 – Val Grays Border Collie Rescue
2 – Second Chance Eastleigh
3 – Cristina Romanian Rescue

We have opened a separate PayPal account for donations:
marian.sheppard@hotmail.com

This will be overseen by my niece Sophie Newman and other family members.

Please leave a message as to where you would like the money to go to (1/2/3 or a combination of them).

Please also send a personal message as when my time does come all messages will be displayed in place of any flowers.

It is my 70th Birthday on 12th December 2016 so please make it special by helping to give me the gift of knowing I'm still helping, and let me go in the knowledge of what I have achieved.

I am also having a little party/get together for my 70th which will be at the Rowans hospice in Purbrook on 12th December, which will be in my room, everyone is welcome and I am allowed visitors all day so please pop in if you are around to help me celebrate in style.

Love to you all
Marian"

Andrew and I had never met Marian although she lived quite close to us and was currently in a Hospice not too far away. The twelfth of December fell on a Monday so neither Andrew nor I could make it for Marian's party, but we both felt that someone who had put their whole life into rescuing dogs and had been actively part of Fleur's life-saving treatment, at least should be shown the respect of a visit. So, on Sunday, November 11th 2016 we found ourselves all jumping into the car and heading across to where Marian was resting. A call to the Hospice before setting off confirmed that Nero and Fleur would be very welcome. I was especially pleased to be able to take Nero, as he had a great affinity for people, especially for those feeling poorly, sad or not in a good place.

We entered the Hospice and immediately Nero did what he does best. I'm a firm believer that some dogs just have the most amazing sense for what is going on. I honestly believe that if we had unclipped Nero he would have gone directly to Marian's room...having never been in that building or ever meeting Marian before.

A nurse guided us down the corridor but Nero was on a mission. He needed no guidance. He was up front, pushed open the closed door, straight up to the side of a bed containing a lady neither Andrew or I new and introduced himself the only way he knows. Head between Marian's arm and side, eyes fixed on Marian and a tail wagging but not excitable. This lad had perfected an ability to purvey calm and tranquility, even at the worst of times. Then came Nero's most endearing trait, he extended a big fluffy front paw, never any danger of catching frail skin with claws, and placed it on Marian's chest, exhaling as he did it with a big puff, closing his eyes and taking up residence at Marian's side. Marian seemed to be in a semi sleep, but the effect I believe Nero was looking for occurred. Almost immediately Marian extended her left hand placing it on Nero's wide but soft forehead, stroking through his black and white mane.

Marian's room was adorned with flowers, plants, gifts and cards. She woke up and after introductions we talked about Fleur and her adventures since arriving in the UK. Marian was very much up to speed with Fleur and her journey. She also recounted many stories of dogs she had seen through her many years of dog rescue. Fleur became more comfortable with the whole situation the longer we stayed. Eventually she felt comfortable enough to approach Marian and pay her respects.

It wasn't too long before Marian became tired and was due her medication so it was an appropriate time to bid farewell and leave. In all the time we had been with Marian Nero had remained by her side. A constant calm companion.

An everlasting memory I will take away from visiting Marion was how upbeat and content she seemed to be. Andrew and I have never met Marian's family but they should take heart that this very special lady was fully aware of the circumstances and she was most defiantly taking strength from those final days. It was a privilege and honour to have the opportunity to meet Marian. A true inspiration to dog rescue.

On 14th December we posted the following on Chronicles of Fleur:

'I am so very sorry to inform you all that today a great lady 'Marian Sheppard' passed away.

Marian was a true Ambassador to dog rescue.

Wendy and I were both fortunate to have had the opportunity to visit Marian on 11th December, along with Fleur and Nero. One of life's real heroes, a rescuer of hundreds of dogs.

Marian may have passed on, but her ability to provide for dog rescue continues. Donations in tribute to Marian and her life work to dogs can be made via PayPal to; 'Marian.sheppard@hotmail.com'

Our thoughts are with Marian's family and friends at this time.

Rest in peace Marian, you can now run free on that rainbow bridge with all the dogs passed over.'

For Andrew it was also heart-breaking and he was so far away.

I was stunned. Dumbstruck. Powerless. In that moment I really felt those seven thousand plus miles between me and my dog that I was powerless to breathe life back in to. That distance was amplified by the fact that I now had zero say in the decisions that had already been made. None of the ideas or concepts that I could muster to assist Marti mattered. I wasn't in a position to provide any positive input into Marti's wellbeing. It was too late.

Two thoughts continued to harass me during that sleepless night. The first was that I was never going to see Marti again. Period. Never. She was gone for good. Never again was she going to greet me when I got home. My head was filled with an image. It came from a video that had been taken whilst we were on holiday in Turkey in October, just a few weeks previously. It was the seventh, my birthday and the lady looking after the dogs, Jenny Hopwood, sent through a video. It showed Nero and Marti both wearing party hats while Jenny and Sue Hopwood sang happy birthday. Fleur lay on the sofa uninterested in the festivities. Nero barked happily along whilst Marti looked bewildered about what was on her head. Her face stuck in my head. When we got home from Turkey her greeting was so warm, so excited. The day after I was back on a plane to work and now she was gone. Just like that. Gone.

Jenny recorded that return too, and now those two precious videos are my last memories of Marti. Never again would I be so quick to leave the dogs for any amount of time. Wendy brought Marti's ashes home along with a lock of her fur and a paw print. She was placed in the living room next to a photo of me and her, it was the first time she had shown contentment in such close proximity to me, and the first time we noticed her ears were upright instead of being held back in fear. There she stayed, watching over proceedings as we carried on with the Marti-shaped hole that was now in our lives.

Life did indeed go on. We still had Nero to look after and, of course, Fleur. I was still working away, but that doesn't mean I didn't have my ways of influencing life at home. Fleur had been to a variety of dog shows and events to please her adoring public, so I decided to take the next step and book her on to an agility course.

It wasn't until after booking it that I actually looked into it properly and realised that maybe Fleur didn't have the right demeanour for agility. Trying to get her off the bed was work enough. I did wonder if it was acceptable to put a chicken in the agility ring, Fleur would happily chase a chicken. Then all we needed to do was train the chicken to do the jumps. Maybe it would be easier to just stick Fleur up Wendy's jumper and get Wendy to do the course.

December the fifteenth was the dreaded morning. The morning of the agility class. It wasn't dreaded for me, of course, I was thousands of miles away but for Wendy the day started as good as it could have. Fleur wouldn't get out of bed and neither would Nero. Was this a portent for what was to come that day? Was Fleur just not made for agility? I, along with the rest of Fleur's FaceBook fan club, waited for the update.

We were treated to not only one, but two. Wendy gave her account, but it was the account of Nancy Hudson, the class instructor, that really showed the impact of what Fleur had achieved that day. To put this in to some sort of context, Fleur had obviously never been to any form of training or socialisation classes. Other than the dog shows we had taken her too, she had never been in that environment. Now, on her first time at an agility class Fleur was weaving in and out of poles, balancing on wobble boards and playing all manner of training games with confidence. As Nancy pointed out, this was because of her trust in Wendy. It was Wendy that had instilled that confidence in her that day, and it was a real sign that everything we had put into her had made an impact, and the bond we felt with her was reciprocated.

The lead up to Christmas 2015 was difficult without Marti, but Fleur's progress was a good buffer to counteract our sadness. The agility really wiped her out and she completely flaked out afterwards, but she didn't seem to bounce back. She started to sleep a lot, but Wendy and I just put it down to tiredness, but Wendy's nursing intuition told her something wasn't right. Wendy had always been one of those nurses that could spot trouble before it happened, there had been a number of instances where she would feel that something wasn't quite right with a patient, despite blood tests showing nothing, yet in a short period of time the patient had gone downhill. So, if Wendy had a feeling about one of the dogs, we tended to listen to it.

It was a Thursday night that Fleur first vomited. I was still away, and would be all over Christmas, so it was down to Wendy to deal with, but she kept me updated as much as she could. Initially it was just dismissed as a stomach bug, but Marti was still fresh in our minds at this point, so the worry lingered.

She didn't eat as well as usual that night or on the Friday morning, but the real signal that something was wrong came during her walk. For the first time ever, Wendy had to take Fleur home and walk Nero on his own, Fleur just didn't want to walk. This was extremely unusual, so Wendy called our vet who told her to get Fleur in ASAP. Her bloods came back OK but the X-Ray showed a full stomach, with no foreign body. All the indications were that there was a blocked valve. The vet wasn't happy to leave her so once again Fleur was referred to the RVC. There was a distinct feeling of history repeating.

At the RVC Fleur was kept in for observations, bloods and some pain relief. She was very tender on her abdomen and her stomach was hard and hot to touch, which only increased Wendy's anxiety. It was all so familiar that it was hard for assumptions to not be made. That day both myself and Wendy posted in Fleur's FaceBook group that, once again, we needed prayers for Fleur.

The following day the update came through, and I'm sure Wendy believed the prayers had worked. Fleur was doing well, but they needed to do an ultra-scan and they had mentioned pancreatitis, but in the context of ruling out everything due to her complex history. Whilst Wendy was the one that put the most emphasis on the power of prayer and positive thinking, I felt the urge to write my own post.

'Dear Father Christmas, last month when my wife asked me what I wanted for Christmas I said nothing, I already have everything I wanted. Can I change my mind and ask for one Christmas gift? Can I have my Fleur back at home, safe and well? Thank you'.

Maybe it was because I was so far away, and it was some sort of way of linking back to what was happening at home and implementing the only influence I could possibly have on the situation. Despite my reservations when it came to wishes and prayers, maybe this time someone was listening.

On Sunday, December 20th at 5:30pm. The RVC called with news. The ultra-scan had come back normal and their diagnosis was pancreatitis. The upshot was; Fleur was going home. When Wendy collected her, she had a shaved abdomen and three shaved paws, which was more than likely the reason for her whimpering. Over the previous year Fleur had developed a definite regal grace to her presence, and this new haircut definitely didn't fit into that persona.

Regardless of how she looked, she was home. She was safe, and she was going to be OK. For most owners a stomach problem and potential pancreatitis wouldn't be something that caused a huge amount of undue stress. However, for us, having dealt with what she had dealt with since Fleur's arrival, whenever there was a sniff of illness it was a stress trigger, and when these issues relate to her stomach these triggers began to stack and the stress increase. When you are burned by fire, you automatically pre-empt future burns whenever you go near fire. Whenever Fleur had stomach issues, we began to pre-empt the worst possible scenario.

It may not have been the best way to lead into Christmas that year, but it did demonstrate Fleur's utter strength to overcome whatever is thrown at her. She had had one of the most traumatic eighteen months any dog could have and yet she still dealt with life's hurdles in her stride.

Strides were on my mind at that point. As Fleur had started agility training, I of course assumed she would be selected for Crufts agility and I was sat in my room trying to formulate some script about how unjust it was that she wasn't going to be present at Crufts agility 2016 when I read a post from Val on FaceBook. Fleur had been invited to be on the rescue stand at Crufts alongside Icey, a Scruffts finalist and fellow Romanian rescue and a little dog named Rolo.

New Year is always a time for looking back and reminiscing about the year that has passed. For us it was a time to evaluate Fleur's journey. From seeing that picture shared on the Valgrays page, the almost constant set-backs to Fleur coming over to us and her multiple fights for life this little dog had earned every single breath she took, every step she took and every single bit of love and adoration she had been given from us and those that had followed her story. She had made an impact on so many people's lives that this was a fitting end to the year that her impact was taking her to the biggest event in the doggy calendar.

Fleur was going to Crufts.

Chapter Seventeen

STARDOM FOR FLEUR

~ • ~

SOME ARE BORN great and some have greatness thrust upon them. Well, Fleur wasn't born great but…let us allow Andrew to continue the story.

Saturday, March 12th 2016 came around pretty quickly. Early 2016 hadn't brought anymore big dramas with it and most of it was spent looking forward to the 12th March. Then, suddenly, it was upon us. The preparations had started the day before with Wendy primping, bathing, combing, brushing and fluffing Fleur who took it all with absolute pleasure. Thankfully all I had to do was pop my head in, nod my approval and head back out to cricket. Pretty cushy deal.

My smugness soon washed away when the alarm rang at 04:45 on the Saturday morning. Groggily I began to get myself ready for possibly the most exciting day of Fleur ownership thus far. I was the last one to get ready but, polishing my head and dying my beard a very specific shade of rosebush with a hint of silver is no easy task. That wasn't what made us late, however. That was the star herself, Lady Fleur, who point blank refused to get out of bed, to the point that I had to carry her from the bed to the car. I couldn't help but think how much I preferred this instance of carrying her to the car than the last time I had had to do it.

Two hours later, and a stop at the services 20 miles from the event, a services which was teeming with dogs. We arrived at the NEC and headed towards Hall 3 where Valgrays was set up. Fleur can be a little indifferent in situations where there is an influx of dogs, and that was most definitely what we were walking in to; but we needn't have worried as Fleur pranced through the NEC like she had been born to it without a care in the world.

We were soon on the stand and joined Icey, Holly and Rollo providing an eclectic mix of dogs and a resounding example of the sheer determination of dogs to survive, and the love and determination of those that dedicate their lives to saving them. The day passed mainly in a blur of visitors and me gabbling on and on to anyone who listen. What does stick in my head is looking up to see Fleur's Romanian saviours.

I was dumbfounded, flabbergasted and staggered to see Alina, Ramona and Radu standing in front of me. Somehow Val and Nickie had pulled off the heist of all heists and arranged this surprise visit. Needless to say, there was a whirlwind of 'Oh my goodness', hugs and cuddles for Fleur, who dealt with everything with her now usually poise and grace.

It was fantastic to see how much Fleur's story had touched people, but also to be able to spread the world about rescue and the plight of other dogs in Romania but one of the utter highlights was watching Val and Icey strut their stuff as finalists in the Golden Oldie category of the Scruffts finals. This was the first time I had ever heard of Scruffts. Sponsored by James Wellbeloved, it's the cross-breed equivalent of Crufts where non-pedigree dogs compete to win heats in different categories and the final is held at Crufts. It looked like fun and there was pang of inspiration as I watched Val and Icey walk proudly around the ring.

As we watched Wendy leaned over to me and said, "That could've been Fleur."

She was right. Fleur had a sweet and laid-back nature and one hell of a story to tell. Just to test the water I asked if we should enter Fleur the following year. The answer was a resounding yes and pretty quickly I had registered our interest on the Scruffts website. It didn't take long to get a reply and on April the 11th 2016 we were in the car headed to our first Scruffts heat in All About Dogs in Newbury.

Well, eventually we were. Once Fleur had stopped snoring and dragged herself away from her bed. In fact, I don't think she actually stopped snoring on the way to the car, it just depleted in its intensity. This wasn't a given, we weren't automatically in the heat. There was a cut-off point, and as Wendy hadn't let up telling me all week, if we didn't get there early enough we would miss the cut-off. As a joke I mentioned we should just camp and be done with it. Wendy was all for

More tears in the Morris home

it, but thankfully my selective deafness meant I didn't need to brush off the tent pegs.

There was a bitter wind that morning and with Wendy's nerves we bounced from toilet to toilet before we queued at 10:00am. By 10:30am we were registered and went off on our merry way to return for 12:30pm when everything was to kick off. Time was easy to lose at All About Dogs especially when you had a dog that was famous within doggy circles. We met a number of Fleur fans, which was always a pleasure and still a shock to see just how far her story had spread. On top of that we got to promote Valgrays and meet up with other Valgrays rescues such as Lynda Lewis and her three Valgrays rescues Dieter, Frankie and Ozzie. It's a small world.

When we did return, they were still taking entries. It's just as well we didn't camp, or the air would have been a deep shade of blue. Fleur was in the first category, 'Prettiest Bitch' so we got stuck right in. We did. Fleur absolutely bombed. The early morning had obviously taken its toll on Fleur who fell asleep on the ring floor. Full on, snoring, dribbling sleep. As you may have guessed, she didn't win that category.

We needed to change tack, so we did a lap of the showground, including all of the toilets we had already seen, and a cardboard burger and Fleur had a new lease of life, so it was back into the ring for the 'Best Rescue' category. Thankfully Fleur managed to keep her eyes open this time round as the judge walked dramatically up and down the row of dogs. Third place was awarded. Second place was awarded. A little more dramatic wandering and then…

He stopped in front of Fleur. She'd done it, she had won her category, we couldn't believe it! In the next category of 'Good Citizen' fellow Valgrays alumni Dieter brought it home and got first place. Two Valgrays winners! What a fantastic afternoon and a real achievement for Fleur, demonstrating just how far she had come in terms of confidence. We all piled back into the car happy, shattered and eagerly looking forward to the next Scruffts heat at Discover Dogs at the Excel in London on the 22nd of October.

The summer passed in a mixture of Facebook posts, dog shows and everyday life. We entered Fleur into local shows to try and give her more experience of the ring in a quieter, less pressured situation and to give us more experience too. In all honesty it's quite likely we were much more nervous than she was. We knew what was coming, she was happily living moment by moment.

Fleur had always liked her sleep, and the busy summer schedule had taken its toll on her but that was to be expected. As summer morphed into early autumn Fleur didn't recover as we would have expected to. She remained lethargic and then other symptoms began to manifest. She became snappy with dogs she had previously played with, regurgitating her food and her weight began to decline. When she got up from being lay down there was far too much of her coat left behind. These combined with Fleur's mood changes were a real combat indicator that something wasn't right. Wendy's nurse intuition kicked in and we contacted our vets.

The worst part? Food. Or the lack of it. After Fleur had given her blood for the screening she wasn't permitted to eat until the results came through. Of course, routine in our house was pretty strict and both dogs knew that after their walk came food. Fleur would always sit patiently waiting whilst Nero barked his head off. On the way back from that walk I was already questioning how I was going to manage not feeding her whilst Nero happily chowed down. As if she wasn't going through enough and now she couldn't eat? Poor Fleur. So, I explained the situation to both Fleur and Nero, upon which they both left the kitchen and went to bed. Maybe I was over thinking it?

Her blood tests showed she had a vitamin B12 deficiency and she was given antibiotics, but she continued to regurgitate her food and her mood was still unstable. The vets were concerned that there could be something else, something underlying such as Grey Collie Syndrome, or Canine Cyclic Neutropenia, a stem cell disease seen mainly in very young dogs which usually means they don't live beyond two to three years. Once again Fleur was referred back to the RVC.

It seemed that whenever this poor dog was just starting to enjoy her life fate came in and knocked her for six. In dog years she was still barely out of adolescence, and yet she had been faced with more mountains to climb than most dogs get during their whole lives. Just when we thought the ground was flat and we could move forward without climbing, we were headed back to Potters Bar.

The RVC told us they felt Fleur needed a bone biopsy to be tested for infection, Leukemia/blood cancer and heritage/genetic problems. The 'C' word always hit hard, but we knew how strong Fleur was and what she had already fought through. It was with a heavy heart that we posted the update to FaceBook, not knowing what kind of journey we would be in for now.

Fleur remained lethargic and we made sure she had plenty of attention and cuddles and prayed that the bone biopsy would be the beginning of the end of the tests and poking and prodding. We hoped that this was just an infection, a side effect of her previous medical history and we could give her some antibiotics and move on.

On October 6th 2016 I left the RVC with Fleur's collar and lead in my hand, but no Fleur. It was far too reminiscent for my liking, but I was buoyed by the knowledge that she was in safe hands with people that understood her. Plus, on meeting her the vet exclaimed;

"Ah, so this is the famous Fleur. Pleasure to meet you."

Evidently her reputation precedes her, but at least we knew that they understood what Fleur had been through.

As the vet promised, at 5pm we received a phone call. Fleur had undergone all of the tests she needed without sedation. She had been a willing, model patient. It's hardly surprising, invasive veterinary procedures were the one thing Fleur had a history of exposure too. It was her equivalent of socialisation training. Most dogs grow up getting used to other dogs, people, play. Fleur grew up getting used to poking, prodding, injections and pill popping.

A few days later we all, including Nero and the dogs we were looking after, Skye and Maisse, went to collect Fleur from the RVC. Fleur would be forgiven for confusing the RVC for the grooming parlours given that every time she left she had a new and creative hairstyle, like a canine Toni and Guy. The consultant came and spoke to us to give us the news. A Vitamin B12 deficiency. That was all, and it was better than any best-case scenario we could have hoped for. She would need life-long B12 injections, but she could go about her life as normal. Or as normal as life got for the now famous Lady Fleur of Valgrays.

We all left the RVC on a cloud, a cloud that was leading us straight to the Scruffts semi-final at Discover Dogs.

Wendy, of course, was also much relieved. Once again, Fleur had come through her latest trial.

Sometimes life has a very peculiar but oddly satisfying sense of irony that simply can't be ignored. On Saturday October 26th 2016 we made our way to Discover Dogs at the Excel. The car was filled with a nervous energy, apart from Fleur who had no idea what was coming, despite my chats with her. It was on this journey that something struck me, it was this day two years ago that we put ourselves forward to adopt Fleur. That tiny, weak bag of bones was now on her way to represent all Romanian rescues and Valgrays as Best Rescue in the Scruffts semi-final. A lump came to my throat as I realised just how far she had come and what she had conquered to get there.

The nerves weren't just coming from the fact we had to navigate another show ring in front of heaven knows how many people, this time we were doing it in front of a Channel 4 camera. Fleur had been caught on camera before, at last years' Scruffts where she was caught walking with Icey and they had remembered Fleur. So, no pressure then, just a national camera team.

One of the film crew, Jaz, met us in the car park and gave us a rundown of what they wanted to capture. It was a surreal feeling, to be told where and how to walk. We (Fleur, Andrew and I) were to walk into the entrance and stop for a brief chat. Easy, right? As we walked towards the camera I felt like a superstar. A superstar with trembling hands and a heart that was threatening to explode through her jacket.

We did as we were instructed and moved into the Excel with a throng of people, where Jaz beckoned us over. We were asked questions and I took the opportunity to air Fleur's amazing story, plus it acted as a good pre-show warm up. Interview over, we were free to go into the exhibition and explore.

It wasn't long before our prior learning kicked in and Andrew's anxiety rose. The last time we were at Discover Dogs, Fleur hadn't been happy with the rubber matting that is placed on the floors to protect them from the hordes of people walking in and out. On top of that, the room we needed to be in had been up two flights of stairs. Ordinarily Fleur wouldn't give two hoots about the stairs, but the business and crowdedness (including two pugs in tutu's) of the venue meant Fleur wasn't happy about climbing them. Her anxiety had been so pronounced that Andrew had had to pick her up and carry her.

By now we had had Fleur for a long time, we knew how she worked and what helped her and in situations like these all she needed was to lean into your leg, to know that you were there. She would look up to you as if all she needed to know was that you were there with her and she would then walk on. That's what happened at Discover Dogs that day. Fleur looked to us for her confidence and she headed forwards. No need for lifting her up or carrying her up any stairs. She coped with the humans, dogs, voices, loud PA announcements and music. Two years to the day and Fleur's confidence and bond with us was stronger than ever.

We found the chill-out area for the dogs and before long Andrew was half in the crate with Fleur where he happily stayed whilst I and Val and Nickie from Valgrays wandered around the show. Later we took Fleur to the ring where she would be strutting her stuff in front of the semi-finalist judges, a way of breaking her in gently and getting her used to the arena beforehand; plus, she got to have a go on a few of the agility jumps which for Fleur, now a fully-fledged agility lover, was always a bonus.

All too soon, but also not soon enough, the time came. There were fifteen semi-finalists in the 'Best Rescue' category and we were the first ones up. Fleur and I took our seated position on the edge of the ring with the fourteen other dogs and owners. In the stands I could see Andrew videoing us live with a big cheesy grin and thumbs up like a cross between Homer Simpson and Wallace from Wallace and Gromit.

And so, it began. The judge, Maria Scott, came to us and asked about Fleur and her story. Every time I tell Fleur's story I well up, and it was all I could do not to cry whilst relaying the story to Maria and the surrounding crowds. By the end of it I was completely emotionally spent and that must've come across because when I finished, Maria, who had been on the floor fussing Fleur, stood back up with tears streaming down her face. I assumed that was a good thing. Hopefully.

With that she moved on to the next dog and that was it. There was nothing more we could do. Fleur lay back on the floor and I lay with her as Maria made her way through the other fourteen stories. I stroked her silky ears and whispered to her that no matter what happens, she was our superstar and she had already won in life. Then the boards came out.

Third place was awarded. Then second. The previous heat came flooding back and I dared to wonder; what if...

Maria's voice boomed over the PA – 'Lady Fleur of Valgrays is the worthy winner of Scruffts Best Rescue 2016'

She had done it! Our beautiful, brave, strong and ever gracious girl had gone and done it. She had won her category and cemented her place in the

Scruffts 2016 final. I was shocked, excited, proud and every other emotion all in one. There was a roar of rapturous applause and congratulatory cheers lead by the Valgrays contingent. Fleur responded very aptly by letting out a loud bark as her name filled the room.

Somewhat ironically, Fleur won a year's supply of James Wellbeloved food as they sponsored the event, but because of her intestine issues Fleur's diet was restricted and she couldn't eat it. So, in her honour, the food was donated. Half want to Ramona's in Romania and half went to Valgrays. A fitting tribute and a way of Fleur giving back to those that had ensured she had got to this point. Two years previously Fleur had been given one percent chance of survival, and now she was heading to the Scruffts final. I think I may have actually glowed with pride.

There wasn't much time to stand around and bask, however, and as soon as the ring cleared the Kennel Club came for an interview whilst the whole thing was filmed for Channel 4. It was exciting and overwhelming to think how many people were going to hear Fleur's story, but this wasn't the end.

Fleur's story was featured in our local papers with the headlines 'Fleur Battles the Odds to Win Scruffts. Award' and 'Dog Rescued from Romania Reaches Scruffts Final'. As the following days passed it really hit home. Fleur was in the final. She stood a chance at winning Nation's Best at Crufts. Competition was tough, but she was there, and she was in with a chance.

The previous years' Scruffts had come complete with a documentary filmed by Channel 4, which had included Icey and a brief glimpse of Fleur having a wee. The programme had done well and, buoyed by its success, Channel 4 had decided to beef it up for 2016 and carry out filming in between the Scruffts semi-finals and the grand finale at Crufts 2017.

November 2016 rolled around and Mentorn Media, who were making the programme, came to the Morris house to film Fleur with the intent of getting her back story from her forever home. I was expecting this big Hollywood style film crew to turn up with cameras and sound equipment with a huge entourage. What we actually got on the day was the director, Andrew (nice and confusing), and his equipment. Lots of equipment.

Fleur wasn't fazed one iota and we all sat on the sofa and spoke about life before heading to the recreation ground for a walk where we met up with Fleur's boyfriend, Ruben, and his owner Brenda. At the same time Andrew carefully and quietly captured Fleur's every move on camera, being conscious not to cause any undue stress. Fleur was her usual graceful, accommodating self and showed all aspects of her personality from sedateness to cuddly and loving to tearing around like a headless chicken.

With that 2016 turned into 2017 and whilst Fleur's following grew, and her page continued to attract followers and messages of support the days passed without incident. We were still preparing ourselves for the final at Crufts and the excitement didn't dissipate. On the 31st January we were once more on the motorway headed back to the RVC, but this time Fleur was fit and healthy and Mentorn Media were in tow. It was the day before Fleur's second 'Gotcha Day' and, as so many things seemed to be with Fleur, it was yet another reminder of her incredible journey and the people she had touched along the way.

This time Andrew (Papa Morris) was able to join us, just to make things nice and confusing. We met Andrew (Mentorn Andrew) and Lucy just outside Potters Bar and all headed to the RVC together where we met Vicky Viscombe and Andrew (good grief) Phillips, the surgeons who had operated on Fleur and saved her life. We were interviewed in a small side room but then we were shown around the clinic, including the room I was in when I first came, and Fleur was taken from me. We were taken around the 'behind-the-scenes' rooms and then into the room where I remembered giving Fleur's medical history.

Everything came flooding back as we walked around the clinic discussing what had happened to Fleur at that time. All of the emotions that I felt, the fear, the overwhelming sadness and the worry washed over me again, but it did make me appreciate where we were that day, how far we had come to get there. We need to remember the dark times to appreciate the light we live in and as I looked down to Fleur her face symbolised hope and this was a time to celebrate life, not dwell on what could have been or what was in the past.

A lot of the interview focused on the medical aspects of what Fleur had endured. The intense invasiveness of the surgery that she experienced in order to save her life and the sheer seriousness of her illness came to light during those conversations. The sheer intensity of the infection Fleur had when she was brought in, how far it had spread, came to light and Vicky made it clear how slim she had thought her chances were. There had been frank pus all the way through her tissues and in to the abdomen which was stuck together in a ball. All the leaks had to be plugged and then a massive abscess had been discovered that was full of pus too. It was here that the seriousness of her infection was most apparent, and Andrew Phillips explained how pessimistic he was about Fleur's recovery.

At this point a heavy sadness fell over the room, a real tangible realisation of exactly how ill Fleur had been. Sad eyes fell on Fleur just as she rolled around happily on the cold, tiled floor; a charming habit she had developed. Everyone smiled, and it summed exactly what Fleur symbolised, and how she affected those she came in to contact with. From depressing illness, she fought her way to charming goofiness and she brought a smile to the face of everyone she met. That day in the vets when everyone was touched by the heart-wrenching sadness of her story, she brought a smile to everyone's face with her innocent silliness.

Of course, we couldn't leave the practice without somehow showing our gratitude for everything they had done for Fleur, not only during that first major surgery but for everything they had done since. Without them we wouldn't have a Fleur to be taking to the Scruffts final, or a beautiful member of our family. What on earth do you give someone who has had such a huge positive impact on your life and a dog you care about so deeply? Why, a Fleur Stool Chocolate Cake, obviously.

That was it for the filming until the final at Crufts. To think, the whole nation would hear and see Fleur's story. We knew she had a huge following already thanks to social media and Beverley Cuddy's articles in Dogs Today, but this definitely felt like a step up in Fleur's exposure.

Fleur needed to look her best on her big day so on February 11th we took her in to Sue's Grooming Room in Finchampstead. As had become the norm now, Sue knew of Fleur's story, having been told by Rob King who had come to photograph Fleur nearly two years previously. In fact, Rob came by that day to take some stunning candid shots of Fleur whilst she was being pampered and primped. Little did I know that these pictures were then to be featured in yet another article, this time for Dogs Monthly where Fleur was hailed as the 'Kate Moss of canines' and was the first dog ever to be featured on the cover of both Dogs Today and Dogs Monthly. Up until this point Fleur had mainly been featured in dog specific news and publications, but that was all about to change.

On Tuesday, February 21st Jasmyn from Mentorn Media arrived at the Morris house for some last-minute filming. Most of it was spent nervously packing for Birmingham, mainly for Fleur. I packed three bags for Fleur alone. A day bag, a food bag and a toy bag. It was worse than going on holiday with a baby. Jasmyn made a passing comment that a photo of Fleur on her princess bed would make a great photo for TV Times.

Two hours after Jasmyn left the phone rang. It was The Kennel Club telling me that both TV Times and Radio Times wanted to cover Fleur's story. What? I agreed and awaited the calls from each magazine, whilst eagerly texting friends, family, and pretty much everyone I had ever met.

The following day both magazines called me and interviewed me for a write up for the run up to Scruffts and to coincide with the documentary. As if I wasn't already excited enough for the final, now I was practically bouncing off the walls. Then came another call from Radio Times asking if they could come and photograph Fleur for a feature in their magazine, and then TV Times called asking for the photograph of the scared, yellow Fleur under the chair that started this whole thing off.

It was February 27th when the Radio Times photographer visited, along with a myriad of equipment. Fleur is a natural in front of the camera and lived up to her Kate Moss comparison, though it could have been all the treats she was receiving. She turned on her flirty Fleur mode and cuddled up to the photographer before we headed out to the recreation ground. It was a dull drizzly day but that didn't stop Fleur working it for the camera. One photo in particular really struck me. It was me and Fleur sat together on a bench and she looked so relaxed and so regal, as if she had had the same life as all the other dogs out and about that day. From that terrified, weak, yellow dog under a chair to this proud, beautiful dog who had touched and was loved by so many. My heart swelled three sizes looking at that photograph.

It may not have been 'OK' or 'Hello' magazine, but for us it was huge. It was national, and it would open up a world of possibilities for Fleur and us to give back to those who had given us so much. In March the Radio Times featured a full double spread on Fleur and her story and in the same week she was featured in TV Times. The media coverage had really upped Fleur's popularity and people connected with her story. She was quickly becoming the favourite to win at Scruffts with over 400 likes on the Crufts FaceBook page. The pressure was beginning to build as March 11th loomed ever closer. The big day was almost upon us and Fleur had as much buzz around her as an X-Factor finalist.

The day of the final came around quickly. The days leading up to it had been filled with talk of clothing options, mainly from me, Andrew was less concerned. But then, he wasn't going to be on national TV. I would talk about anything and everything to do with the show non-stop from the moment I woke to the time we went to bed. There was a distinct buzz in the house, the kind you get leading up to a big event like a wedding or a family holiday. It was all a little surreal but mostly exhilarating as an electricity surged through the house.

Everything was going to plan and the support around Fleur was looking incredibly promising. The Scruffts social media put the finalists on their FaceBook page and Fleur was by far and away the favourite. Whilst other finalists were getting between 35–40 votes Fleur was heading to over 450. My God, she could really do this. We could have a Scruffts finalist in our midst. This little dog that had battled so much to become the nation's canine sweetheart, who become a poster dog for Romanian rescues could now go and win a national dog show. The real icing on top of the cake, proof that she really was as strong and as special as we had always believed, and that everyone else believed it to.

We had already had the Radio Times and TV Times and interviews, Fleur was all over social media and Dogs Today/Dogs Monthly and then we were asked to go on This Morning with all the other finalists. This was big. This Morning is one of the most watched TV shows and that kind of exposure would be immense, however we were to go on with all the other finalists and they had made it clear it was all or nothing. As it got closer to the show being filmed, one of the other finalists pulled out and it didn't go ahead. Instead we were replaced with a woman in the bath with her dog on the show. Yes, we thought the same.

Despite this, Fleur had had a huge amount of media exposure, much more than any other finalist and there was a definite belief that she was a shoe in. She had this in the bag. It wasn't just us either, everyone had the same feeling. We weren't just being big-headed or cocky, all the information pointed to Fleur winning so the excitement in the Morris household was intense.

We had both always been very conscious of ensuring we gave back to those that had believed in Fleur, those that had offered prayers, thoughts, time and money to help and to get here where she was. Scruffts was the perfect opportunity to do this so we made some Fleur based gifts to give out. We had some cups that had Fleur's beautiful face on, some had chocolates in and were all packaged up with cellophane and ribbon. They had been kept up on a high shelf, knowing the dangers chocolate posed to dogs and their digestive system.

On the Tuesday, two days before Scruffts, I worked a half day, so I came home early as usual, but, unusually, as soon as I opened the door Fleur shot out and delivered a violent stream of hosepipe diarrhoea. This in itself wasn't that unusual for Fleur due to the damage done to her intestines, however the urgency and the silver flecks of chocolate paper that were interspersed within the brown liquid were worrisome. In the living room my fears were justified, three cups were laying on the floor and wrappers were scattered all over the place!

So, with 48 hours to go until the final Fleur was rushed to the vets once more. Panic started to set in. It was too close to Fleur's big day for this to be happening. This was her moment to stand in front of the crowds, to be seen by the nation for what she was and to show them what she stood for. She had already climbed so many hurdles to get to this point, surely, she deserved a break now? Surely, she deserved her time in the spotlight given how hard she had fought for it?

Ever the nurse, my first thoughts (aside from 'Oh crap, literally') went to the cause. I investigated exactly how much Fleur had eaten, knowing it would help the vets' diagnosis. There were three cups on the floor, and each cup contained ten chocolates. A total of thirty potentially ingested chocolates. That wasn't good. That was more than enough to cause some serious issues.

Thankfully, on further investigation I calculated that Fleur couldn't have eaten more than eight of those thirty. One small bonus was those eight weren't purely chocolate, because of the centres they had s they weren't as dangerous. At the vets she was given a Vitamin B jab and an injection of antibiotics. Only time would tell if it would pass, but thankfully it was nowhere near as serious as it could have been. For once it appeared Fleur had a reprieve, a bit of luck. hopefully it as a sign of what was to come.

Then, it was here. The day of the final. Nerves and elation were in equal measure as he laid our heads down the night before in an attempt to sleep. Sleep was never going to come easy, at least it wouldn't for me. Although Andrew was excited, he still had the infuriating ability to sleep, regardless. It didn't help that we were in a strange bed rather than our own. Crufts is held in Birmingham, so it would have been a long day if we had travelled from home. Instead, we opted to stay in a hotel.

The morning of Crufts I woke up first and took Fleur out for a toilet break and a quick walk to get her ready for the day ahead. We had been told to film Fleur getting into the car and our journey to Crufts, which was fine until Andrew informed me that he would be the one filming on my phone, which meant I had to drive. Like I wasn't nervous enough already?

As had happened at the semi-final, Jasmin had asked if they could film us walking in and talk to us as we entered. We parked up and telephoned Jasmin to let her know we were there. We were there. It was happening. This wasn't just another Crufts where we would watch all the other dogs in the ring. This year, we would be in that ring with a chance of coming out of it with a title for Lady Fleur of Valgrays.

We headed towards the entrance, not knowing what was going to happen but with a bright ray of hope guiding us. We telephoned Val and Nicki too, as this was as much their day as it was ours and Fleur's. As we have always said, without them we wouldn't even have Fleur. They have always been integral to Fleur's story, weaving in and out of it like a knitting needle through wool.

We carried out our interview and headed into the melee that was Crufts. Ahead of us was the James Wellbeloved stand which is where we were supposed to be. It was set out on two levels with stairs up to a seating area with comfy sofas. The walls were adorned with all the Scruffts finalists' pictures. We scoured them quickly and there she was. Fleur. Best Rescue, owned and loved by Wendy Morris. Yes, Yes, she was.

Entering the 'backstage' area was exciting, but I was nervous. Fleur had managed the stairs fine this time, as she did at the semi-final but there on the sofa was Biscuit with his owner Joshua. Biscuit is a big black German Shepherd/Border Collie cross, and Fleur isn't a big fan of big black dogs, for whatever reason. On any other day this wouldn't have caused us much issue, we would have managed it as we did everything else but on that day; emotions were heightened and our need to avoid any kind of negative interaction or experience prior to going into the ring was paramount, which meant paranoia was riding up front.

There were no exchanges as we walked Fleur past Biscuit and both Andrew and I breathed a sigh of relief. The last thing we wanted this close to the final was something to freak Fleur out and stop her going into the ring. We were greeted with drinks and encouraged to sit and relax as other dogs and owners arrived, each with friendly hello's and greetings. I had already made FaceBook contact with a couple of them, King Tommy who was the Most Handsome Dog finalist and owned by Monique, and Prettiest Bitch finalist Ginny, owned by Judy. Everyone else seemed to know who was who.

Then came the press call, which was a little more manic. I was interviewed, as I was the one showing Fleur. It was all in my name. Andrew was just there to offer moral support and act as a film crew, which was fine by him. People were interviewed, and photographs were taken. Fleur was never one to shy away from a camera and this part went without any issue. Once that was over it was time for rehearsal.

Rehearsal was to take place in the main arena where the final would be held, so of we went, following members of the James Wellbeloved team between Biscuit and Ginny. Thankfully Fleur's big black dog issues didn't come to the surface, however, her rubber matted floor issues did. Fleur absolutely froze and refused to move. To keep up with the others I had to pick Fleur up and carry her, it wasn't exactly confidence boosting but the show must go on.

The rehearsal itself passed quickly, everyone was told where to stand and it was explained that the judges were to come over and talk to the owners, then the winner would be announced, and everyone would walk off. Sounds simple enough, right? Oh, and we were up first. No pressure. Keep calm. Deep breaths. Oh God.

Rehearsal over, we headed back to the James Wellbeloved stand and Andrew. We were walking behind King Tommy and Monique as they escalated the ramp. As they went up, two other dogs came down and suddenly they both had a pop at King Tommy. More noise than anything else, and King Tommy responded with his own barks and didn't seem overly phased. Fleur, however, did what she usually did when something scary happened and tried to push herself into the small space between me and the barrier of the ramp. Not the best experience for her to have this close to the final. I prayed it wouldn't bother her later.

We returned to the stand and it was obvious that Fleur was flagging. It had been a long morning, but now we had a lunch break. Joshua spoke to me during the lunch break, he had come with his family and as it turned out his brother was a Fleur fan. A traitor in the ranks, but perfectly understandable.

We were then given time to rest, which was handy as it had been a long day already and we still hadn't had the main event yet. Stalls had been set up for each of us to rest in. Biscuit had his own soft cage to rest in and I felt a pang of guilt as I looked down on Fleur's blanket. It looked depressing in comparison, but it was worlds away from the wooden pallet she slept on in Romania.

Everyone interacted with each other and Fleur was tiring. The day had already taken its toll and the clock was ticking closer and closer to 5:30. I just wanted it to get there before she completely flaked out.

Then suddenly, all too quickly, it was time. We were asked to make our way to the main ring and a wall of nerves hit us all. Despite the nerves, I was convinced we would win. Everything that had happened over the past two years or so. All of the pain, the fighting, the sleepless nights, the tears and the laughter. Everything had lead us to this point and we had had such tremendous support from everyone, from family to people we had never even met, that I had no doubt we had this. This was our title. All the other contestants had a consensus that is was between Fleur and King Tommy.

Walking into the huge arena I was hit by a gust of applause and cheers, it felt warm like opening an oven door mid cooking. I searched the crowds for Andrew and there he was, surrounded by a sea of purple rosettes and hopeful, supportive smiles from all of the friends we had made on this incredible journey. I so wanted to win this for them, and for all rescue dogs, Romanian or otherwise.

We all stood there on the stage as their judges made their way to us. As promised, they came to me first. I was sure everyone could see my heart pounding, even in the back row of the audience, it was so pronounced in my chest. It went through my head that we went first in the semi-finals and won those, and we were up first here too. That must be a sign, right?

I answered the judges' questions and they moved on. It didn't seem like thirty seconds had passed before they retired back to make their decision. It was all in their ands now. Everything else kind of faded and it was just me, Fleur and my mind which was racing. We were going to do this. We were about to win Scruffts. Fleur was about to win Scruffts and prove to everyone what a Romanian rescue dog could do, what they could overcome.

Then a finger pointed. It belonged to the judge. I followed it as it moved past us and landed on Joshua and Biscuit. Wait, what? Biscuit had won. My heart absolutely hit the floor. I couldn't believe it. This whole thing had been so built up in the lead up to the competition that it was a huge disappointment. I forced myself to smile as I lead the others out of the ring.

After all of that, of two months of living and breathing Scruffts, all of the press coverage and reports and it wasn't to be. My heart ached. Then I looked down to Fleur. She looked back up at me with those devastatingly beautiful eyes, those eyes that had drawn me in all those months ago. She wasn't bothered in the slightest, her tail still wafted gracefully, and her eyes still sparkled.

Fleur had come from the most horrendous of situations. She had travelled for hours upon hours to get here. She had undergone surgery that only three other dogs had gone through and was given a one percent chance of survival. She was the only dog to ever survive the surgery. Her story had inspired people to raise over £10,000 in 24 hours and since then she had overcome further illnesses whilst settling into a life of which she had absolutely no previous experience.

Fleur may not have won this competition, but she had won everything else. She had championed anything that had been thrown at her and here she was at the final of a national competition being recognised for everything she had achieved. A rosette, a trophy, nor a lifetime supply of dog food could ever demonstrate or do justice to exactly what Fleur symbolised. Her strength, her determination and her unwavering love and devotion.

Scruffts had been a massive high with a crushing low. It was a huge bump back down to earth, but it was time to take stock. Fleur championed and highlighted the cause of Romanian rescue dogs, and she was our champion. She was a champion for so many and that's what mattered. I thought back to the previous night in the hotel. Fleur had gone to sleep on her bed in the hotel room and when I woke she was in bed with Andrew, his arm draped over her. That was what was important. That was what made Fleur, and every dog, special.

Regardless of her result in any show, Fleur was, and is, always our winner. And not only ours.

Out of the blue I received a message from Beverly Cuddy.

"Can I ask you to save the date for May 9th we have something special planned in London for Fleur, would be in the daytime. Hope you are both able to come. X"

I replied:

"will do already booked in the diary"
"Brilliant x" replied Beverly.

A month later another message from Beverley:

"Just checking that you and Andrew and Fleur are still okay to come to the London Pet Show May 9th? Val can come too now, which is great news. What's your address so we can send your passes and more info?"

I sent a reply back confirming and giving her our details we asked if we could mention this on Fleur's Facebook page as some of her follows may be there and meet her and we can say thank you.

Beverly replied:

"You can say that Fleur will be meeting Super vet Noel Fitzpatrick in the super theatre and that if people want to watch and cheer her on we can get 20% off tickets by quoting our discount code"

This was a real WOW. We are going to meet Noel Fitzpatrick, this was when we found out she had been nominated for a Heroic Hound award. This was going to be an amazing day, and Fleur was once again featured in the Dogs Today Magazine:

'Miracle Maker, in the afternoon beloved Romanian survivor Fleur was honoured and the amazing Val Phillips from Valgrays rescue was also applauded for almost 40years of amazing rescue work. One of the Royal Veterinary College vets that had operated on Fleur saving her life

– had travelled to the show to cheer her on, too'.

This was the first time Beverly had actually met Fleur and commentated on how tiny and fragile she was. Vet Vicki had remarked on her amazing will to survive and Val reminded everyone that there had been 1% change of survival, what a miracle.

We remember this day with many fond memories, we took our neighbour Anne who looks after Nero, Marti, Fleur and Babe while we are at work, and another neighbour's daughter whose birthday it was and she had been following Fleur's story.

15 May'15 – London Pet Show Chronicles of Fleur – 'Lights, Camera, Action'
'Well…lots to tell leading up, during and after the London Pet Show at the Excel Exhibition Centre, London.

Andrew was as excited as anyone of course

Before I start – Fleur, Wendy & I would like to offer a HUGE thank you to Beverley Cuddy, Val and Nickie for keeping us all updated and on our toes during the day. It was all run like clockwork.

So, getting ready to receive a Heroic Hound 2015 award is no easy business. First we had to sort out what to wear. Lady Fleur of Valgrays (official title – her Kennel Club Registration says so – #PROUD) was an easy fix; the purple jacket with F.L.E.U.R. spelt out across the shoulders using the sparkly letters Fleur received as a gift and some 'VALGRAYS Border Collie Rescue' sticky transfers did the trick. That is until we arrived and realized the area was roasting and poor Fleur would have cooked in that coat! Never fear – we still had her hand-made 'named' lead and collar neckerchief to fall back on.

Friday night bath time was left to Wendy to splash out. I made some feeble excuse and disappeared out the door with Nero and Marti for a very long walk (how long I hear you ask…just long enough for Wendy to bath Fleur is the answer). We all arrived home to find Fleur doing the standard 'carpet rub' while Wendy was trying to soak up the water from the bathroom floor.

Saturday morning was seamless with the packing up of the car and a long enough walk to entice Fleur to leave a No 6 at home rather than on centre stage of the EXCEL. Our neighbours Anne and Ella also joined us for the day and the road trip, albeit 2 hours, was painless, up until almost arriving at the EXCEL where we become a London road traffic incident statistic...shunted at traffic lights! No injuries, minimal damage, that's what insurance is for and we had a show to get too.

Lady Fleur got straight to work on arrival. It took her very little time to settle in and greet her adoring public.

Val, Nickie and Stacey McEvoy had made the 'VALGRAYS' stand look awesome. At the front were two different issues of 'Dogs Today'. One being the 'Fleur' front cover issue. So it made sense to set up next to these and have Fleur handing them out. She was magnificent...loads of passers-by ended up with a magazine and Fleur selfie. The occasional person did remark on how much the dog on the front cover looked similar to the dog on the 'VALGRAYS' stand... Yup, I'm serious...

By the way – I was introduced to Mr. Moo (a VALGRAYs rescue Border Collie). I love that boy, one day he will be mine... (Just saying).

Most interested people have seen the photos and video of Fleur receiving her award. Personally I think Beverley Cuddy did an amazing job of encapsulating the work carried out by Val, not only the story of Fleur but that of VALGRAYS too. Thank you Beverley for ensuring the legacy continues. We also managed to catch up with the lads from 'House of Hugo' (Leon & Matt Henderson – Rood) and Anneka Svenska who was on the judging panel for the event. Anneka is a well-known celeb who works tirelessly for animals, we were very lucky in that she came over to the VALGRAYS stand and interviewed Val and Wendy. Hopefully this media can be the TV 'air time' Fleur fans have all asked for have and all strived for, utilising Fleur's story in a positive way to educate people in regard to the plight of dogs in Romania.

Of course for the ladies, meeting the Supervet Noel Fitzpatrick put a spring in their step and twinkle in their eyes.

For me, and not detracting from the phenomenal day that we all had, was the opportunist meeting of our very own 'Super Vet' Vicky Lipscomb. Vicky was visiting with her family and by chance came across the VALGRAYS stand (she was unaware that Fleur was also there).

Thankfully Vicky and her family came to the Heroic Hound presentation and we were all able to meet up. For those that are not aware, Vicky is the

More tears in the Morris home

surgeon from RVC who (along with the RVC team) saved Fleur's life. It was fantastic to have the opportunity to meet her again and tell her family how great she is (although they already knew that).

It had become a whirlwind of publicity, appearances and meeting many great people and dogs. We had introduced Fleur to a better life and she had done the same for us.

Chapter Eighteen

FLEUR HAS THE FINAL WORD

~ • ~

SO WHAT WAS Fleur doing trotting through a hospital? All in good time. First of all let us let her complete her story, thus far.

It's so warm. And so light. I stretch full length in my comfy bed as the warm, summer morning sun shines through the window. The room is empty, the people must already be downstairs. My impeccable canine sense of smell makes my nose twitch. I know that smell. Breakfast. A deep yawn and another stretch before I head downstairs.

I pad into the food room, the same room I spent so much time in when I first arrived at home, and I'm greeted by soft, friendly voices and fuss. It feels nice, warm and familiar. I move my head into their hands to try and get as much contact as possible. Then the rope thing is clipped to my collar and I know it's time for a walk. I wag my tail in anticipation; walks are fun. That's when I get to see the other dogs that walk around here and, as long as we avoid the metally things in the floor, there are always new smells and scents to explore.

Plus, if we go to the grass place I can run. Tearing through the grass and feeling the wet dew on my paws fills me with a tingly type feeling and I just want to run faster and faster. After a short walk we get to the grass place and as soon as I hear the clip released from my collar I charge. My paws pound the wet grass hard as the air whips through my fur. I push my nose into it as my legs pound harder. It feels amazing to run because I want to, because I enjoy it, rather than because I'm running from something scary.

The man calls my name, so I stop and run back to him. I know I have to stop running, but I also know what's coming next. I approach him, and I get some contact and a biscuit before he clips my lead back on and we walk home.

When we get home, I know it's time for the best part, the bowl. It's always full and always tasty. I barely remember what hunger pains are these days. I sit quietly and wait. I can feel my mouth getting wetter as the saliva builds in anticipation. Here it comes. Here it comes. Mmm.

When the food's gone it's back to bed. Which bed depends on how I feel. There are so many sleeping spots to pick from I try and vary it. Most of the morning I snooze happily, lazily. I might get up and find someone to cuddle in to if the mood takes me but I'm free to do as I please, generally. I feel so free when I run, but now I feel a freeness all the time. I'm free to go about my day without the constraints of fear or pain. I know where my meals are coming from and I know I can sleep without worrying about what will happen when I do. If only Shimeka and the deformed-leg dog had been as lucky. I wondered for a moment where the deformed-leg dog was, if her life was as good as mine was. I hoped with all my heart that it was.

Back when everything hurt, and I was in the chemical smelling rooms and the cage rooms I had no idea what was to come next. I didn't know what kind of life awaited me, but I'm happy that I clung on to find out. The memories stay with me and sometimes when I close my eyes I still see the man hacking at that poor dog's legs, or I feel the deformed-leg dog's warm body lying next to me and the cage mesh on my skin but right now, lying fully stretched on my bed in the direct light of the warm sun I'm not a street dog anymore, I'm Fleur. I'm the dog that refused to die.

I wondered where we were going when I was taken to another building I had never seen before. I was curious but my curiosity turned to worry just fr a moment. I could smell chemicals again. No! Surely…no, what am I thinking of? My humans wouldn't bring me here unless there was a very good reason. They have never let me down yet, I…I…trust them. Yes, that's the word – trust.

I was allowed to walk through this big building and we went along hallways and through big rooms with lots of beds. Some people didn't seem to notice me but most of them looked at me surprised. I don't know why, I'm just a dog, they must have seen one before.

Fleur has the final word

Then we came to another big room with lots of other small rooms sort on inside it and lots of beds again. They must need a lot of rest here.

These humans are mostly very small, like pups. It reminded me about when I was a pup but I quickly put that out of my mind. These human pups did not look very happy. Perhaps that was what I was here for, to make them happy.

I could hear the bigger humans talking and I kept hearing them mention my name as if these young humans were going through the same sort of illness that I had been through.

I hope not, it was not good. One of the young humans is reaching out to me. Perhaps if I lick his hand and let him know everything will be alright, it might reassure him.

There, his hand is clean now and he looks as if he might be…yes, he is. I have seen humans look like that before when they seem to be happy.

So that's why they brought me here. I'm to lick their hands and make them happy.

Hello, I'm Fleur. I used to be ill too. But I'm alright now. I'm Fleur, I was in a place like this – lots of times and people looked at me worried. They probably look at you worried too.

It's OK though. They do some amazing things, you feel better after a while and everyone is happy again. That's what will happen to you.

If you get scared just think of me, remember my name. I'm Fleur.

ENDS

In loving memory of Nero and Marti.